General Editor: Robert Rietty

LUIGI PIRANDELLO

Collected Plays

Volume One

HENRY IV
THE MAN WITH THE FLOWER IN HIS MOUTH
RIGHT YOU ARE (IF YOU THINK YOU ARE)
LAZARUS

JOHN CALDER PUBLISHER · LONDON
RIVERRUN PRESS · NEW YORK

This edition first published in Great Britain in 1987 by
John Calder (Publishers) Limited

And in the United States of America in 1987 by
Riverrun Press Inc

Reprinted 1998 by John Calder Publisher

British Library Cataloguing in Publication Data
Pirandello, Luigi
    Collected plays.
    Vol. 1
    I. Title   II. Rietty, Robert   III. Pirandello
    Luigi [Enrico IV, *English*] Henry IV
    IV. Pirandello, Luigi [L'Uomo del fiore in
    bocca. *English*] The man with the flower in
    his mouth   V. Pirandello, Luigi [Cosi e se
    vi pare. *English*] Right you are (if you think
    you are.
    852'.912   PQ4835.17
    ISBN 0-7145-4110-9

Library of Congress Catalog No. 85-61656.

Typeset in 10/11pt Times by Gilbert Composing Services
Printed and bound in Canada by Webcom

CONTENTS

INTRODUCTION

Surprisingly little seems to be known in England about Luigi Pirandello who died in 1946, and of whom *The Times* said: 'It is largely to him that the theatre owes its liberation, for good or ill, from what Desmond MacCarthy called "the inevitable limitations of the modern drama, the falsifications which result from cramming scenes into acts and tying incidents down to times and places." ' Only a few of his major works have been published in English to date and as a result there is a tendency to classify Pirandello as a purely intellectual writer, prone to 'cerebral gymnastics' and most difficult for an actor to intrepret. Those who find him so might first study a little the life of the man and in so doing they may reach a better understanding of Pirandello the dramatist.

Pirandello was born at Caos in Sicily in 1867. He studied letters at Palermo University and later in Rome. For many years he taught at a girls' school, living in comparative poverty and growing steadily unhappier in his work. His marriage ended in disaster when his wife became mentally unbalanced and had to be sent to a mental institution. His literary efforts began with poems, short stories and later he wrote novels; he did not start writing seriously for the theatre until 1915 at the age of forty-eight, after which he gave to the stage no fewer than forty-three plays in Italian and several in Sicilian.

For a number of years he was in charge of his own theatrical company, which had as its leaders Ruggero Ruggeri and Marta Abba, and many of his plays were written as tailor-made articles for them and for the rest of his group. Despite the severe lack of finance, he never succumbed to writing plays which conformed to the style and idiom of the more successful dramatists of his time. He deliberately created anti-heroes. His protagonists are like 'soldiers who have been beaten in their first battle and have no belief in the future!'

Having lost a considerable sum of money with his own company, and become greatly disillusioned because his native Italy considered him 'too original for the box office', (often his plays were translated and performed abroad long before they saw the footlights in their own language) and already in his seventies, Pirandello suddenly announced that Europe had grown too old for him, that it could boast of only one other young brain (Bernard Shaw), and that he would take himself off to a country of new ideas—and then journeyed to America.

Pirandello was a fiery, passionate man who had reached his own particular outlook on life through adversity and years of tortured wondering at the true significance of reality. His primary concern was with the illusions and self-deceptions of mankind and the nature of identity. His works grew—as Eric Bentley points out—'from his own torment, and through his genius they came to speak for all the tormented and potentially to all the tormented, that is, to all men.' He delighted in creating an unusual but logical situation—developing it seemingly illogically—and by continually tossing the coin until both sides had been clearly revealed, managing to convince his audience that his unconventional and not very credible treatment was in fact wholly logical and convincing.

Many of his plays were written in the style known to the Italians as 'grottesco': comedies developed tragically or tragedies developed comically. Nearly all spring from intensely dramatic situations—situations in which passion, love and tragedy make their presence strongly felt.

In England theatre productions of his works have been few and far between, and this may be due partly to the fact that producers and actors, when faced with a play of his, sometimes assume: 'He is going to be far too difficult for the audience so it will be up to us to put that right!' By approaching the text with the preconceived notion that a particular interpretation must shine like a beacon between author and audience in order to elucidate matters, one often succeeds merely in confusing the issue further. There have been examples of this author's brilliantly cynical humour, behind whose mask we are meant to see our own selves, being deliberately distorted to the level of unacceptable farce in an attempt to 'clarify'.

If Pirandello's plays were approached more simply, were permitted to play *themselves* more, and did not have the Latin sentiment and human compassion ironed out by their interpreters, perhaps the fear that one may not be able to follow him would be removed from the minds of many of our theatre-goers. It would be found that his comedies, as Kenneth Tynan wrote: 'wear their fifty-odd years as if they were swaddling clothes', and his works might then find themselves a niche in our commercial theatre.

In presenting the complete dramatic works of Luigi Pirandello, we have attempted to hold to the line of simplicity in translation, avoiding the temptation of so many adaptors to reconstruct the author's statements in the light in which they themselves see them. Many translations offered to us have been by people with little or no knowledge of Italian, who have relied on a commissioned literal translation which they have rephrased in their own style. This is a method which should be severely frowned upon.

ROBERT RIETTY

HENRY IV

Enrico IV

1922

Translated by
Robert Rietty and John Wardle

CHARACTERS

HENRY IV
MARCHESA MATILDE SPINA (Donna Matilde)
FRIDA, her daughter
THE YOUNG MARQUIS CARLO DI NOLLI
BARON TITO BELCREDI
DOCTOR DIONISIO GENONI
LANDOLF (Lolo) ⎫
HAROLD (Franco) ⎪ Four young men employed
ORDULF (Momo) ⎬ to pose as the
BERTOLD (Pino) ⎭ Emperor's 'Counsellors'
GIOVANNI, an old butler
TWO MENSERVANTS dressed in 11th-century costume

The action of the play occurs in an isolated country villa in Italy during the 1920s.

ACT I	The Throne Room
ACT II	Another room in the villa
ACT III	The Throne Room

Enclosed by square brackets in Act I there is a short passage which Pirandello suggested should be omitted in performance in order not to hold up the action.

ACT I

The large hall of the villa. It has been furnished and decorated with great care to suggest a hall that could be the throne room of HENRY IV *in the imperial palace at Goslar. But conspicuous among so much which is antique are two life-size modern portraits in oil. They hang at the back of the room, not much above a ledge in carved wood which runs the whole length of the back wall. The ledge is wide and protrudes so that people can sit on it, as on a long bench. The portraits are on either side of the throne, which is in the middle of the wall. The portraits represent a man and a woman, both young and in fancy dress, the man as* HENRY IV, *the woman as* MATILDE OF TUSCANY. *There are two doors on the right and one on the left.*

When the curtain rises, the TWO MENSERVANTS, *as if startled, jump up from the ledge, on which they have been sprawling full length, and, picking up their halberds, post themselves at the foot of the throne to right and left, afterwards standing there like a couple of statues.*

After a few seconds HAROLD, LANDOLF, ORDULF *and* BERTOLD *come in by the second door on the right. They are young men who are paid by the* MARQUIS CARLO DI NOLLI *to pretend to be 'Privy Counsellors', that is to say vassals of the sovereign who belong to the inferior section of the aristocracy at* HENRY's *court. They are accordingly dressed like German knights of the eleventh century.* BERTOLD, *whose real name is* FINO, *is just starting on the job. The other three, although showing him the ropes, are amusing themselves at his expense. The whole of this opening scene should be acted with feverish vivacity.*

3

LANDOLF (*to* BERTOLD *as if continuing an explanation*): And this is the throne room.

HAROLD: At Goslar.

ORDULF: Or, if you like, at the Hartzburg Castle.

HAROLD: Or at Worms.

LANDOLF: We're kept jumping from one place to the other, according to what particular historical scene we're playing.

ORDULF: Might be Saxony.

HAROLD: Lombardy.

LANDOLF: On the Rhine.

1ST MANSERVANT (*remaining still, moving only his lips*): Psst! Psst!

HAROLD: Yes?

1ST MANSERVANT (*rigid as ever, and sotto voce*): Is he coming or not? (*Referring to* HENRY IV).

ORDULF: He's asleep. Take it easy.

Both menservants relax. The second, after letting out a sigh of relief, stretches himself out on the ledge again.

2ND MANSERVANT: You might have said so!

1ST MANSERVANT (*going down to* HAROLD): Give me a light, will you.

LANDOLF: A-ah! No pipes in here!

1ST MANSERVANT: Don't worry, it's only a cigarette. (HAROLD *produces his lighter.*)

1ST MANSERVANT *lights his cigarette and goes to sprawl on the ledge.*

BERTOLD (*he has been taking things in, half in admiration, half in bewilderment*): But—this room—these clothes . . . I don't understand. He is HENRY IV of France isn't he?

The others laugh at this.

LANDOLF (*egging his companions on to make fun of* BERTOLD): Henry of France! Listen to the man!

ORDULF: So you thought he was Henry the Fourth of France, did you?

HAROLD: Henry IV of Germany, my dear chap. Salic

Dynasty and all that.

ORDULF: The great and tragic emperor.

LANDOLF: Henry IV of Canossa. We wage a terrible war here—between State and Church, day after day.

ORDULF: Empire against Papacy.

HAROLD: Antipope against Pope.

LANDOLF: Kings against anti-kings.

ORDULF: **And** we fight the Saxons.

HAROLD: **And** all the rebel princes.

LANDOLF: Even the Emperor's own sons.

BERTOLD (*holding his head as if to shield it from this avalanche of information*): Of course, of course! I see it now. No wonder I couldn't understand when I found myself in this costume and saw this room. I was right, wasn't I? No one wore anything like this in the sixteenth century.

HAROLD: Sixteenth?

ORDULF: We're bang in the middle of the eleventh!

LANDOLF: Work it out for yourself. If we're outside Canossa, on the 25th of January 1071, then . . .

BERTOLD (*more and more bewildered*): Canossa! But good lord, that place is just a ruin now, isn't it?

ORDULF: It certainly is if you still think you are at the French court!

BERTOLD: But then, I've studied the wrong history!

LANDOLF: My dear fellow, we are four hundred years ahead of you. As far as we're concerned, you aren't even born yet.

BERTOLD (*flaring up*): They damn well ought to have told me it's Henry IV of Germany and not France he's turned himself into. They gave me a fortnight to swot all the facts. God knows how many books I've been cramming—and all for nothing.

HAROLD: But didn't you know when you were going to take poor old Tito's place here, that you were going to play Adalbert of Bremen?

BERTOLD: Adalbert of where? No one told me a blasted thing.

LANDOLF: Well, you see, when Tito died, the young Marquis di Nolli . . .

BERTOLD: That's right. **He's** the chap who engaged me. Why the blazes couldn't he have told me . . .

HAROLD: He may have thought you knew.

LANDOLF: He didn't want to take on anyone else in Tito's place. He thought the three of us who were left would be enough. But **he** started shouting 'They've driven Adalbert away from me.'—You see, he didn't realise poor Tito was dead, and as he thought of him as Bishop Adalbert, the old man assumed he'd been driven away from Court by his rivals the Bishops of Cologne and Mainz.

BERTOLD: I don't understand what you're talking about!

ORDULF: Now take it easy, old boy, take it easy.

HAROLD: The worst of it is we don't know who you're supposed to be, either.

BERTOLD: You don't know who I'm to play?

ORDULF: Well—Bertold, I suppose.

BERTOLD: Bertold who? And **why** Bertold?

LANDOLF: Because **he** started shouting: 'They've driven Adalbert away from me, so now I must have Bertold. I want Bertold.'

HAROLD: We didn't know what he was talking about. We'd never heard of Bertold.

ORDULF: But now you are here . . . so Bertold you are!

LANDOLF: You'll be fine in the part.

BERTOLD (*concerned, making for the door*): Oh no, thank you very much! I'm off.

The others laugh while HAROLD *and* ORDULF *pull him away from the door.*

HAROLD: Easy, easy!

ORDULF: You don't need to look like the original Bertold, even if there was one.

LANDOLF: And if it's any comfort to you, we don't know who **we** are, either. He's Harold, he's Ordulf, I'm Landolf. These are the names he's given us, and we're used to it now. But who knows who we really are. Just names from that period. That's all you'll be too. Just a name from that time. Poor old Tito was the only one we really knew existed. He was

the Bishop of Bremen. He managed to look like one too. He
played the part beautifully.

HAROLD: He never stopped reading about his character.

LANDOLF: And the way he used to dominate His Imperial
Majesty too! Took him in hand, guided, advised him like a
tutor or counsellor. If it comes to that, we're counsellors as
well—'Privy Counsellors', but that's only because it's down
in the history books that Henry IV was hated by his great
nobles because at his Court he surrounded himself with
young men belonging to the petty aristocracy.

ORDULF: Which is us.

LANDOLF: Exactly. Royal small fry! Devoted enough; a bit
dissolute; gay . . .

BERTOLD: Have I got to be gay?

HAROLD: Well . . . shall we say cheerful! Like us.

ORDULF: It's now always easy, believe me!

LANDOLF: It's all such a pity really. Because everything's
here. With these costumes we could mount a lovely
production of some historical play, the kind of thing that
goes down so well in a theatre. And not just one. A dozen
plays. The story of Henry IV could be really well presented.
But what's the use! All four of us and those two clowns there
(*Indicates the* MENSERVANTS)—when they're standing to
attention at the foot of the throne—we're all here with
nothing to do . . . no one to direct us . . . like in a real play. It's
as if—how can I put it?—as if we were all form and no
content. We're worse off than the actual privy counsellors of
the real Henry IV, because, well, I know no one gave them
parts to play either, but at least they didn't know they were
supposed to be acting! What they did they just did. It wasn't
acting, it was simply their life. They looked after their own
interests and didn't give a damn about anyone else! They
sold investitures and heaven knows what. Whereas we—here
we are all dressed up in this fine throne room—with nothing
to do. Like six puppets hanging on the wall, waiting for
someone to take us down, give us our moves and tell us what
to do and say.

HAROLD: Oh come off it. Don't exaggerate! At least we have

to know how to answer him correctly! Don't we? If he says something to you and you aren't quick on your cue with the right answer . . . God help you.

LANDOLF: Well yes, I admit that.

BERTOLD: Oh—that's fine! And how am I to know the right answers when I've been swotting up Henry IV of France and suddenly I'm supposed to know all about Henry IV of Germany?

The three others again laugh.

HAROLD: It's up to you to make up for lost time pretty quick.

ORDULF: Never mind, we'll help you.

HAROLD: You'll find a mass of books in there. You'd better start looking through them.

ORDULF: Yes, you'll soon get the hang of it.

HAROLD: Look at that picture over there. (*He spins* BERTOLD *round to show him the portrait of* MARCHESE MATILDE *on the wall at the back*.) Who's she, for instance?

BERTOLD: That woman? Well, if you ask me, she seems out of place here. Modern paintings among all these antiques!

HAROLD: You're quite right. As a matter of fact, there weren't any pictures here at first. There are niches in the wall behind those two. Statues in the style of the period were going to be put there, but the idea was dropped; so now these two paintings are there to cover up.

LANDOLF (*breaking in*): They certainly would be out of place if they were just paintings.

BERTOLD: What are they then? **Aren't** they portraits?

LANDOLF: Yes if you go and touch them, you'd say they **are** paintings. But to **him** (*Meaning* HENRY IV, *he gestures impressively towards the right*), **he** never touches them   so to him they are just . . . (*He shrugs, searching for the word*).

BERTOLD: Well, what are they to him?

LANDOLF: They're—Mind you, this is only my own idea, but I don't think I'm far out. They're images. Images like—well, reflections in a mirror. This one (*Points to the portrait of* HENRY IV) shows him alive as he is today in this throne room, which is in the style of the 11th century. Surely you can understand? If you were put in front of a mirror now, as you are, in medieval dress, it would still be the real, living you of today dressed up in period costume that you'd see, wouldn't it? Well then, it's as though there were two mirrors right here, reflecting back at us living images which . . . oh, don't you worry, you'll see, you'll see. As you'll be living with us, it'll all come to life.

BERTOLD: I think it'll drive me mad!

HAROLD: What if it does? You'll find it fun!

BERTOLD: How did you get to learn all this?

LANDOLF: My dear fellow, you don't come back through eight hundred years of history to your own time without bringing a bit of experience with you.

HAROLD: Come on, we're wasting time. Don't worry. Trust us; we'll fill you in in no time.

ORDULF: You'll soon learn in this class.

BERTOLD: Well, for God's sake start teaching me at once. At any rate give me the main points.

HAROLD: I'll give you a few hints. He'll give you others . . . and in no time . . .

LANDOLF: We'll join all your loose ends and get you connected. Before you know where you are, you'll be a thoroughly convincing and qualified puppet. Now, let's get on with it (*Takes him by the arm to lead him out.*)

BERTOLD (*resisting and looking at the woman's portrait*): No, wait a moment. You haven't told me who she is. Is she the Emperor's wife?

HAROLD: No. The Emperor's wife is Bertha of Susa, sister of Amedeus the second of Savoy.

ORDULF: And the Emperor can't stand her. He wants to be young with us, so he's thinking of divorcing her.

LANDOLF (*meaning the portrait*): She's his bitterest enemy— Matilda, Marchesa of Tuscany.

BERTOLD: Oh, I know! The one who played host to the Pope . . .

LANDOLF: That's it. At Canossa.

ORDULF: Pope Gregory the seventh.

HAROLD: Yes, our scarecrow. Come on. We'd better be going.

All four are making for the door on the right by which they came in, when the door on the left opens and GIOVANNI, *the old butler, enters. He wears evening dress.*

GIOVANNI (*in a hurry and very agitated*): Here . . . psst! Franco! Lolo!

HAROLD (*stopping and turning*): What do you want?

BERTOLD (*astonished that* GIOVANNI *should come into the throne room in modern dress*): But what—'s **he** doing here?

LANDOLF: A man from the twentieth century! Go away!

ORDULF: He's an emissary of Gregory VII. Get out!

HAROLD: Go on!

GIOVANNI (*defending himself and highly irritated*): Now stop it, will you!

ORDULF: You can't come in here.

HAROLD (*emphatically*): Get out!

LANDOLF (*to* BERTOLD): It's all sorcery, you know! This is some demon conjured up by the Wizard of Rome. Draw your sword! (*He makes as if to draw his own.*)

GIOVANNI (*shouting*): Will you stop fooling! The young Marquis has just arrived, with a lot of other people.

LANDOLF (*rubbing his hands*): Oh good! Any women?

ORDULF: Old or young?

GIOVANNI: There are two gentlemen . . .

HAROLD: But what about the women?

GIOVANNI: The Marchesa Spina and her daughter.

LANDOLF (*incredulously*): What?

ORDULF: The Marchesa? Did you say . . .

GIOVANNI: Yes, yes, the Marchesa!

HAROLD: And who are the men?

GIOVANNI: I don't know.

HAROLD (*to* BERTOLD): They'll be coming with some papal information, you'll see.

ORDULF: All of them envoys from Gregory VII. Well, it will be a bit of a break anyhow.

GIOVANNI: Will you let me finish!

HAROLD: Then get on with it!

GIOVANNI: I think one of the two gentlemen is a doctor. The other is . . .

LANDOLF: Oh—not another doctor!

HAROLD: Bravo, Bertold, you've brought us luck. Now we'll have some fun.

LANDOLF: We'll show this doctor what's what!

BERTOLD: It looks to me as if I've landed right in the soup!

GIOVANNI: Will you listen! They want to come in here. In this room

LANDOLF (*astonished and appalled*): What! Her? The Marchesa in here!

HAROLD: In that case it looks as if we're going to get more than we bargained for!

LANDOLF: I'd say this is where the real tragedy begins!

BERTOLD: Tragedy? Why?

ORDULF (*indicating the portrait*): Because she posed for that portrait of Matilde.

LANDOLF: Her daughter is engaged to the young Marquis di Nolli.

HAROLD: What are they doing here? (*To* GIOVANNI.) Do you know?

ORDULF: If **he** sees her there'll be hell to pay.

LANDOLF: Perhaps he won't recognise her any more.

GIOVANNI: If he wakes up you'd better keep him busy in there.

ORDULF: Oh yes? Don't be funny. How?

HAROLD: He'll go mad!

GIOVANNI: Damn it, by force if necessary! And that's an order! Off with you.

HAROLD: You're right. Let's hope he hasn't woken up yet.

ORDULF: Right, we're going, we're going!

LANDOLF (*to* GIOVANNI, *as he goes off with the rest*): Will you **please** tell me what it's all about?

GIOVANNI (*calling after them*): Lock the door after you and hide the key! (*Pointing to the other door on the right.*) And that door too!

LANDOLF, HAROLD, ORDULF *and* BERTOLD *go out by the second door on the right.*

GIOVANNI (*to the* TWO MENSERVANTS): You two as
well. Out! That way. (*He points to the first door on the right.*)
Lock the door and take the key.

The TWO MENSERVANTS *go out as directed,* GIOVANNI
then goes to the door on the left and opens it to admit the
MARQUIS DI NOLLI.

DI NOLLI: Have you given everyone their orders?
GIOVANNI: Yes, my lord! It's all under control.
DI NOLLI: Good.

DI NOLLI *goes out again for a moment to ask the others to join
him. The first to enter are* BARON TITO BELCREDI *and*
DOCTOR DIONISIO GENONI, *then* DONNA MATILDE
SPINA *and her daughter,* THE MARCHIONESS FRIDA.
GIOVANNI *bows and goes out.* DONNA MATILDE *is about
forty-five; still beautiful and elegant, although it is evident that
she modifies the inevitable ravages of time. The effect of this
make-up is to make her look something like a Valkyrie. Her
mouth however is sad and extremely beautiful—in disturbing
contrast with her other features. She has been a widow for many
years, and has as her friend* BARON TITO BELCREDI, *whom
neither she nor anyone else ever takes seriously, it would seem.
What* TITO BELCREDI *really means to her he alone knows, so
he can afford to laugh if she appears not to know herself. He even
manages to smile when others are amused by her jokes at his
expense. Slim, prematurely grey, though a little younger than the*
MARCHESA, *he has a curiously bird-like head. He would be
extremely lively if his supple agility (which makes him a
formidable swordsman) were not, as it were, sheathed in a kind of
sleepy, Arab like languor, which betrays itself in his nasal and
drawling voice.* FRIDA, *the* MARCHESA's *daughter, is
nineteen. Overshadowed by her imperious and rather too
spectacular mother, she lacks vitality, and in her obscurity she
resents the gossip caused by her mother's behaviour—which
humiliates her more than her mother.* FRIDA *has had the luck to
become engaged to the* MARQUIS CARLO DI NOLLI; *a young
man with a strict conscience. He is tolerant of others, but
dedicated to, and obsessed with, doing the little he believes he can*

that will be of value to society; though perhaps in reality he is not too sure himself just what it is he can do. In any case he is concerned by the various responsibilities he feels are weighing him down. It is as if others, good luck to them, may gossip and amuse themselves, but not he; not because he wouldn't like to but simply because he can't. He is dressed in strict mourning for the recent death of his mother. DOCTOR DIONISIO GENONI has the rubicund and uninhibited face of a satyr, with protruding eyes and a little pointed beard, which shines like silver; he has good manners and is nearly bald. They enter showing traces of concern and almost apprehensively, though at the same time all (except DI NOLLI, of course) look about them with interest. At first they speak in low tones.

BELCREDI: Magnificent. Really magnificent.

DOCTOR: Most interesting. His mania is consistent and logical even to the extent of surrounding himself with the right things. Significant, yes, indeed. Magnificent.

DONNA MATILDE (*who has been looking round for her portrait, sees it and moves towards it.*): Ah, there it is! (*She contemplates it from the right distance, and experiences mixed feelings.*) Yes, there it . . . But . . . How extraordinary! Frida, Frida! Come here and look.

FRIDA: Ah . . . your portrait.

DONNA MATILDE: No! It isn't me! It's you!

DI NOLLI: Didn't I tell you!

DONNA MATILDE: I wouldn't have believed it could be so like her. (*She feels a shiver in her spine and tries to shake it off.*) Frida: (*She puts an arm round* FRIDA *and draws her close beside her.*) Don't you see yourself in me, there?

FRIDA: I don't know . . .

DONNA MATILDE: You don't see the resemblance? How can you possibly miss it? (*She turns to* BELCREDI.) Tito, you look: and tell her.

BELCREDI: No thank you. I refuse to look—on principle!

DONNA MATILDE: Idiot! He thinks he's paying me a compliment. (*She turns to the* DOCTOR.) Doctor, you tell her. (*the* DOCTOR *walks towards the picture.*)

BELCREDI (*pretending to prevent him, surreptitiously*): Psst!

No, Doctor! For God's sake keep out of it!

DOCTOR (*puzzled but smiling*): Why?

DONNA MATILDE: Pay no attention to him. Please come and look. He's insufferable.

FRIDA: He never stops playing the fool. Didn't you know?

BELCREDI (*as the* DOCTOR *resumes his approach*): Watch your feet, watch your feet, Doctor! Your feet!

DOCTOR: My feet? Why on earth should I?

BELCREDI: You've got hob-nailed boots.

DOCTOR: Nonsense.

BELCREDI: Yessir! Mind you don't crush those—tiny glass slippers.

DOCTOR (*laughing*): Rubbish! After all, there's nothing astonishing in a daughter resembling her mother.

BELCREDI: Crash! Now you've done it!

DONNA MATILDE (*overdoing her anger*): What has he done? What on earth are you talking about?

DOCTOR (*mildly*): I thought it was just a harmless truth.

BELCREDI (*answering* DONNA MATILDE): He told you there was nothing to be astounded at, and you appeared to be thunderstruck! I must confess I fail to see why. Isn't it natural that a portrait of you painted all those years ago should be like your daughter as she is now?

DONNA MATILDE (*exasperated*): What a fool you are! Don't you see it's just because it *is* so natural. Because that (*meaning the portrait*) isn't my daughter at all. It's a picture of me. And what so took me aback was to see my daughter when I was expecting to see myself. And (*she is now angry again*) my reaction was genuine. Don't you dare doubt it!

After this outburst—an embarrassed silence. Rather surprisingly, it is FRIDA *who breaks this silence.*

FRIDA (*quietly*): Oh God! Must we always have these arguments about the least little thing?

BELCREDI (*also quietly—and apologetically*): I'm not doubting your mother's sincerity. But what puzzles me is that while this resemblance to you sends your mother off at the deep end, you seem totally unconcerned.

DONNA MATILDE: Well, of course. Because she can't recognise herself in me as I was at her age; whereas I can easily recognise myself in her as she is today.

DOCTOR: Very true. Because a portrait catches a moment and fixes it for ever; for the young lady this is a remote moment and one with no association; whereas for the Marchesa it must recall a host of things that are not in the painting . . . gestures, glances, smiles . . .

DONNA MATILDE: Exactly!

DOCTOR: Naturally you can see yourself again now in your daughter.

DONNA MATILDE: But **he** (BELCREDI) always has to sneer at any genuine emotion I feel—just to infuriate me.

DOCTOR (*dazzled himself by the light of his own explanation, turns to* BELCREDI *and proceeds to lecture him enthusiastically*): Resemblance, my dear Baron, often comes from things we can't explain. And this accounts for the fact that . . .

BELCREDI (*cutting the lecture short*): That someone might even see a resemblance between you and me, my dear Professor.

DI NOLLI: Please—enough of that! We've wasted enough time as it is! (*But he points warningly to the two doors on the right to suggest that someone may overhear unless voices are kept low.*)

FRIDA: We certainly have. When **he's** about (*indicating* BELCREDI) that always happens.

DONNA MATILDE (*quickly*): That's just why I didn't want him to come.

BELCREDI: When I give you so much cause for amusement! There's ingratitude for you!

DI NOLLI: Tito, please! Enough! You know the Doctor is here on serious business and I'm very worried about it.

DOCTOR: Quite, quite. Now first let us get one or two points clear. Donna Matilde, may I ask how this portrait comes to be here? Did you give it to him?

DONNA MATILDE: Certainly not. I could never have done it then. I was Frida's age—and not even engaged. No, I gave it away three or four years after the accident. Your mother begged me to, Carlo.

DOCTOR: And she was **his** sister? (*He nods his head towards the doors on the right, indicating* HENRY IV.)

DI NOLLI: Yes, Doctor. And this visit of ours today is to discharge a debt—a debt I owe my mother. She died a month ago. Otherwise Frida and I would now be cruising on our honeymoon.

DOCTOR: So you put that off?

DI NOLLI: Well, naturally. But the point I'm coming to is that my mother died in the firm belief that her brother—she adored him, you know—was almost cured.

DOCTOR: What made her believe that?

DI NOLLI: I think it was his unusual manner towards her, just before she died.

DOCTOR: Unusual, you say? Well now, it would help me if you could be more explicit. Did your mother tell you what he said to her?

DI NOLLI: Unfortunately not. All I can tell you is that she came home terribly upset after her last visit to him. It appears he had been unusually gentle towards her, as if he sensed somehow that he would not see her again. On her deathbed she made me promise never to neglect him, to see that he should be checked regularly . . . by a specialist.

DOCTOR: I see. Good. Now I must explain something. Often, you know, the merest trifles are enough to . . . This portrait, for example . . .

DONNA MATILDE: Really, Doctor, I don't think we ought to attach too much importance to that. The only reason it affected me as it did was because it's so many years since I've seen it.

DOCTOR: But that is not what I . . .

DI NOLLI (*also interrupting*): It's true, Doctor. That painting has been there a good fifteen years.

DONNA MATILDE: Longer. More like eighteen.

DOCTOR: Do excuse me, but neither of you knows yet what I am trying to ask. I'm relying to a considerable extent, a very considerable extent, on these two portraits. They were painted, I take it, before the famous . . . the, hm, the most unfortunate—cavalcade. Am I right?

DONNA MATILDE: Yes, of course.

DOCTOR: That's to say while he was perfectly sane. What I want to know is, was it his suggestion that you should have your portrait painted?

DONNA MATILDE: Oh, no, Doctor. Most of us who took part in the pageant had one done—just as a souvenir.

BELCREDI: Yes, I had mine done too—as Charles of Anjou.

DONNA MATILDE: As soon as our costumes were ready.

BELCREDI: Because, you see, at first the idea was to hang them all together, in the drawing-room of the villa where the pageant was being held—so as to have a record of the whole thing. But then everyone wanted to keep his own.

DONNA MATILDE: And, as I told you, I handed over mine—not without some regret—when his mother . . . (*Indicating* DI NOLLI.)

DOCTOR: Do you know whether or not **he** requested it?

DONNA MATILDE: Not so far as I know. Possibly—or it may just have been his sister's idea of helping him. She was very fond of him.

DOCTOR: I see. Another thing: was the pageant **his** idea?

BELCREDI (*quickly*): No doctor, it was mine.

DOCTOR: Really?

DONNA MATILDE: Don't listen to him, it was poor Belassi's.

BELCREDI: Belassi's! What are you talking about!

DONNA MATILDE (*still to the* DOCTOR): Count Belassi, poor man. He died a few months later.

BELCREDI: But Belassi wasn't even there when . . .

DI NOLLI (*concerned at the prospect of another argument*): For heaven's sake, doctor, do we have to establish whose idea it was?

DOCTOR: Well, it would certainly help me to . . .

BELCREDI: It was mine, mine, I tell you! Not that I'm proud of it—when I think of the result. Listen, doctor: it came about like this: I remember it perfectly. I was in the club, one evening early in November, looking through a German illustrated magazine—just for the pictures, you understand, because I don't speak German. There was one picture which showed the Kaiser in some university town where he was a student. I can't remember it's name.

DOCTOR: Bonn, Bonn.

BELCREDI: Bonn, yes, that was it, Bonn. He was on horseback and dressed up in that queer outfit that German students wore in medieval times. Behind him, also on horseback, was a bunch of other students—noblemen, of course. It was that picture which gave me the idea. You see, at the club we were already thinking of getting up some sort of pageant on a big scale for the next carnival. So I suggested this historical cavalcade.—I meant it to have a definite shape and purpose—that each of us should represent a particular historical personage—from any century; king, emperor, prince—and have his lady, queen, empress, whatever she was, beside him. And the horses would be in armour of course if it was right for the period. Well, everyone was keen on my suggestion.

DONNA MATILDE: I can only say, my invitation came from Belassi.

BELCREDI: If he said it was his idea he was lying. I tell you he wasn't even in the club that night I made the suggestion. For that matter, neither was **he**. (*Alluding to* HENRY IV.)

DOCTOR: And I suppose **he** chose to represent Henry the Fourth.

DONNA MATILDE: Yes, because I had said I would like to go as the Marchesa Matilda of Tuscany, simply because that's my own Christian name.

DOCTOR: I—er—I'm afraid I don't quite see the connection.

DONNA MATILDE: I'm not surprised. Neither did I at first. But then he said in that case he would be at my feet like Henry the Fourth at Canossa. Well, I know about Canossa, but the truth is I remembered the story only vaguely. So when I looked it up afterwards in order to get the background to the woman, I wasn't exactly pleased to find that I was supposed to be a highly loyal and zealous friend of Pope Gregory VII, taking part in a fierce struggle against the German Empire. But then I understood why he wanted to be

beside me in the procession as Henry IV—because I'd
chosen to appear as his deadly enemy.

DOCTOR: But I still don't understand . . .

BELCREDI: Good lord, doctor, because he was paying court
to her, and she, of course—

DONNA MATILDE (*violently*): Yes, yes, indeed! Especially
just then!

BELCREDI (*with a gesture towards* DONNA MATILDE *for
the* DOCTOR's *enlightenment*): You see! She just couldn't
stand him.

DONNA MATILDE: Oh, that's not true! I didn't dislike him.
Quite the contrary. But you see, as soon as a man wants me
to take him seriously . . .

BELCREDI (*completing it for her*): He gives you striking proof
of what an ass he is.

DONNA MATILDE: No, my dear. Not in his case. He wasn't
nearly such an ass as you.

BELCREDI: But I've never asked to be taken seriously.

DONNA MATILDE: You're telling me! But he couldn't be
teased. (*To the* DOCTOR, *in a different tone.*) Doctor, one of
the misfortunes of being a woman is suddenly to find a pair
of eyes staring at you with the intense promise of eternal
love! (*She laughs rather shrilly.*) There's nothing more
ridiculous. If men could only see themselves with that 'I'll
love you for ever' look! It's always sent me into fits of
laughter. And he couldn't take that! But I must confess, and
I **can** now, after more than twenty years; when I laughed at
him, it was partly to shake off a feeling of fear. Because I
could tell he meant that promise! And that would have been
very dangerous for me.

DOCTOR (*alert with professional interest and concentrating on
a clue*): Ah! I would be particularly interested to know why
you say dangerous?

DONNA MATILDE (*lightly*): Because he wasn't like the rest.
And because I was always—I still am—what shall I call
it?—(*She searches for an unpretentious word.*) impatient of
solemn and over-earnest people. But then I was so young,
you see. I wanted to have my fling, and I felt that to give up

all that would have needed more courage than I possessed.
So I laughed at him too. Afterwards I regretted it. I even
hated myself for it, because I seemed to be laughing at him in
exactly the same way as all those stupid people who made
fun of him.

BELCREDI: Almost as much as they do me.

DONNA MATILDE: People laugh at you, my dear, because
you pretend to be humble! It was very different with him.
And then, people laugh at you to your face.

BELCREDI: Better than behind my back, at any rate.

DOCTOR: Please, please, may we get back to the point.
From what you tell me I gather he was . . . shall we say
excited?

BELCREDI: Yes, doctor, he was, but in an odd way.

DOCTOR: How?

BELCREDI: Quite coldly, almost icily, I'd say.

DONNA MATILDE: Nothing of the sort! He seemed odd
only because he wasn't blasé like the rest of you. He was . . .
he was vital . . . ardent . . . excited . . .

BELCREDI: **Over** excited more likely. But I'll take my oath,
doctor, that sometimes he'd suddenly get a glimpse of
himself at the height of his excitement. As though he could
suddenly see himself from outside. And I'm certain it
worried him a lot. Sometimes he'd be so furious with himself
that he was positively comic.

DONNA MATILDE (*in surprised agreement*): That's true.

BELCREDI (*to* DONNA MATILDE): And I'll tell you why. I
think he would have that flash of lucid perception an actor
experiences when he's playing a role, and this would
instantly detach him from his own personal feeling, which
would then seem to him—not affected, because it was
sincere—but something which he felt it was necessary . . .
how can I put it? . . . to 'intellectualise' . . . in order to
compensate for the real heartfelt warmth he felt he lacked.
And so he improvised, exaggerated, let himself go . . . as it
were, to . . . to stop seeing himself from outside, as I said. To
others it made him seem inconsistent, erratic and—yes, I'll
be frank—sometimes ludicrous.

DOCTOR: And would you say anti-social?

BELCREDI: Not in the least! He was a great one for arranging tableaux vivants, dances, charity shows—just for the fun of it. And he was a damn good actor, I can tell you.

DI NOLLI: And since his madness—he's become quite brilliant. Terrifying.

BELCREDI: He always was. Since that accident when his horse threw him—

DOCTOR: He fell on his head I believe?

DONNA MATILDE: It was horrible, horrible! He was right beside me, and then the horse reared, and there he was on the ground with the horse about to trample on him.

BELCREDI: But at first we didn't think he was seriously hurt. Of course it stopped the procession and things got a bit disorganised—everyone trying to make out what had happened, but by then he'd been carried into the villa.

DONNA MATILDE: You couldn't tell he was hurt. Not a scratch or a drop of blood.

BELCREDI: Everyone thought he'd just fainted.

DONNA MATILDE: And about two hours later he . . .

BELCREDI: I do wish you'd let me finish, I'm coming to that. Yes, about two hours later he came into the drawing room of the villa, where we all were.

DONNA MATILDE: His face was terrible. That's what I noticed at once.

BELCREDI: That's not true. No one realized anything, doctor, I give you my word.

DONNA MATILDE: **You** didn't, of course! You were all behaving like lunatics.

BELCREDI (*with a laugh*): Because we were all acting out our roles; it was part of the game.

DONNA MATILDE: So you can imagine how terrified we were when it dawned on us that he wasn't acting . . . that he was in grim earnest.

DOCTOR: Ah? . . . you mean that by then . . .

BELCREDI: Yes, I'm telling you! He came and joined us. We thought he'd recovered and, seeing what we were doing, had started to play **his** part too, to **act** like the rest of us, or rather, a great deal better, because I've told you what a good actor he was. We thought he was just fooling, you see.

DONNA MATILDE: And some of them in fun began to lash at him with their whips.

BELCREDI: And then—he suddenly unsheathed his sword (after all he was armed like a king) and he hurled himself at some of the men. God, it was terrifying.

DONNA MATILDE: I shall never forget that scene. Our own frightened faces behind our masks—and that awful mask of his which wasn't a mask any longer. It was madness itself.

BELCREDI: Henry IV! Henry IV to the life, and in a fit of fury.

DONNA MATILDE: You know for a whole month he had thought of nothing but that masquerade. It came into everything he did and thought, like an obsession.

BELCREDI: The research he put into it! Down to the smallest details.

DOCTOR: That explains it all. The fall and concussion affected his brain, and what was previously play-acting became reality in his mind. He became—permanently—the person he had been impersonating. Yes. Such accidents can cause people to become unbalanced; or even to go mad.

BELCREDI (*to* FRIDA *and* DI NOLLI): You see, my dears, the tricks life can play on us. (*to* DI NOLLI.) You were four or five when it happened, Carlo. (*to* FRIDA.) And to your mother, Frida, it seems that you have taken her place in that picture, yet it was painted before she even dreamt of bringing you into the world. I've got grey hair—and as for him, poor devil . . . (*Points to the picture of* HENRY IV.)—A blow on the back of the head—and bang . . . he's Henry IV for ever.

DOCTOR (*he has been lost in thought, but now raises his hands and spreads his fingers wide, by way of claiming attention—as if to embark on a scientific explanation*: Now, ladies and gentlemen, what it comes to is this—*he is interrupted by a very angry* BERTOLD *who bursts in from the upper door on the right.*)

BERTOLD: I'm sorry, I didn't mean to . . . (*He stops short, seeing their alarm at his sudden appearance*).

FRIDA (*taking refuge behind the nearest chair*): Oh God, he's here!

DONNA MATILDE (*drawing back in alarm and holding one hand in front of her eyes so as not to see him*): Is it him? Is it him?

DI NOLLI (*quickly*): No, no, calm down.

DOCTOR (*bewildered*): Well who the dickens is he?

BELCREDI: Just an escaping puppet.

DI NOLLI: He's one of the four young men we keep here to humour him in his delusion.

BERTOLD: I beg your pardon, my lord.

DI NOLLI: I should think so! I gave orders that the doors were to be locked and that no one was to come in here.

BERTOLD: Yes, my lord, but I couldn't stand it any longer. I'm giving notice.

DI NOLLI: Oh. You're the new one? You came this morning?

BERTOLD: That's right my lord, and I'm leaving now. I can't take it.

DONNA MATILDE (*to* DI NOLLI *apprehensively*): What does this mean? I thought you said he was perfectly calm now.

BERTOLD (*cutting in*): Oh it's not **him**, your ladyship. It's those other three. Here to humour him you said, my lord? A fat lot of humouring they do! If you ask me, they're the ones who are nuts. I arrive here this morning, and instead of helping me, they . . .

LANDOLF *and* HAROLD *now appear in the same doorway. They seem hurried and upset, but they stop on the threshold to ask permission to enter.*

LANDOLF: May we come in, please?

HAROLD: My lord . . .

DI NOLLI: Oh, come in, come in, for heaven's sake! What **is** all this? What's going on?

FRIDA: I'm getting out of here. I'm frightened.

DI NOLLI (*restraining her*): Frida, please.

LANDOLF (*pointing to* BERTOLD): Marquis, this idiot . . .

BERTOLD: Thanks very much; but this idiot's chucking it.

I'm through.

LANDOLF: Well, I can't say I'm sorry.

HAROLD: He's ruined it all—running out like this!

LANDOLF: It's sent him (HENRY IV) into a rage. We can't
   hold him back much longer. He's ordered us to put him
   under arrest and says he's going to sentence him from the
   throne. What do you want us to do?

DI NOLLI: Do? Lock that door, go and lock it at once!

LANDOLF *closes and locks it.*

HAROLD: But Ordulf can't possibly manage him there on his
   own.

LANDOLF: What about announcing you've arrived, my
   lord? It might take his mind off what's happened. That is, if
   it's settled how we are to present you . . .

DI NOLLI: Yes, yes, that's all arranged. Doctor, are you ready
   to see him now?

FRIDA: I won't. No, Carlo, don't make me! I'm going!
   Mother, you come with me, please, please!

DOCTOR: I say, he's not armed, is he?

DI NOLLI: Of course not, doctor. Frida, darling, don't be so
   childish. After all, you wanted to come.

FRIDA: I didn't. It was Mother.

DONNA MATILDE (*firmly*): And I'm staying. What do we
   do?

BELCREDI: Is it really necessary for us to dress up like this?

LANDOLF: Absolutely   essential,   Baron—unfortunately.
   Look at us. (*Indicating his own costume.*) If he saw you all in
   modern dress, there'd be hell to pay.

HAROLD: He'd think you'd come from the devil.

DI NOLLI: Just as they look dressed up to you, so he'd think
   we were masquerading in these clothes.

LANDOLF: He'd think it was all the work of his mortal
   enemy.

BELCREDI: You mean Pope Gregory VII?

LANDOLF: Yes. He says he's a pagan.

BELCREDI: The Pope? That's a good one.

LANDOLF: Yes, Baron. He says he conjures up the dead,

accuses him of practising black magic. He's scared stiff of him.

DOCTOR: Persecution mania.

HAROLD: He'd be in a terrible rage.

DI NOLLI (*to* BELCREDI): But it isn't necessary for us all to see him, only the doctor. The rest of us can wait outside.

DOCTOR: You mean . . . leave me alone with him?

DI NOLLI: You won't be alone. There'll be these three. (*Indicating the young men.*)

DOCTOR: But didn't the Marchesa want to . . .

DONNA MATILDE: Of course. I want to be here too. That's why I've come—to see him again.

FRIDA: But why, Mother, why? Oh, do come with us!

DONNA MATILDE (*arrogantly*): Allow me to do as I please. I tell you this is why I have come. (*to* LANDOLF.) I shall be Adelaide, his mother-in-law.

LANDOLF: Good. The Empress Bertha's mother. That's excellent. It will be enough, Marchesa, if you wear the ducal crown and a cloak to hide everything else. Harold, go and get them.

HAROLD: Wait a bit. What about this gentlemen? (*Meaning the* DOCTOR.)

DOCTOR: Oh, yes. Didn't we say I should be a Bishop . . . Bishop Hugo of Cluny?

HAROLD: Abbot, I think you mean, sir. Abbot Hugo of Cluny.

LANDOLF: But Hugo's been here a lot.

DOCTOR (*disconcerted*): What?

LANDOLF: Doesn't matter. It's a quick disguise . . .

HAROLD: We've often used it before.

DOCTOR: But . . .

LANDOLF: There's no danger he'll remember. He's more interested in the clothes than the people wearing them.

DONNA MATILDE: That's just as well for me too, then.

DI NOLLI: Come, Frida, we'll go. Tito, you come with us.

BELCREDI: No—if she stays I stay.

DONNA MATILDE: But I don't need you. Really.

BELCREDI: I may not be of much use, but I want to see him

too. What's wrong with that?

LANDOLF: If I may say so, I think it might be as well if you did stay, Baron. Three might be better than two.

HAROLD: How are we going to dress him?

BELCREDI: Haven't you got something handy?

LANDOLF: I know. A Cluniac monk.

BELCREDI: What might that be?

LANDOLF: The Benedictine habit they wear in the Abbey of Cluny. You'll be a monk in attendance on Monsignore. (*to* HAROLD.) Right. Go and see to it. (*to* BERTOLD.) And you too, and don't let him see you for the rest of the day. No, wait! He'll (*slight gesture towards* HAROLD.) give you the clothes and you bring them back here. (*to* HAROLD.) And you go to **him** (HENRY IV.) and announce the arrival of the Duchess Adelaide and Monsignor Hugo of Cluny. Got it?

HAROLD: Right. Come on, Bertold.

HAROLD *and* BERTOLD *go out by the first door on the right*

DI NOLLI: We'll disappear then. Come, Frida. (*He and* FRIDA *go out, left.*)

DOCTOR (*to* LANDOLF): I hope that as Hugo of Cluny I shall be well received?

LANDOLF: Don't worry. The Monsignore has always been treated here with the greatest courtesy. And you too, Marchesa. He'll welcome you. He's never forgotten the time he was kept waiting in the snow for two days—frozen stiff—and it was only thanks to you two that he was finally admitted to the Castle of Canossa and the presence of Gregory VII, who all that time had refused to receive him.

BELCREDI: And what about me, if you don't mind my asking?

LANDOLF: You, Baron? I think you'll have to stay respectfully out of the way.

DONNA MATILDE (*in nervous irritation*): Go away altogether you mean.

BELCREDI (*quietly, but angry*): You've got yourself into a state!

DONNA MATILDE: I am what I am! Leave me alone!

BERTOLD *returns with their costumes.*

LANDOLF: Ah, here are your costumes. Thanks, Bertold. This is your cloak, Marchesa.

DONNA MATILDE: One moment. Let me take my hat off. (*She does so and holds it out for* BERTOLD *to take.*)

LANDOLF (*to* BERTOLD): All right; take it away. (*Then, offering to fit the crown on* DONNA MATILDE.) May I?

DONNA, MATILDE: Good heavens, isn't there a mirror in here?

LANDOLF (*pointing to the door on the left*): There are several out there. Perhaps you'd rather put it on yourself.

DONNA MATILDE: I would prefer to. Give it here. I won't be a second. (*She takes back her hat from* BERTOLD *and goes out with him. He takes the crown and the cloak. In the meanwhile the* DOCTOR *and* BELCREDI *get into their Benedictine garb as best they can.*)

BELCREDI: I must say I never thought I'd turn into a Benedictine monk. This madness of his must be costing a fortune!

DOCTOR: I'm afraid madness is expensive!

BELCREDI: When you've a fortune to go with it!

LANDOLF: Yes, gentlemen, we've a whole wardrobe out there, all costumes of the period, copied to perfection from actual dresses of the day. It's my special responsibility; I go to all the theatrical costumiers. We spend quite a lot.

DONNA MATILDE *re-enters wearing the cloak and crown.*

BELCREDI (*in admiration*): Oh, magnificent! Truly regal.

DONNA MATILDE (*bursts out laughing at the sight of him*): My God what a sight! You look like an ostrich dressed up as a monk!

BELCREDI: What about the doctor?!

DOCTOR: What does it matter?

DONNA MATILDE: The doctor doesn't look so bad, but you really look ridiculous.

DOCTOR (*to* LANDOLF, *considerately changing the subject*): Do you often get visitors up here?

LANDOLF: It depends. Sometimes he'll issue a command that a certain person he brought to see him. Then we have to find someone who's willing to act the part. Ladies too.

DONNA MATILDE (*not pleased with this information, but not wishing to show it*): Really? Ladies too?

LANDOLF: Yes, Marchesa. At first there were a lot.

BELCREDI (*laughing*): That's wonderful. Were they dressed up too?

LANDOLF: Yes, but they were not the sort of ladies you would approve of . . .

BELCREDI: You mean 'welcome' pinned across them. I see. (*to* DONNA MATILDE, *miraculously*.) Did you hear that, Marchesa?

The upper door on the right opens and HAROLD *enters. He first makes a gesture of warning the others to stop talking, and then he announces solemnly:*

HAROLD: His Majesty the Emperor.

Enter first the TWO MENSERVANTS, *who take up their posts one each side of the throne. Then comes* HENRY IV, *followed by* ORDULF *and* HAROLD *who walk slightly behind him.* HENRY IV *is nearly fifty, extremely pale, and already grey at the back of the head; but at the forehead and temples he is fair, where he has used an obvious dye. In comic contrast to his tragic pallor is a doll-like dab of colour on each cheek. Over his royal robes he wears the sackcloth of a penitent, as at Canossa. His eyes have an agonised fixed stare. This tortured look is at odds with his general bearing, which is that of one who wishes to display humble repentance almost too obviously as though he wanted people to realize the humiliation is far from deserved.* ORDULF *bears the imperial crown in both hands.* HAROLD *has charge of the sceptre with the eagle and the orb with its cross.*

HENRY IV (*bowing first to* DONNA MATILDE *and then to the* DOCTOR): Your Grace . . . Monsignore. (*He sees* BELCREDI *and is about to bow to him too, but turns to* LANDOLF *and asks in an uneasy undertone.*) Who is that? Peter Damiani?

LANDOLF: No, Sire, he is only a monk from Cluny who came in attendance on the Abbot.

HENRY IV (*turns and scrutinises* BELCREDI *with growing mistrust, and then, noticing that* BELCREDI *is looking irresolutely from* DONNA MATILDE *to the* DOCTOR, *as if asking for a clue as to how he should behave, he draws himself up and shouts*): It is Peter Damiani! There is no need for you to look at the Duchess in that manner, Father. (*He turns quickly to* DONNA MATILDE *as if to fend off some danger.*) I swear to you, my lady, I swear to you that my heart has changed towards your daughter. I confess that if Damiani here had not come to forbid me in the name of Pope Alexander, I would have repudiated her. Oh, yes, there were some who were ready to support me in the divorce. For the price of 120 farms the Bishop of Mayence would have agreed. (*Sensing an unspoken warning from* LANDOLF, *and almost muttering to him.*) Yes, yes, I know. This is no time for me to be speaking ill of the bishops. (*Humbly, he turns back to* BELCREDI.) Believe me, I am grateful to you now, Peter Damiani, truly grateful that you prevented it. My life has been one long humiliation—my mother, Adalbert, Tribur, Goslar—and now this sackcloth you see me wearing. (*His tone suddenly changes as if—in a lucid moment, he were giving himself directions on how to play his part.*) No matter. Clearness of mind, perspicacity, firmness of attitude and patience in adversity. (*Now he addresses everyone on a note of sober penitence.*) I must put right the wrong I did. I humble myself before you, Peter Damiani. (*He bows deeply and remains in that position, as if gripped by a sudden suspicion which forces him to add in a threatening tone, half against his will.*) Provided of course it was not you who invented the obscene lie that my sainted mother committed adultery with Bishop Henry of Augsburg.

BELCREDI (*as* HENRY IV *still remains bowed, but with a finger pointing at him in accusation, he puts both hands on his breast in denial*): I never said such a thing. Never!

HENRY IV (*rising*): No? Truly? (BELCREDI *shakes his head,* HENRY IV *stares at him for a moment.*) I don't think you are capable of it. (*He goes to the* DOCTOR, *gives his sleeve a little friendly tug, and asks with a sly smile.*) It's always the mysterious 'them' to blame, isn't it, Monsignore.

HAROLD (*in a prompting whisper*): Yes of course! Those rapacious bishops.

DOCTOR (*trying to carry off the part, but looking at* HAROLD *for approval*): What's that? The bishops? Oh, yes, yes, of course.

HENRY IV: Nothing ever satisfied them. I was just a poor little boy, Monsignore, playing with toys to pass away the time. I did not know I was a king. I was six when they took me away from my mother. They made use of me against her and even against the power of the dynasty. They profaned everything. Thieves all of them, each one greedier than the other—Hanno worse than Stephen, Stephen greedier than Hanno.

LANDOLF (*softly, changing the subject*): Your Majesty . . .

HENRY IV (*quickly turning to him*): Yes, you are right. This is not the time to talk ill of the bishops. But Monsignore, this infamous libel on my mother goes beyond everything! (*He looks at* DONNA MATILDE, *and his tone softens.*) And I cannot even weep for her, my lady. You will understand for you have a mother's heart. About a month ago she came all the way from her convent—just to visit me. Now they tell me she is dead. (*A long pause filled with emotion, then he smiles sadly.*) And I cannot even weep for her, because, if you are here now and I wear *this (he looks down at the sackcloth)* that means I'm only twenty-six years old.

HAROLD (*gently*): In that case she must still be living, Your Majesty.

ORDULF: Still in her convent.

HENRY IV: True, true! I can postpone my grief for another time. (*Almost conquettishly he draws* DONNA MATILDE's *attention to his dyed hair.*) Look! My hair keeps its gold. (*Then quietly, as if in confidence.*) That is just for you. I don't really need it, though I admit a little external evidence is useful. It defines the boundaries of time, if you follow me, Monsignore! (*He turns again to* DONNA MATILDE,

staring at her hair.) Ah, but I see that you too, Duchess . . .
(*He winks and gestures expressively.*) Ah . . . you Italian
women! (*As much as to say 'artificial', but not in contempt,
rather in mischievous admiration.*) God forbid that I should
be disillusioned or even surprised. We all wish for the
impossible. None of us can bear to admit that some
inscrutable and fatal power sets limits to our will. We are all
born and we all must die. Did you ask to be born,
Monsignore? I did not. And in between birth and
death—neither of which is of our desiring—so many other
things happen which we all regret, but which we are
powerless to do anything about. We can only resign
ourselves to the inevitable.

DOCTOR (*just for something to say while he studies him
attentively*): Too true, too true.

HENRY IV: And if we refuse to resign ourselves, out come the
hopeless desires. A woman wishes she were a man—an old
man wants to be young again. None of us either lies or
pretends. There is so little one can say. We are all of us
genuinely and unshakeably convinced that our fine conception of ourselves is the true one. But, Monsignore, while you
stand firm in your own conception, grasping your holy habit
with both hands, down your sleeve, something is slipping
away, slithering like a snake. Life, Monsignore, life! You're
astounded to see it escaping like that, before your very eyes.
You're furious, angry with yourself. And full of remorse—
especially remorse! That was the worst part of it for me,
Monsignore: the remorse! Seeing a face which I recognised
as my own, yet it was so horrible I was forced to turn my eyes
away. (*He turns to* DONNA MATILDE.) Has it never
happened to you, my lady? Have you always been the same
in your own eyes? Were you always above reproach? What
about that particular day when you . . . (*He pauses, staring
hard at her.*) How could you do such a thing? (*His glance is so
intent that she turns pale.*) I see you know what I refer to. But
don't worry, I shan't tell anyone. And as for you, Peter
Damiani . . . how could you befriend such a man?!

LANDOLF: Your Majesty . . .

HENRY IV (*quickly*): Don't worry. I won't say his name! I
know how it upsets him. What do you think, Damiani? Let's
hear **your** opinion. I say we all—no matter what opinions
others may have—we all hold firmly to our own conception
of ourselves—just as some people, when growing old—dye
their hair. What does it matter if this dye does not fool
you—and you are aware it's not my real colour. You, my
lady, certainly don't dye your hair in order to deceive
others—or even yourself . . . but in order . . . shall we say . . .
to cheat your image in the mirror—just a little. I do it for
fun—you do it in all seriousness. But I tell you that—
however serious you may be—you too are wearing a mask!
And I don't mean the venerable crown on your head—
before which I bow—or your ducal robe. I simply mean the
memory you wish to retain forever: and the memory of the
beautiful golden hair which was once your pride and
delight—and which you'd like to make permanent by
artificial means. Or of the dark hair—if your hair was dark . .
The fading image of your youth. On the other hand, you
Peter Damiani—look on the memory of what you
were—and what you *did* as merely a figment of a past
life—like a dream. Isn't that so? Well—that's how it is for me
too . . . a dream—and when I think of it now—I understand
it less than ever. What of it? It's not so astonishing, Peter
Damiani: the way we live today will seem like that
tomorrow. (*Suddenly—in anger—he grasps the sackcloth he
is wearing.*) And as for this sackcloth . . . ! (HAROLD *and*
ORDULF *are alarmed by the fierce glee with which he seems
about to tear it off, and rush to restrain him.*) By God! . . . (*He
backs away from them and takes off the sackcloth, shouting.*)
Tomorrow at Brixen twenty-seven German and Lombardian
bishops will sign with me the deposition of Gregory
VII—He's no pope, he's an evil monk!

ORDULF: For heaven's sake, Your Majesty!

HAROLD (*encouraging him to put the sackcloth on again*): Sire,
you shouldn't say such things!

LANDOLF: The Monsignore and the Duchess came to
intercede for you. (*Surreptitiously he signals to the* DOCTOR

to say something.)

DOCTOR (*confused*): Ah, yes. Yes, of course. To . . . to
intercede for you.

HENRY IV (*suddenly contrite, almost terrified, allowing the*
THREE YOUNG MEN *to help him back into the sackcloth*
and pulling it to him convulsively): Pardon, oh pardon,
Monsignore, pardon! Pardon, my lady . . . Already I feel the
weight of the excommunication upon me. (*He bends down,*
shielding his head with his hands, as if expecting something to
crush him. He remains like that for a moment, then whispers
confidentially to LANDOLF, HAROLD *and* ORDULF.)
Somehow, I don't know why, I can't humble myself before
him. (*With a furtive gesture towards* BELCREDI.)

LANDOLF (*sotto voce*): But why do you persist in taking him
for Peter Damiani, Sire, when we have told you he is not?

HENRY IV (*with a frightened look at* BELCREDI): Are you
sure?

HAROLD: He's just a poor monk, Your Majesty.

HENRY IV (*sadly and with a sigh of frustration*): Ah, we can't
control ourselves when we react instinctively. As a woman,
perhaps you can understand me better than the others.

N.B. PIRANDELLO SUGGESTS THE FOLLOWING PASSAGE IN BRACKETS
SHOULD BE OMITTED IN PERFORMANCE:

HENRY IV: [This is a solemn and decisive moment. I could
now, as I speak, accept the help of the Lombard
bishops—kidnap the Pope, and lock him up here in the
castle; I could rush to Rome and elect an anti-pope; I could
make an alliance with Robert Guiscard—Gregory VII
would be lost! But I resist the temptation, and, believe me, I
am wise to do so. I recognise the spirit of our times, and the
majesty of one who bears himself as a true Pope. Do I sense
you want to laugh at me? You'd be unwise to do so. It would
prove you had not understood that I wear this penitent's
sackcloth for political reasons. I tell you, tomorrow our roles
could be reversed. Then what would you do? Would you
scoff at the Pope because he was a prisoner? No. We'd be

equals then. I—masquerading as a penitent today—he as a prisoner tomorrow. And woe to him who does not understand how to wear his mask, be he King or Pope. Perhaps he seems to be acting a little too cruelly at this moment. Yes, maybe that's all it is.]

HENRY IV: My lady, your daughter Bertha ... I told you my heart has changed towards her ... (*He turns on* BELCREDI *with sudden anger, as if the man had contradicted him, and shouts in his face:*) Changed, changed! Because of the love and devotion she has shown towards me at this terrible time. (*He tries to curb his anger and groans with remorse. Then turns to* DONNA MATILDE *in gentle and sad humility.*) She has come with me, my lady; she's down there, in the courtyard. She chose to follow me on foot like a beggar woman. And she is cold, frozen, after two nights in the open ... in the snow. You are her mother. That alone should move you to mercy and to join with the abbot here (*indicating the Doctor*) in pleading to the Pope for my pardon. If he'd only grant me an audience.

DONNA MATILDE (*trembling, and almost inaudibly*): Of course. At once.

DOCTOR: We'll plead with him, Your Majesty.

HENRY IV: And another thing. (*He beckons them to come close, then adds secretively.*) It is not enough that he should receive me. You know there's nothing he cannot do. Nothing! He can even call up the dead! (*He beats his breast.*) I'm a witness to that! He's a master of magic! Well, Monsignore, my lady—my real punishment is in myself (*he taps his breast, then points to his portrait, as if in fear*) or rather in THAT! For I can't free myself from this magic. I am repentant now, and I swear to you both that I shall remain penitent until he has received me. But I beg you, after he has lifted my excommunication, you must implore the Pope to grant me one other thing in his power—to separate me from that (*he points to the portrait again*) so that I may live my own life, for he makes it impossible for me! I can't go on being twenty-six years old for ever, my lady! I beg this for your daughter's sake as well, so that I may love her as she deserves, and as I yearn to do now that she has proved her devotion to me. I have finished. That is all. I am in your hands. (*He bows.*) My lady! Monsignore! (*He is about to leave by the doorway through which he entered, but, noticing* BELCREDI *has crept forward to listen, and imagining he is going to steal the imperial crown from the throne, he runs to pick up the crown, stuffs it under his sackcloth, and—a sly smile on his lips and in his eyes—turns to bow to each, then goes.* DONNA MATILDE—*overwrought—collapses into a chair, on the point of fainting.*)

CURTAIN

ACT II

Another room in the villa, next to the throne room, austerely furnished in antique style. To the right, about eight inches above floor level, there is a raised platform with a wooden rail and supporting pillars. There are steps leading up to it from the front and side. On the platform are a table and five small period chairs. The main entrance is at the rear.

To the left are two windows looking out on the garden, to right a door to the throne room. It is late afternoon on the same day as Act I.

DONNA MATILDE, *the* DOCTOR *and* TITO BELCREDI *are in the room. The two men are in the middle of a conversation, but* DONNA MATILDE *stands apart, gloomy in expression and evidently annoyed by what the other two are saying, though she cannot help listening to them, because in her present state of uneasiness everything they say interests her in spite of herself, preventing her from working out something which has just occurred to her and which both shocks and attracts her. Because of this she instinctively feels a need not to follow out her thoughts so that she does not miss a word of their talk.*

BELCREDI: You could be right, doctor. I was only giving you my impression.

DOCTOR: I don't say you're wrong, but I think it's no more than an impression.

BELCREDI: And yet, he said so himself—quite clearly. Didn't he, Marchesa?

DONNA MATILDE (*distracted*): Said what? Oh, yes, he did. But not for the reason you think.

DOCTOR: He saw through our disguise—your robe (*To the* MARCHESA.), our Benedictine habits. It's all too childish.

DONNA MATILDE (*interrupting him, indignantly*): Childish! What do you mean, doctor?

DOCTOR: From one point of view. Let me explain, dear lady. Medically speaking, it is more complex than you can possibly imagine.

DONNA MATILDE: It's perfectly clear to me.

DOCTOR (*with the indulgent smile of the expert to the amateur*): I appreciate that, but one needs to understand the psychology of mad people. You can be quite certain a madman is aware—fully aware—of any disguise worn in his presence, and that he sees through it, and yet he accepts it: just as children, for whom it's both game and reality. That's why I say all this is childish. But at the same time it is extremely complex—for he must, you see, be perfectly conscious of being an image, confronting himself—that framed image in there! (*Meaning the portrait in the throne room.*)

BELCREDI: He said so himself.

DOCTOR: Precisely. An image before which other images appear: ours, do you follow me? Now in his mania—which is sharply perceptive and in its way logical—he has quickly detected the difference between our images and his. That is to say that our images are a pretence. That made him distrustful. Every madman protects himself by means of

constant and unremitting suspicion. But that's all. It's too
much to expect him to appreciate that we are playing this
game—his game—for his own sake. And **his** game seems to
us all the more tragic for—suspicious as he is—he felt
challenged to expose it—do you follow me? Yet part of **his**
game was to appear before us wearing make-up and dyed
hair and then saying he had done it for fun.

DONNA MATILDE (*breaking out again*): No, doctor, no!
That's not it! That's not it at all!

DOCTOR: What is it then?

DONNA MATILDE (*her voice vibrant with conviction*): I am
perfectly certain that he recognised me!

DOCTOR   (*together*): ⎱ Impossible, impossible!
BELCREDI   ⎰ Oh, come!

DONNA MATILDE (*with still more conviction and intensity*): I
tell you he recognised me! When he came close to me, and
stared straight into my eyes—he recognised me!

BELCREDI: But he was talking about your daughter . . .

DONNA MATILDE: No—me! He was talking about me!

BELCREDI: Well perhaps, when he said . . .

DONNA MATILDE (*in full steam, regardless of* BELCREDI):
About my own dyed hair. But didn't you notice how quickly
he added 'Or, of your brown hair—if your hair was brown.'
He remembered perfectly well that in those days my hair **was**
brown.

BELCREDI: Oh, nonsense!

DONNA MATILDE (*paying no attention to him, turning to the*
DOCTOR): My hair really **is** brown, doctor, like my
daughter's. That's why he began talking about her.

BELCREDI: But he doesn't known her—he's never seen her.

DONNA MATILDE: That's just it! Oh, you never understand
a thing! By my daughter he meant me—me as I was then.

BELCREDI: God—this madness is catching!

DONNA MATILDE (*with quiet scorn*): **Must** you be such a
fool?

BELCREDI: But you were never his wife. In his lunatic world
it's your daughter who is married to him: Bertha of Susa.

DONNA MATILDE: Exactly. Because I'm no longer dark, as

he remembers me, but blonde, like this. And I presented myself to him as Adelaide, the mother of Bertha. My real daughter doesn't exist for him—he has never seen her—you said so yourself. How should he know whether she's blonde or brunette?

BELCREDI: But he was only generalising when he said 'dark'. Just as people do when they describe their remembrance of youth . . . as dark or fair. He was generalising. But as usual, you have to go and dramatise the whole thing. Doctor, she says I shouldn't have come, but she's the one who should have stayed away.

DONNA MATILDE (*at first perceptibly shaken by* BELCREDI's *argument, she seems thoughtful for a moment then recovers herself and insists, because of her doubts*): No—no he meant me. All the time he was talking to me, with me, about me . . .

BELCREDI: I like that! You say he was talking about you all the time! Didn't you hear him attacking **me**? Did you think he meant **you** when referred to Peter Damiani?

DONNA MATILDE (*challengingly, and with embarrassing frankness*): Who knows? Can you tell me why he took a dislike to you from the first moment? You and you only. Immediately.

The tone of her question makes it clear that the implied answer is 'Because he realised that you are my lover.' BELCREDI *understands immediately and shelters behind a fatuous smile.*

DOCTOR: If I may suggest . . . The reason could also be that only the Duchess Adelaide and the Abbot of Cluny were announced. So when he saw a third person with them who had not been announced, he immediately became suspicious.

BELCREDI: Exactly, and because of that, he took me for an enemy—Peter Damiani. But she will have it that he recognised her . . .

DONNA MATILDE: There is no doubt about it. I saw it in his eyes, doctor. That unmistakeable look of recognition that comes into someone's eyes when they really do remember you. It may only have been for a split second, but it was there.

DOCTOR: We can't rule it out: a lucid moment perhaps . . .

DONNA MATILDE: Perhaps. But then . . . everything he said seemed full of regret for my youth and his—for the horrible thing that happened, and which left him stuck with that mask. That mask from which he longs to escape—but he simply can't.

BELCREDI: Right. So that he can love your daughter— or you, if you insist—because he seems to have been touched by your feeling for him.

DONNA MATILDE: Which is very real, believe me.

BELCREDI: So we see, Marchesa. So real, a mystic would label it a miracle.

DOCTOR: May I be allowed **my** say? I don't deal in miracles because I'm a doctor. I listened very carefully to everything he said, and I repeat that the elasticity of perception which characterises all forms of consistent mania is in his case very—how can I put it?—relaxed. In other words, the elements of his mania are no longer rigid. I think that just now he is slowly readjusting himself beneath his outer personality through experiencing sudden surges of memory, which pull him (and this is very encouraging) not out of a state of incipient apathy, but rather from smooth complacency into moods of reflective melancholy, which show— believe me, they do—really considerable cerebral activity. Well, now this violent shock we have planned for him . . .

DONNA MATILDE (*turning to the window, and speaking like a complaining invalid*): Why isn't the car back yet? It's been three and a half hours!

DOCTOR (*startled*): What's that you say?

DONNA MATILDE: The car, doctor, the car! It's been more than three and a half hours.

DOCTOR (*getting up and looking at the clock*): So it has. More than four by this clock.

DONNA MATILDE: It should have been back in half an hour at the most. But, as usual . . .

BELCREDI: Perhaps they can't find the dress.

DONNA MATILDE: But I told them exactly where it was!

(*Impatiently*.) Frida would . . . Where **is** Frida?

BELCREDI (*leaning out of the window*): I expect she's in the garden with Carlo.

DOCTOR: He'll be calming her fears.

BELCREDI: She's not afraid, believe me, doctor. She just thinks it's a bore.

DONNA MATILDE: Well, please don't argue with her. I know what she's like.

DOCTOR: We must be patient a while. Remember, it will all be over in a moment, but we must wait till it gets dark. As I was saying, if we succeed in giving him a shock, and if by means of this violent shock we break the already slackened threads which still bind him to his fantasy, in this way giving him back what he begs for ('I can't go on being twenty-six for ever, my lady', he said.)—if we give him release from this punishment which he himself terms a punishment: well, in short, if we manage to make him regain in a flash an awareness of the passage of time . . .

BELCREDI (*at once*): He will be cured. (*Ironically*.) We'll have set him free.

DOCTOR: Like a watch that has stopped at a particular time. Yes, we hold that watch patiently in our hands till that precise time comes round again, and then give it a shake, hoping it will start up again and keep the correct time—even though it had stopped for so long.

At this moment DI NOLLI *enters from the main door.*

DONNA MATILDE: Oh, there you are, Carlo. Where's Frida?

DI NOLLI: She's coming; she'll be here in a moment.

DOCTOR: Is the car back?

DI NOLLI: Yes.

DONNA MATILDE: Good. With the dress?

DI NOLLI: It's been here some time.

DOCTOR: Excellent. Excellent.

DONNA MATILDE (*trembling*): Where is the dress? Where is it?

DI NOLLI (*with a shrug and a wry smile—he is taking part against his will in a game which he considers to be in bad taste*): You'll see soon enough. (*He points to the door by which he entered.*) There you are.

BERTOLD *appears on the threshold and ceremoniously announces:*

BERTOLD: Her Highness the Marchesa Matilde of Canossa.

FRIDA *enters, looking magnificent and extremely beautiful in the eleventh-century costume her mother wore as the Marchesa Matilde of Tuscany. She is the living image of the portrait in the throne room*

FRIDA (*with assumed condescension, as she passes the bowing BERTOLD*): Of Tuscany, of Tuscany, please! Canossa is just one of my castles.

BELCREDI (*struck with admiration*): Just look at her! She's transformed!

DONNA MATILDE: It's me! Don't you see? Stop, Frida. You see?—my portrait come to life.

DOCTOR: Yes, yes. Absolutely perfect. She **is** the portrait.

BELCREDI: Yes, there's no doubt about it. And such style!

FRIDA: Don't make me laugh for goodness sake or I'll burst. What a tiny waist you had, Mother! I had to breathe out before I could squeeze into the thing.

DONNA MATILDE (*fussing with the dress*): Wait a bit . . . Stand still! These pleats might let out. Is it really so tight as all that?

FRIDA: It's cutting me in two! Do let's get it over with quickly, for heaven's sake!

DOCTOR: We have to wait till nightfall.

FRIDA: Oh, no, please! I can't hold out till then!

DONNA MATILDE: But why did you put it on so soon?

FRIDA: I simply had to. The temptation was irresistible.

DONNA MATILDE: You might at least have let me know. I could have helped you. It's all crumpled. Oh, dear!

FRIDA: I know, Mother. But they're old creases. They'd be difficult to get out.

DOCTOR: Don't worry, Marchesa. The illusion is perfect. (*His gesture suggests she should take up a position a little in*

front of her daughter without entirely masking her.)
Look—stand about here—a little distant from her. Good.
Just a little further forward . . .

BELCREDI: To hint at the passage of time?

DONNA MATILDE (*to* BELCREDI): Twenty years after!
It's frightening.

BELCREDI: Let's not exaggerate.

DOCTOR (*embarrassed and trying to set things right*): No, no,
no, not at all. I meant . . . I mean it's because of the
costume—I want to see how . . .

BELCREDI (*with a laugh*): Oh, the costume. That's not twenty
years, doctor. More like eight hundred. It's an abyss. Do you
really think he can leap over it in one go? (*He points first to*
FRIDA, *then to the* MARCHESA.) From here to there?
You'll have to pick up the pieces afterwards. Now
look—let's all think seriously. For us it's just a matter of
twenty years, two costumes, and a masquerade. But for him,
as you yourself have told us, doctor, time has stood still. If he
is living in Frida's day with her—eight hundred years ago—I
tell you the sheer vertigo of the leap will be such that when he
drops down here among **us** . . . *The* DOCTOR *shakes his
head.* You disagree?

DOCTOR: I do. Because, my dear Baron, life will carry on.
This life here—**our** life—will immediately become real for
him too. It will take hold on him at once, tear away illusion
and reveal to him that the eight hundred years you talk about
are merely twenty. It's a trick . . . in a way like the Masonic
initiation: the leap into space, which seems vast, but is really
only the depth of a stair tread.

BELCREDI: Well put, doctor, but I'm not convinced. Look at
Frida and the Marchesa. Who is the more advanced? The
young people think they are, but they're wrong. We're ahead
because we've lived longer.

DOCTOR: If only our past didn't force us so far apart from
each other.

BELCREDI: But it doesn't. How should it? If Frida and Carlo
have to go through what we have already; grow old, making
more or less the same stupid mistakes that we've made . . .

This is the common fallacy; that we leave this world by a door ahead of the one by which we entered life. It isn't true. As soon as we are born we begin to die, so whoever is born first is ahead of everyone else, and the youngest of all is Adam! Look at the Marchesa Matilda of Tuscany there! Eight hundred years younger than us all.

DI NOLLI: Stop playing the fool, Tito.

BELCREDI: You think I'm fooling?

DI NOLLI: Yes. Ever since we came here.

BELCREDI: How can you say that! When I've even dressed up as a Monk.

DI NOLLI: You forget that we came for a very serious purpose.

BELCREDI: Serious for the others—I agree. Serious for Frida here, for instance . . . (*Breaks off and turns to the* DOCTOR.) But doctor, honestly, I still haven't understood what it is you want to do.

DOCTOR (*ruffled*): Well, you'll see. Just leave things to me. I know what I'm doing. When the Marchesa is dressed like that too.

BELCREDI: Why? Has she also got to . . .

DOCTOR: Of course, of course. We have another dress for her out there for when it comes into his head that he is in the presence of the Marchesa Matilda of Canossa . . .

FRIDA (*although talking quietly to* DI NOLLI, *she notices the* DOCTOR'*s mistake*): Tuscany, Tuscany.

DOCTOR (*irritably*): Oh, what's the difference!

BELCREDI: I see! Now I begin to follow . . . If he finds himself confronted with two of them . . .

DOCTOR: Exactly. Two of them. And then . . .

FRIDA: Doctor (*Taking him aside with* DI NOLLI.) I would like you to explain something to us.

DOCTOR (*hurrying over*): Certainly, certainly. Delighted to explain anything.

BELCREDI (*quietly to* DONNA MATILDE): I say you know, look here . . .

DONNA MATILDE (*facing him squarely*): Now what's the matter?

BELCREDI: Are you really set on all this? I mean taking part in this showdown? It's an extraordinary thing for a woman to do.

DONNA MATILDE: For some women perhaps.

BELCREDI: No, no, my dear, for any woman. It's quite a sacrifice.

DONNA MATILDE: Even if it is, I owe it him.

BELCREDI: Oh come off it! You know perfectly well no one's going to think any worse of you for that.

DONNA MATILDE: Then where's the sacrifice?

BELCREDI: Because even if others don't care—it certainly offends me.

DONNA MATILDE: And who cares a fig about you?

DI NOLLI: I think we'd better get started, don't you. Bertold—go and call one of those three men.

BERTOLD: Yessir. (*Goes out through the main door*).

DONNA MATILDE: First we have to pretend to take leave of him, don't we?

DI NOLLI: That's right. I'll send one of those three to let him know you're going. (*To* BELCREDI.) You needn't bother. You stay here.

BELCREDI (*shakes his head ironically*): No, of course, I needn't bother. I needn't bother!

DI NOLLI: I don't mean it that way. I want to avoid his getting suspicious again, that's all.

BELCREDI: Oh yes of course—just leave me out altogether.

DOCTOR: We must make him certain, absolutely certain that we have gone away.

LANDOLF *and* BERTOLD *enter from the door on the left.*

LANDOLF: May we come in?

DI NOLLI: Yes, come in, come in. Now then, your name is Lolo, isn't it?

LANDOLF: Lolo, or Landolf, as you please.

DI NOLLI: Good. Now listen: the doctor and the Marchesa will take their leave of him, formally.

LANDOLF: Very good, my lord. All they need to say is that they have prevailed on the Pope to receive him. Right now he's pacing up and down his room, groaning repentance for all he's said, and despairing of forgiveness. I'm afraid I have to ask you to put on your costumes again.

DOCTOR: Yes, yes, of course. We were just going to. Come along. (*To* DONNA MATILDE.)

LANDOLF: Just a moment. May I make a suggestion? Could you add that the Marchesa Matilda of Tuscany begged you to persuade the Pope to give him an audience?

DONNA MATILDE: That means he **did** recognise me!

LANDOLF: No, madam. It doesn't. It's just that he fears the hostility of this Marchesa because she entertained the Pope in her castle. Mark you—I find it strange in view of the fact . . well—I happen to know a little of the history of that period—although I'm sure not as much as you . . . There's no mention anywhere of Henry IV having been secretly in love with the Marchesa of Tuscany?

DONNA MATILDE (*promptly*): Not a word. On the contrary, he hated her.

LANDOLF: I thought as much. But he says he was once in love with her; he's always saying that. And now he's afraid that she senses this secret love of his and that her contempt for it may make her influence the Pope against him.

BELCREDI: Then it's up to you to persuade him there's no longer any hostility on her part.

LANDOLF: Excellent. I'll do that.

DONNA MATILDE (*to* LANDOLF): I agree. (*Then to* BELCREDI.) In case you don't know, it's historical fact that the Pope gave way only because the Marchesa and the Abbot of Cluny pleaded for him. (*maliciously.*) And another thing, my dear Belcredi, it may interest you to know that when this pageant started I meant to use that historical fact in order to show him that I was by no means so averse to him as he thought.

BELCREDI: Well done, Marchesa. You certainly know your history.

LANDOLF: Indeed. And at that rate madam could spare herself the trouble of a double disguise and be presented with Monsignore as the Marchesa of Tuscany.

DOCTOR (*protesting at once*): Oh God no!—The confrontation must come as a shock! It must be sudden. That would ruin everything. Come now, Marchesa, we must be ready. You'll be the Duchess Adelaide again—mother of the Empress. And we'll take our leave of him. It's imperative he believes we've gone. Now let's not waste any more time. There's so much to do.

The DOCTOR, DONNA MATILDE *and* LANDOLF *go out by the door on the right.*

FRIDA: I'm beginning to feel frightened.

DI NOLLI: Not again, Frida.

FRIDA: I wouldn't be if I'd seen him first.

DI NOLLI: But you're worrying unnecessarily. Believe me.

FRIDA: Are you sure he's not violent?

DI NOLLI: Of course. He's as gentle as a lamb.

BELCREDI (*ironically, with mock sentimentality*): But oh **so** sad. Didn't you hear he's in love with you?

FRIDA: Thank you very much. That makes it worse.

BELCREDI: He won't do you any harm.

DI NOLLI: It will all be over in a moment.

FRIDA: I know, but I have to be in the dark . . . with him . . .

DI NOLLI: Only for a moment. And I'll be close by. The others will be just the other side of the door, ready to rush in. You see, as soon as he's face to face with your mother, you'll have nothing more to do.

BELCREDI: I'm afraid it'll all be a waste of time.

DI NOLLI: Now don't you start! It sounds like an excellent cure to me.

FRIDA: I agree. I'm sure it'll work. I feel all excited.

BELCREDI: But madmen, my dears, (even though they themselves are not aware of it) often possess a kind of happiness we are unable to grasp.

DI NOLLI (*irritated*): Happiness? What on earth are you talking about?

BELCREDI: The inability to reason.

DI NOLLI: What's reason got to do with it?

BELCREDI: Because he'll have to use his reason when he sees

Frida and her mother, if our plan is to work. Remember—it's we who thought up the whole thing: not he!

DI NOLLI: But where does reasoning come into it? We are merely confronting him with a double image of someone he's invented himself, as the doctor says.

BELCREDI (*a sudden outburst*): You know, I've never understood why those people take degrees in medicine.

DI NOLLI: Who?

BELCREDI: Psychiatrists.

DI NOLLI: Well what on earth should they take degrees in?

FRIDA: Exactly! If they're going to become psychiatrists!

BELCREDI: Yes, but in law, my dear, in law. It's all poppycock! And the more they drivel the better they're taken to be. 'Analogical elasticity!' 'Awareness of the perspective of time!' And the first thing they all say is that they can't work miracles—just when a miracle is the very thing one needs. But they know very well that the more they tell you they aren't magicians, the more you'll be impressed by them. Oh no—they don't work miracles . . . but they always manage to land on their feet!

BERTOLD (*who has been looking through the keyhole of the door on the right*): They're coming. They're coming this way.

DI NOLLI: In here?

BERTOLD: And I think he's coming too. Yes, he is, he is!

DI NOLLI: Right. We'll get out. Come on. Quick. (*He turns to* BERTOLD.) No, not you. You stay here.

BERTOLD (*not liking it*): Must I?

He gets no answer. DI NOLLI, FRIDA *and* BELCREDI *go out quickly through the main exit, leaving him anxious and bewildered. The door on the right opens. The first to enter is* LANDOLF, *who stops, turns, and bows swiftly. Then come* DONNA MATILDE, *in ducal robe and crown, as in the first act, and the* DOCTOR, *as the Abbot of Cluny, with—between them—*HENRY IV *in complete imperial regalia.* ORDULF *and* HAROLD *bring up the rear.*

HENRY IV (*continuing a conversation*): How on earth could I be so cunning when they say I'm obstinate.

DOCTOR: Oh, no! Not obstinate! Good lord, no!

HENRY IV (*with a strange smile*): Then in your opinion I really am cunning?

DOCTOR: No, no . . . neither obstinate nor cunning!

HENRY IV: Monsignore! (*He pauses, and then continues in a tone of gentle irony as if to indicate that matters could not quite be like that.*) Monsignore, as obstinacy and cunning hardly go together, I was hoping that since you deny me the one, you would at least concede me a little of the other. I assure you I need it. But if you are resolved to keep it all for yourself . . .

DOCTOR: Are you inferring that I am cunning?

HENRY IV: Oh no, Monsignore, not in the least. What a strange question. If you will excuse me I would like a word in private with her grace the Duchessa. (*He leads DONNA MATILDE a little apart and asks urgently but in a whisper.*) Do you really love your daughter?

DONNA MATILDE (*puzzled*): Of course . . .

HENRY IV: And do you wish me to atone to her with all my love and devotion for the grievous wrong I have done her? Though you must not believe that I have been dissolute, as my enemies say.

DONNA MATILDE: I have never believed that.

HENRY IV: Then is that what you wish me to do?

DONNA MATILDE: What?

HENRY IV: To love your daughter again? (*He looks at her intently and then adds suddenly in a tone that expresses both warning and fear.*) Whatever you do, don't make friends with the Marchesa of Tuscany. Don't make friends with her!

DONNA MATILDE: But I told you she begged and implored the Holy Father for your pardon as urgently as we have done.

HENRY IV (*with a shudder, quietly*): Don't tell me! Don't tell me! In the name of God, madam, can't you see how it upsets me!

DONNA MATILDE (*she looks penetratingly at him, then speaks softly, confidentially*): You still love her?

HENRY IV (*dismayed*): Still? How can you know? No one

knows. No one must.

DONNA MATILDE: Perhaps she knows, since she has begged so hard for you.

HENRY IV (*stares at her, before speaking*): So you do love your daughter? *Brief pause, then he turns to the* DOCTOR, *with a laugh:* Yes, Monsignore, it's true I scarcely knew I had a wife until after . . . late in the day. Very late. And even now, I hardly ever think of her. I can't really believe in her existence. It may be a sin . . . but she has no place in my heart. The strange thing is that her mother doesn't really care for her either. Admit it . . . all she can talk of is the other woman! . . . (*He grows more and more exasperated.*) And with a persistence that I am utterly at a loss to understand.

LANDOLF (*respectfully*): Perhaps, Your Majesty, she does that to make you feel you are mistaken in your opinion of the Marchesa of Tuscany. (*Immediately embarrassed at his words.*) I mean of course, the opinion you held before.

HENRY IV: So you too feel she acted like a friend to me.

LANDOLF: She is doing so now, Your Majesty.

DONNA MATILDE: Exactly. That's why . . .

HENRY IV: I understand. It's clear you don't believe I love her. (*Raises his hand to deter her from interrupting.*) Oh yes, oh yes. He one has ever believed, not even suspected it. So much the better. Now enough of it. (*Again stopping her.*) Enough! (*He turns to the* DOCTOR. *His mood changes.*) Monsignore . . . have you heard under what conditions the Pope is prepared to revoke my excommunication? They have nothing, nothing whatever to do with the reason for imposing it in the first place. Tell Pope Gregory that he and I will meet again at Brixen. And you, my lady, what message would you wish me to send to your daughter, should you chance to meet her in the courtyard of the Marchesa's castle? Tell her to come here. Let us see if I can keep her here, as wife and Empress. Many women have come before me, pretending to be your daughter—the wife I knew I had—yes, and even sought sometimes—I was not ashamed of her. But they all—these women—who said they were Bertha, Bertha of Susa—they all, I cannot say why, giggled as they said it.

(*Confidentially.*) You see—in bed—both us of naked . . . Well, why not, for heaven's sake! A man and a woman, what is more natural? At such a time we lose awareness of who we are, with our clothes dangling on hangers . . . like ghosts—like dreams . . . (*His tone changes though remaining confidential.*) You know, Monsignore . . . in my view, dreams are no more than stirrings of the sub-conscious which we are unable to chain within the bounds of sleep. They come to us sometimes when we are awake too, and they frighten us. At night I am really scared of them when they take shape before me . . . like mocking figures who have jumped off their horses. Sometimes I'm even afraid of my own blood pulsing through my veins in the silence of the night—like footsteps in a far off room. But, forgive me, I have kept you standing here far too long. I wait upon your ladyship. My respects, Monsignore. (*He accompanies them to the main doorway, bidding them goodbye and acknowledging their bows. MATILDE and the DOCTOR go out. He closes the door, then turns around abruptly, completely changed.*) The clowns! Buffoons! (*He laughs*) It's like playing a piano with colours instead of notes. Touch the keys and—white, red, yellow, green appear. And as for that other idiot . . . Peter Damiani. I caught him out nicely! He didn't dare show his face again. (*As all this pours from him in a feverish torrent, he walks about excitedly. Looking around, his attention is caught by BERTOLD, who is both dumbfounded and terrified by this sudden transformation. HENRY IV pulls up in front of him, derisively pointing him out to the other three.*) Look at this imbecile here, staring at me with his mouth open! (*He shakes him by the shoulder.*) Don't you understand? Don't you see how I force them to dress up and solemnly appear before me at will. They are only petrified that I might tear off their masks and reveal their disguise for what it is! As if it wasn't I who made them put it on in the first place and dance the fool before me.

LANDOLF: What!   (*Looking at each
HAROLD: What's he—   other in
ORDULF: Good lord, what's he saying?   amazement.*)

HENRY IV (*turns on them imperiously*): That's enough! I'm
bored with it all! (*Then he quickly goes on as if he can neither
shake it off nor believe it.*) My God, the impudence of it! To
come before me, dragging her lover with her! And
pretending to be so compassionate in case their appearance
should upset a poor lunatic who's already detached from life
. . . from this world. Did they imagine **he** would submit to
their persecution—if it weren't that he could secretly laugh
at it all?! They always expect everyone to behave as **they**
would wish . . . that every second of each day will be lived out
as they dictate? That's not persecution?!—Oh no . . . that's
merely their way of thinking . . . of feeling! Well—to each his
own. Even you! But what **is** your way? To be sheep?
Uncertain, feeble? So that they take advantage of that . . . to
make you submit to their will, so that you feel and see as they
do! But that's part of their illusion. For, after all, what do
they succeed in imposing on you? Words . . . words . . . which
everyone understands and uses in his own way. That's how
so-called current opinion is formed. And heaven help
anyone who some fine day finds he's been labelled with one
of these words which everyone repeats. 'Mad', for instance,
or 'half-wit'. But, tell me, how would you take it if you
discovered someone was busy trying to persuade others that
you are as he sees you—to have you classified for all time in
their minds as mad. 'Mad'! I am not telling you this now that
I'm pretending to be mad . . . but before I fell from my horse
and got concussion. (*He stops suddenly as he sees the others
become agitated and nervous.*) Why do you look at each other
like that? (*He mimics their expression.*) Well?—have you
made up your minds? Am I or am I not? Have it
whichever way you want! Very well—I **am** mad! (*His
expression becomes frightening.*) On your knees, by God! On
your knees! (*He forces them to kneel, each in turn.*) I order
you to kneel in front of me, and touch the floor with your
forehead—three times! Every one must bow before madmen. (*As he stares at the four kneeling figures his savage
merriment turns to scorn.*) Get up you sheep! Why did you
obey me? You could have put me in a strait jacket. To crush a

man like that . . . with a single word! To use words so
callously . . . like swatting a fly . . . yet that single word can
destroy a man for ever. Dead weight. Do you seriously
believe Henry IV is still alive?—Yet I can give you orders.
You are alive . . . which is how I want you to be. Do you
imagine this is all a practical joke? The dead dictating to the
living! Yes—in here—it **is** a joke . . . a game . . . But go
outside, into the living world. Day is dawning. Time lies
before you. 'This day which is about to begin . . . we will
shape it ourselves' you say. But will you? You'll go on
observing every custom . . . all the old traditions! And when
you open your mouths, you'll repeat the same old platitudes.
Do you call that living? You're just chewing the cud left by
the dead! (*He stops in front of* BERTOLD, *who by now is
completely stunned.*) You don't understand a thing, do you?
What's your name?

BERTOLD: Me? Oh—er—Bertold.

HENRY IV: Idiot! What do you mean 'Bertold'. Just between
you and me . . . what's your real name?

BERTOLD: Well—er—to tell you the truth, it's Fino.

HENRY IV (*he turns on the others, noticing them making
warning signs to* BERTOLD): Fino, eh?

BERTOLD: Yessir, Fino Pagliuca.

HENRY IV: I've heard you call each other by your real names
so often when you're by yourselves. You're called Lolo,
aren't you?

LANDOLF: Yes, sir. (*In delighted realisation.*) Oh, thank
God, then you're . . .

HENRY IV (*brusquely*): What?

LANDOLF (*immediately faltering*): Nothing, I mean . . .

HENRY IV: That I'm not mad? Of course I'm not. Can't you
see?—Now we can all laugh behind the backs of those who
believe I am. (*to* HAROLD.) Your name's Franco, I know.
(*to* ORDULF.) And yours is—wait a bit . . .

LANDOLF: Momo.

HENRY IV: Yes, that's it—Momo.

LANDOLF: But then . . . oh God! . . .

HENRY IV: Then nothing! We five can have a good, long

laugh together! (*He laughs loudly himself while the others look at each other in dismay and ask each other: 'Is he cured?' 'Is it true?' 'Do you think he's really sane?'*) Stop whispering! (*to* BERTOLD.) You didn't laugh, did you? Are you still angry with me? Don't be. I wasn't talking about **you**. You see it suits everyone that certain people should be considered mad—it's an excuse for locking them up. And do you know why they want them locked up? Because they can't bear to hear them talk. Suppose I were to say of those people who just left that one's a whore, one's a dirty libertine, and the third's an imposter. 'Not true—not true' people would say. No one would believe it. But they'd all stand there listening to me in horror. I'd like to know why if what I say isn't true. Of course no one would believe a word of what a madman says! Yet that wouldn't stop them listening to me with their eyes wide open in fear. Why? Tell me why? You see I'm quite calm now.

BERTOLD: Perhaps because—because they think that . . .

HENRY IV: No, no, no, my dear boy, look me straight in the eye! I'm not saying it **is** true—don't be alarmed. Nothing is true. But look into my eyes.

BERTOLD: Well then?

HENRY IV: You see? You see yourself . . . there's fear in your eyes—because at this moment I seem mad to you. There's the proof of what I'm saying! (*He laughs loudly.*)

LANDOLF (*emboldened by exasperation*): What proof?

HENRY IV: Your dismay when you think I'm mad. You do believe it. You believed it all along—didn't you? Yes or no? (*He holds their gaze and realizes they are frightened.*) You see? You're terrified. You feel the earth might give way under your feet, taking away the very air you breathe. Believe me, I understand you my friends: how else can you feel before a madman? Before a man who shakes to the foundations everything you've built up within and around yourselves. But that's to be expected. Madmen construct without logic—good for them—or with a cockeyed logic of their own. Totally inconsistent. Never the same two days running. You hang on to your own beliefs. They don't. They are wholly capricious. To you certain things are not possible. For them—everything is possible. "But that's not true," you say. Why? Because it's not true for you—or you—or you—or a hundred thousand like you. But then let's examine what does seem real to those hundred thousand, whom no one considers mad. What a wonderful show they make with their common agreement and their wonderful logic. When I was a child, I believed that the reflection of the moon in a puddle was the real thing. So many things seemed real to me. I believed whatever they told me—and I was happy. God help you if you don't cling with all your might to what seems true to you today—even if what you believe tomorrow contradicts what was true for you yesterday. God help you if your thoughts get fixed on that terrible thing which can readily drive you out of your mind. If you were to find yourselves as I once did: looking into someone's eyes—and seeing yourself mirrored there: and suddenly realize it's not really yourself! No, you see yourself as a beggar at a gate you may never enter. Whoever is able to—it will not be you with your inner world of things you alone can see and touch—but someone you don't even know . . . seeing and touching **you** in his own impenetrable world.

A long pause. It has grown darker, and now—in the gloom, the masqueraders seem to have become even more perplexed and alarmed, increasingly removed from the great Masquerader—a lonely figure, absorbed in the contemplation of a terrible sadness—not his alone—but of all mankind. Then he shakes off his mood—and looks around as if he could not see the others present.

HENRY IV: It's got dark in here.

ORDULF (*promptly*): Would you like me to get the lamp?

HENRY IV (*ironically*): Oh yes, the lamp. Do you think I don't know that as soon as I've turned my back on you and gone off to bed with my oil lamp, you switch on the electric light for yourselves—here and in the throne room too? I pretend not to notice.

ORDULF: Oh, well in that case, shall we . . .

HENRY IV: No, no, it would blind me. I want my own lamp.
ORDULF: Right. It's just behind the door. (*He goes out through the main door and returns at once carrying an antique oil lamp.*)
HENRY IV (*takes the lamp and points to the table on the platform*): Good. A little light. Sit there: round the table. No, not like that. Not so stiff. More relaxed. (*He arranges them in position. To* HAROLD.) You like this . . . (*to* BERTOLD.) And you like this . . . That's better. And me here . . . (*Turning his head to face a window.*) We ought to be able to order a nice moonbeam. She's a great help to us, the moon. To me at all events. I need her a lot. I'm often lost to everything else, looking up at her from my window. To look at her up there, who would believe that she knows eight hundred years have passed and that I, seated at my window and gazing at her like any poor nobody, cannot really be Henry IV? But look: what a magnificent picture we make! 'Nocturne': the Emperor with his trusty counsellors. Don't you like it?
LANDOLF (*in an undertone to* HAROLD, *not wishing to break the spell*): Do you realize . . . if we had known it was all make-believe . . .
HENRY IV: What was make-believe?
LANDOLF (*hesitant and apologetic*): Oh nothing. It's just that . . . well, this morning I was saying to Bertold here while we were showing him the ropes . . . that it was a pity that, dressed as we are and with so many other fine costumes in the wardrobe . . . and . . . and a hall like the throne room . . .
HENRY IV: Well? What was a pity?
LANDOLF: Oh . . . er . . . just that we couldn't . . .
HENRY IV: Play this out for real?
LANDOLF: Well, we thought . . .
HAROLD (*coming to his assistance*): That it was all true.
HENRY IV: And isn't it? Don't you believe it **is** true?
LANDOLF: Well if you say that . . .
HENRY IV: I say that you are a pack of fools! You ought to have acted out the fantasy for yourselves, not just for me and any occasional visitors; but like this, as you are now, natural

and yourselves. Day after day, for no one but yourselves. (*He takes* BERTOLD *affectionately by the arm.*) Of course your part in the fiction would have been just to eat and sleep here and scratch yourself if you felt an itch. (*He turns back to the others.*) But you ought to feel that you are truly living in the year 1100 here in the court of your Emperor Henry IV. And you should tell yourselves that at a distance of eight centuries from our own remote, buried history—way ahead in time, men of the twentieth century are torturing themselves in agony and anxiety to find out what lies in store for them and what their future will bring. While you, meantime are here—with me—in history. However sad my lot, whatever bitter events have shaped my life, it is all history. Nothing can change it. Nothing. It is all fixed for ever. And you may sit there in peace and quiet—observing how every effect follows obediently on its cause with perfect logic. Every event takes place—precisely and coherently—in each tiny detail. The satisfaction of history is all there for you to enjoy.

LANDOLF: Magnificent! Magnificent!

HENRY IV: Magnificent, yes, but now it's over. Now that you know, I can no longer go on. (*He picks up the lamp and is about to go to bed.*) Nor, for that matter, could you, if you have not understood the reason I've lived like this till now. Oh God—I'm sick of it. (*Almost to himself, in restrained anger.*) By God I'll make her sorry she came here! Dressing up as my mother-in-law! And **he** as an Abbot!—Dragging a doctor along with them to examine me. Hoping to cure me?—the fools! But I must at least have the pleasure of slapping one of them in the face. That clown! Famous swordsman is he? He'll run me through? We shall see, we shall see. (*There is a knock at the door.*) Who is it?

VOICE OF GIOVANNI: Deo gratias.

HAROLD (*joyfully—at the thought of playing yet another joke*): Oh, it's Giovanni, coming to play the little old monk as usual.

ORDULF (*rubbing his hands*): Oh, good! Let's make him go through the old routine!

HENRY IV (*suddenly stern*): You fool! Don't you understand?

How dare you make fun of a poor old man who plays his part only out of love for me?

LANDOLF (*to* ORDULF): It must seem for real, don't you understand?

HENRY IV: Exactly. For real! That is the only way to stop truth becoming a mockery. (*He goes to the door, and admits* GIOVANNI, *who is dressed as a humble friar carrying a scroll of parchment under his arm.*) Come in, Father, come in. (*He assumes a tone of tragic gravity and gloomy resentment.*) All the evidence of my life and reign which was favourable to me was deliberately destroyed by my enemies. The only thing which has survived is this account of my life put down on paper by a humble monk who is devoted to me.—And you'd make fun of him? (*He turns affectionately to* GIOVANNI *and invites him to sit at the table.*) Sit here, Father. Here. Take the lamp. (*He places the lamp he's carrying on the table, near to* GIOVANNI.) Now write, Father.

GIOVANNI (*unrolls the parchment and prepares to write from dictation*): I am ready, Your Majesty.

HENRY IV (*dictating*): The peace decree proclaimed at Mainz benefited the poor and the oppressed as much as it frustrated the wicked and powerful. (*The curtain begins to fall.*) It brought wealth to the farmer, hunger and poverty to the latter . . .

CURTAIN

ACT III

The throne room is dark. The back wall is just visible. The canvases have been removed from the two picture frames, and in their place stand FRIDA, *in the Marchesa of Tuscany costume she wore in Act II, and* CARLO DI NOLLI, *dressed as* HENRY IV. *Both have assumed the exact postures of the portraits.*

When the curtain rises the stage seems empty. Then the door on the left opens and HENRY IV *enters carrying the lamp and turning to call back to the* FOUR YOUNG MEN *who supposedly are in the adjoining room with* GIOVANNI, *as at the close of Act II.*

HENRY IV: No. Stay there. I can manage. Good night.

He closes the door and, weary and dispirited, begins to cross the hall, making for the door up Right, leading to his personal apartments. As soon as FRIDA *sees that he has gone a little way past the throne, she whispers from her niche—she is scared and not far from fainting.*

FRIDA: Henry!

He stops abruptly, as if he felt a knife in his back and, turning in alarm to peer at the wall behind him, instinctively raises an arm, as if to defend himself.

HENRY IV: Who's there?

It is not really a question, but an exclamation of fright, expecting no reply from the darkness and terrible silence of the hall. He is struck with the sudden fear that perhaps—after all—he really is mad.

Although his frightened reaction does nothing to calm her own fears, FRIDA *nevertheless calls him again . . . a little louder.*

FRIDA: Henry!

But, while doing her best to play the part she is supposed to, she cannot help craning forward a little from her niche and looking towards the other to make sure DI NOLLI *is still there.*

HENRY IV shouts out in horror and drops the lamp. Covering his head with his hands, he tries to flee.

FRIDA (*jumps from the frame to the ledge screaming like a mad woman*): Henry! Henry! Oh, I'm scared! I'm scared!

Meanwhile DI NOLLI *also leaps onto the ledge and from there to the floor. He runs to* FRIDA, *who continues to scream uncontrollably and is on the point of fainting. From the door on the left all the others rush in—the* DOCTOR, DONNA MATILDE *(also dressed as the Marchesa of Tuscany),* TITO, BELCREDI, LANDOLF, HAROLD, ORDULF, BERTOLD, GIOVANNI. *One of them promptly switches on the electric light, which has a strange effect in the room and comes from bulbs hidden in the ceiling.* HENRY IV *stands watching. Although jolted out of his momentary terror by this unexpected invasion, his whole body is still shaking. The others pay no attention to him, but crowd solicitously round* FRIDA, *who, held by* DI NOLLI, *is also still trembling and sobbing. Everyone talks confusedly.*

DI NOLLI: It's all right, Frida, I'm here. Everything's all right.

DOCTOR: Well, it's over. Good.

DONNA MATILDE: He's cured, Frida! Don't you see? He's cured.

DI NOLLI (*incredulous*): Cured?

BELCREDI: It was all a joke! Nothing to be worried about!

FRIDA: I'm scared. I'm scared!

DONNA MATILDE: But there's nothing to be frightened of. Look at him. He wasn't mad at all.

DI NOLLI: Are you telling us he's cured?

DOCTOR: So it appears, although in my opinion . . .

BELCREDI: But he **is**, he **is**! They told us all about it. And they should know. (*He means the* FOUR YOUNG MEN.)

DONNA MATILDE: Yes, he's been all right for some time. He confessed it to them.

DI NOLLI (*as angry as he is astonished*): But only a moment ago . . .

BELCREDI: It was all an act. He only wanted to have a laugh at our expense. And in good faith, we . . .

DI NOLLI: I can't believe it! Do you mean he even deceived his own sister right up to her death?

During this exchange, HENRY IV *has remained apart, looking at each in turn as they rain abuse on him, for clearly they believe it has all been a cruel joke. The look in his eyes would indicate that*

*he is contemplating revenge, although he has not yet decided the
shape of that revenge. DI NOLLI's accusation has stung him
deeply and he decides to behave as though the fiction they have
created were actually true. He shouts at his nephew:*

HENRY IV: Go on! Don't stop!

DI NOLLI (*startled*): Go on? What do you mean?

HENRY IV: It is not only **your** sister who is dead.

DI NOLLI: **My** sister! I said **your** sister . . . whom you
compelled to come here as Agnes your mother, right to the
end.

HENRY IV: And was she not **your** mother?

DI NOLLI: Of course she was my mother!

HENRY IV: For me your mother died centuries ago, and far
away. You all jump down from your niche up there . . . as
though you had just been born. How would you know that I
might have mourned her for years—in secret—even though I
am dressed as you are.

DONNA MATILDE (*in consternation, looking at the others*):
What's he talking about?

DOCTOR (*studying him closely, with concern*): Gently, gently,
for God's sake!

HENRY IV: What am I talking about? I am asking you all if
Agnes was not the mother of Henry IV. (*He turns to* FRIDA
as if she really were the Marchesa of Tuscany.) You—of all
people—ought to know, Marchesa.

FRIDA (*terrified, clinging to* DI NOLLI): No! I don't, I don't,
I don't!

DOCTOR: It's his madness coming back. You must avoid
exciting him.

BELCREDI (*contemptuously*): Madness my foot! He's play
acting again!

HENRY IV (*quickly*): Am I? It's **you** who have staged this
scene, and emptied those niches. And as for him . . . standing
before me as Henry IV.

BELCREDI: This stupid game has gone on long enough!

HENRY IV: Game! Do you suppose it's a game?

DOCTOR (*angrily*): Don't provoke him, for God's sake!

BELCREDI (*ignoring the doctor's plea*): I know it is. They admitted it. (*Indicating the* FOUR MEN.)

HENRY IV (*turning to look at the* FOUR YOUNG MEN): You? Did you say it was a game?

LANDOLF (*nervous and embarrassed*): No, no. Truly. We only said you were cured.

BELCREDI: Oh, for crying out loud let's put an end to this once and for all! (*to* DONNA MATILDE.) Don't you think the sight of you and him (DI NOLLI) is becoming intolerable? It's so childish!

DONNA MATILDE: Oh, shut up! What does it matter who's wearing what if he's really cured!

HENRY IV: Yes, I am cured. (*to* BELCREDI.) But that doesn't mean the story is ended quite so simply. (*Aggressively.*) Do you realize that for twenty years no one has ever dared to appear before me dressed like you and this gentleman here? (*The* DOCTOR.)

BELCREDI: I know. Actually this morning I dressed up before you as . . .

HENRY IV: As a monk.

BELCREDI: And you took me for Peter Damiani. And I didn't even laugh—because I believed that . . .

HENRY IV: . . . that I was mad. And does it make you laugh now that you know I'm sane, and you see her dressed up like that? Aren't you forgetting that in my eyes, the way she looks now . . . (*He breaks off with a sudden gesture of contempt.*) Oh never mind. (*He turns swiftly to the* DOCTOR.) You're a doctor?

DOCTOR (*startled*): Eh? Yes—yes, I am.

HENRY IV: And it was your idea to dress her up as the Marchesa of Tuscany? Do you realize, doctor, that you ran the risk of plunging my mind back into that abyss of darkness . . . by making those paintings come to life and jump out of their frames! (*His gaze falls on* FRIDA *and* DI NOLLI, *and then it shifts to the* MARCHESA *and finally he looks at the clothes he is wearing.*) Excellent, excellent. Two perfect facsimiles. Bravo, doctor! Splendid shock treatment. But to Belcredi it just seems a carnival out of date, doesn't it?

(*He now turns to face* BELCREDI.) Well, I'll get rid of my own fancy dress now. Then I can come away with you, can't I?

BELCREDI: With me? You mean with all of us.

HENRY IV: Where shall we go? To the club? Tails and white tie? Or shall we just spend a cosy evening together at home with the Marchesa?

BELCREDI: Wherever you like. I'm sure you won't want to stay on here alone now, living in this world of make-believe you've created since that unlucky carnival. I'm still wondering how on earth you managed to keep it up all these years after you recovered.

HENRY IV: Well, you must realize, doctor—after I fell from my horse and cracked my head, I really was mad—for I don't know how long.

DOCTOR: I see. For a long time, you say?

HENRY IV: Yes, doctor, a long time, about twelve years. (*It is a quick, almost parenthetical reply, and he promptly resumes his conversation with* BELCREDI.) Which means, my dear Belcredi, that after that cavalcade I didn't know a thing about what was happening in your world—how circumstances were changing, what friends were letting me down, who had stepped into my shoes, or stolen the heart of the woman I loved. I didn't know who had died—who had moved away . . . and all that was far from a joke for me—even though you imagine it was.

BELCREDI: No . . . no . . . I didn't mean that. I was talking about **afterwards**.

HENRY IV: Oh really? Oh yes, afterwards. One day . . . (*He turns to the* DOCTOR.) You know, doctor, I'm a very interesting case—truly, you should make a close study of me. (*He begins to shudder as he speaks.*) One day . . . without warning . . . my mind started to clear . . . Heaven knows how . . . . and I began to see straight again. As first I wasn't sure if I was dreaming. I found myself touching things . . . to see if they were real—and, yes, they were . . . I was awake at last. And now, he's right (*indicating* BELCREDI), let's throw off the masquerade . . . the nightmare! Open all the windows and let in the fresh air. Let us breathe in life. Come, let's run outside. (*He pulls himself up suddenly*.) But where to? And to do what? To have everyone point at me secretly and say 'Look—there's Henry IV' . . . not as I am now, but arm in arm with you—among my dearest friends.

BELCREDI: Why should they? What makes you think that?

DONNA MATILDE: They wouldn't dare . . . they know it was due to that accident.

HENRY IV: But they said I was mad even before it happened. You know that Belcredi. You opposed anyone who said I wasn't.

BELCREDI: Oh come now. That was only in fun.

HENRY IV: And look at my hair now. (*He points out the hair at the nape of his neck*.)

BELCREDI: Well I'm going grey too!

HENRY IV: But there's a difference! I went grey as Henry IV. . . here, and I didn't know it. I noticed it suddenly one morning. It was a terrible shock! Because it made me realize that not only my hair had gone grey . . . I was grey inside. My life was finished. In ruins. I was like a hungry man arriving at a banquet which was already over.

BELCREDI: Yes, but other people . . .

HENRY IV (*cutting him*): I know! They couldn't be expected to wait for me to be cured. Not even those who crept up behind me and viciously stabbed my horse until it bled.

DI NOLLI (*stunned*): What's that? What did you say?

HENRY IV: They jabbed my horse to make it rear up—and I fell off.

DONNA MATILDE (*horrified*): It's the first I've heard of this!

HENRY IV: Perhaps that too was 'only in fun'! . . .

DONNA MATILDE: But who did it? Who was behind us?

HENRY IV: Does it matter? All those who were going to the feast and who have been kind enough to save me a few flabby morsels of pity, perhaps even a scrap of remorse sticking to their dirty plates, Marchesa. (*Abruptly*.) Now, doctor, don't you think my case is really new in the annals of lunacy? I preferred to remain mad—I found everything was here to

hand for this novel pleasure—to live my madness out . . .
completely aware of what I was doing, and in this way to
revenge myself on the stone which played havoc with my
head. Solitude, this solitude—squalid and empty though it
seemed when my eyes were reopened—made it possible for
me to dress up again in the colour and splendour of that
distant carnival day when you . . . (*He looks at* DONNA
MATILDE, *indicating* FRIDA *to her.*) Yes, you Marchesa—
had your triumph. And I would oblige all those who came
before me to play out that masquerade of long ago which for
you, but not for me, was the whim of a day. I could make it
become a permanent reality here, with everyone dressed in
costume . . . A throne room, and my four privy counsellors . . .
all traitors! (*Turning on them suddenly.*) I wonder what you
thought you had to gain by letting them know I am cured. If I
am cured, then I no longer have need of your services—so
you're now without a job! It was certainly mad of me to
confide in you. Ah yes, but it's now my turn to play the
traitor! Do you know that until this strange turn of events,
they planned to go on acting this charade with me behind
your backs! Yes—the joke was on all of you! (*He laughs
loudly. The others laugh feebly, with the exception of* DONNA
MATILDE.*)
BELCREDI (*to* DI NOLLI): You hear that?
DI NOLLI (*to the* FOUR YOUNG MEN): Is that true?
HENRY IV: But we must forgive them! This, you know
(*grasping his clothes*) is obviously and intentionally a
caricature of that other masquerade which goes on all the
time—and in which we participate involuntarily every
minute of our lives . . . (*indicating* BELCREDI) when we
dress up as who we think we are. As for these four young men
. . . we must forgive them, since they don't realize that the
clothes with which they cover themselves carry their own
personality. (*Again to* BELCREDI.) You soon get used to it,
you know. It's not difficult to walk about like this . . .
pretending to be a tragic character in a drama . . . especially
in a room like this. You know, doctor, I remember once
seeing a priest . . . I'm sure he was Irish . . . quite a handsome

man, too . . . asleep on a bench in a park, in the November sun, with his arm behind his head. He was lost in the golden delight of that sunny warmth which must have seemed to him like a breath of summer. I'm sure that at that moment he completely forgot he was a priest—forgot even where he was! He was dreaming . . . of heaven knows what! And a cheeky little boy came by, carrying a flower he'd torn up by the roots; and as he passed the priest, he tickled his neck with the flower. The priest opened his eyes—and I saw that they were laughing—laughing with the blissful joy of his dreams . . . . but he was quite unaware of that. Then he sat up—and suddenly he was the priest again—and as he became aware of his cassock—his eyes became serious. As serious as the expression you've seen in my eyes. Because Irish priests defend the seriousness of their Catholic faith with as much zeal as I defend the sacred rights of hereditary monarchy. I am cured my friends . . . because I'm perfectly aware I play at being mad—and I do it quite calmly. The trouble with you is you live out **your** madness in a state of constant agitation—without seeing it for what it is.

BELCREDI: Oh I see . . . so what it boils down to is that **we** are the madmen now!

HENRY IV (*trying to restrain his anger*): If you and the Marchesa were not mad—would you have come to see me here?

BELCREDI: To tell the truth I came because I believed you **were** mad.

HENRY IV (*almost shouting*): And she?

BELCREDI: I can't speak for her. She seems struck dumb by all your talk! She's spellbound by this **conscious** madness of yours. You know, Marchesa—as you're dressed for the role, you could stay here if you want and live out this madness with him.

MATILDA: Don't be insolent.

HENRY IV: Ignore him. He's always like that. He's trying to excite me because the doctor warned him not to. (*To* BELCREDI.) Don't imagine I'm still upset by what happened between us . . . at the part you played with her in the accident. (*To* MATILDE.) Or what part he now plays in your life. My life is **here**. Not like yours. You've grown old in the life you lead. I haven't. Was that what you wanted to tell me—to show me with this sacrifice of yours? . . . dressing up like this on the advice of this doctor? Oh, nice work, doctor! 'What we were then—and what we are now, eh?!' But I'm not a madman in **your** understanding of the word, doctor! I know only too well that **he** (*indicating* DI NOLLI) can't possibly be me—because I am Henry IV—and have been for the last twenty years. She has lived through and enjoyed these twenty years . . . to become . . . look at her . . . a woman I no longer recognise. (*He goes over to* FRIDA.) For me—she will always be like this. You all seem to me like children I can easily scare. And you're scared too, child, aren't you, by the joke they persuaded you to play on me—without realizing that for me—it couldn't be the joke they meant it to be. What a terrible revelation! My dream come to life in you—more vividly than ever. Up there—in that picture frame—you were an image—they have turned you into flesh and blood. And you are mine . . . mine! You're mine by right! (*He grasps her in his arms, laughing madly while the others cry out in fright. They rush to free* FRIDA *from him, but he becomes furious and calls to the* FOUR YOUNG MEN:) Hold them! I order you to hold them!

The FOUR YOUNG MEN *are so mesmerized by him that they automatically try to restrain* DI NOLLI, *the* DOCTOR *and* BELCREDI.

BELCREDI (*freeing himself easily and hurling himself at* HENRY IV): Let her go! Let her go! You're not mad!
HENRY IV (*in a flash, draws the sword from* LANDOLF's *scabbard*): Not mad, eh? Then take that! (*And he wounds* BELCREDI *in the stomach.*)

There is a shriek of horror and the others rush to help BELCREDI, *shouting confusedly:*

DI NOLLI: Are you hurt?
BERTOLD: In the stomach! He's wounded him!

DOCTOR: I told you! I told you!

FRIDA: Oh God!

DI NOLLI: Frida—come here!

DONNA MATILDE: He's mad! He's mad!

DI NOLLI: Hold him!

BELCREDI (*protests as they carry him out through the door on the left*): No . . . you're not mad! He's not mad! He's not mad!

They exit. Their shouts continue in confusion until we hear a sudden piercing scream from DONNA MATILDE. *Then silence.*

HENRY IV (*has remained surrounded by* LANDOLF, ORDULF *and* HAROLD. *His eyes are wild, appalled at the fiction of his own creating which has carried him to the point of committing a crime):* Now . . . yes . . . I've no choice . . . (*He draws them around him, as if to protect him.*) Here . . . together . . . together . . . for ever . . . for ever . . .

CURTAIN

THE MAN WITH THE FLOWER IN HIS MOUTH

L'uomo dal fiore in bocca

1923

Translated by
Gigi Gatti and Terry Doyle

CHARACTERS

The Man with the Flower in his Mouth
A Care-Free Traveller

Towards the end of the play there occasionally appears around the corner the shadow of a woman, dressed in black, in an old hat with weeping feathers.

Translators' notes

'*Un Pacifico Avventore*':
We have translated *Avventore* as 'Traveller' rather than 'customer' or 'client'. Otherwise The Man With The Flower In His Mouth could be taken for the proprietor of the café, which is confusing: perhaps Pirandello really meant it to be ambiguous?

Again, we have translated *pacifico* as 'carefree', even though the traveller is not by circumstance or character 'carefree'. He is only 'carefree' in relation to The Man With The Flower In His Mouth, who is dying. We assume this to be Pirandello's meaning.

In the background an avenue; street lights glimmering through the leaves of the trees. On both sides, the end houses of a street leading into the avenue. Among the houses a dingy all-night café; tables and chairs out on the pavement. In front of the houses, on the right, a street lamp, shining. On the corner of the last house, on the left, at right angles to the avenue, another street light shining. It's just gone midnight. From afar, the occasional haunting strum of a mandolin.

As the curtain rises, THE MAN WITH THE FLOWER IN HIS MOUTH *is sitting at one of the tables, slowly, silently, observing* THE TRAVELLER *at the next table who is calmly sucking a creme-de-menthe through a straw.*

THE MAN WITH THE FLOWER: Well, you're quite a cool customer, I must say. So you missed the last train?

THE TRAVELLER: Missed it by a minute. I arrived at the station and saw it vanish right in front of my nose.

THE MAN WITH THE FLOWER: You could've run after it!

THE TRAVELLER: Yes, I suppose it is a bit of a joke. If only I hadn't had all those damned parcels, packets and packages with me . . . for Christ's sake, more loaded up than a mule I was! Women! Shopping here . . . shopping there . . . There's no end to it. Do you know, it took me three whole minutes after I got out of the taxi, just to arrange all those loops around my fingers. Two packets for every finger.

THE MAN WITH THE FLOWER: Must've been a fine sight! You know what I'd have done in your place? I'd have left the whole lot in the taxi.

THE TRAVELLER: Oh, yes! And what about my wife? And daughters? And all their friends?

THE MAN WITH THE FLOWER: Screams and shouts, eh! I'd have really enjoyed that.

THE TRAVELLER: Maybe you don't know what women are like once they're on holiday!

THE MAN WITH THE FLOWER: Of course I do. Precisely because I do know. (*pause.*) They all say they won't be needing a thing.

THE TRAVELLER: As if that was all. They're even capable of claiming they go on holiday to save. Then, the moment they set foot in one of these little villages round here—the uglier it is, the more plain and simple—the more pains they take to tart it up with all their frippery. Women! But then that's the way they are . . .—'If only you'd pop into town for me, dear! I could do with a thing or two . . . And while you're there, couldn't you just get me this as well . . . and that? And if you don't mind too much (I like the "if you don't mind"), seeing you'll be going that way anyhow . . . '—But my dear, how on earth am I to do all that in three hours?—'Oh, come on, if you took a taxi . . . ' The trouble is that, thinking I'd be away only for three hours, I came out without my keys.

THE MAN WITH THE FLOWER: Nice one. What next?

THE TRAVELLER: I dropped the pile of packets and parcels in the left-luggage at the station and went to eat at a *trattoria*. Then, to let off steam, I went to the theatre. The heat in there was enough to finish me off. When I came out I asked myself: what next? It's already midnight; I'll be catching the four o'clock train. It's not worth spending the money just to get three hours' sleep. So here I am. This café stays open all night, doesn't it?

THE MAN WITH THE FLOWER: Never closes, no sir. (*pause.*) So, you dropped all your parcels in the left-luggage, at the station?

THE TRAVELLER: Why do you ask? Aren't they safe there? They were all wrapped up . . .

THE MAN WITH THE FLOWER: No, no, I didn't meant that! (*pause.*) Well wrapped up . . . yes, I'm sure: with that special flair shop assistants have for gift wrapping . . . (*pause.*) What hands they have! A large double sheet of red, smooth paper, so beautiful in itself . . . so smooth it makes you want to press your face against it. Cool as a caress . . . They spread it out on the counter, and then, with such casual elegance, position the fine, well-folded cloth right in the middle. First they lift up a flap from underneath with the back of one hand; then, with the other hand, fold over the other flap, and then they tuck in the corners with such graceful ease—a little extra touch just for the sake of art. After that they fold the end-flaps into triangles and tuck the points away; they reach out for the roll of string, give a tug to unravel just the right length, and tie up the parcel with such speed that you've hardly time to admire their skill, before you're presented with the package, complete with the loop for you to put your finger through.

THE TRAVELLER: I can see you've spent a lot of time observing shop assistants at work.

THE MAN WITH THE FLOWER: Me? My dear sir, I spend entire days watching them. I can stand in one place for a whole hour, watching them through the shop window. I forget myself while I'm there. I feel as though I were . . . I'd like to be that roll of silk . . . that piece of cloth . . . that red or blue ribbon the young girls from haberdashery measure out by the metre—Have you ever noticed how they do it? They gather it into a figure eight between thumb and little finger, before wrapping it up. (*pause.*) I watch the customers coming out of the shop with the parcel looped round their finger, or in their hand, or under their arm . . . I gaze after them, until I lose sight of them . . . imagining . . .—ah, so many things! You have no idea. (*Pause. Then darkly as though to himself.*) But that's what I need. Just what I need.

THE TRAVELLER: Just what you need? I'm sorry . . . what exactly?

THE MAN WITH THE FLOWER: To attach myself to life like that—I mean, with my imagination. Like a creeper round the railings of a gate. (*pause.*) I can't let my imagination rest, not even for a moment. I must use it to cling, cling to other people's lives . . . —but not to people I know. No, no, that I couldn't do! The mere thought of it

disgusts me—if only you knew—sickens me . . . No, I cling to
the lives of strangers, where my imagination may work
freely. Not capriciously though: on the contrary, I take note
of every little mannerism of one person or another. If only
you knew how my imagination works, and how hard! How
deeply I can penetrate their lives! I see people's homes; I live
there; I see myself right inside them, until I even become
aware of . . . do you know that particular odour that nests in
every home? Yours, mine . . . —But in our own home we're
no longer aware of it, because it's the very odour of our lives.
Are you with me? Yes, I can see you're nodding . . .

THE TRAVELLER: Yes, because . . . I mean to say, you must
get great pleasure from imagining all those things . . .

THE MAN WITH THE FLOWER (*irritated, after having given
it some thought*): Pleasure? Me?

THE TRAVELLER: Yes . . . I mean . . .

THE MAN WITH THE FLOWER: Tell me. Have you ever
been able to see a good doctor?

THE TRAVELLER: Me? No, why, I'm not ill!

THE MAN WITH THE FLOWER: Don't be alarmed! I was
only wondering if you've ever had a look at one of those
good doctors' waiting-rooms where the patients sit, waiting
their turn.

THE TRAVELLER: Ah, yes, once, when I had to take my
daughter who was suffering from nerves.

THE MAN WITH THE FLOWER: Good. I didn't want to
pry. I mean, waiting-rooms . . . (*pause.*) Did you have a good
look? Dark-covered, old-fashioned sofas . . . odd, uphol-
stered chairs . . . Furniture picked up here and there in some
second-hand shop and dumped there for the patients. None
of it really belongs in the house. For himself and for
entertaining his wife's friends, the dear doctor has quite a
different reception room. Elegant, tastefully furnished. How
out of place they would be, those nice chairs and armchairs,
if they were brought out into the waiting-room, where the
patients have to make do with decent, sobre furniture. I'd
like to know if, when you took your daughter there, you
observed carefully the chair or armchair on which you sat,

waiting.

THE TRAVELLER: No, not really . . .

THE MAN WITH THE FLOWER: Of course not. Because you were not ill yourself . . . (*pause.*) But even those who are ill don't always notice these things, wrapped up as they are in their own suffering. (*Pause.*) And yet, how often you see people sitting there, staring at their own finger tracing vague patterns on the polished arm of the chair! Lost in their thoughts, not seeing a thing! (*Pause.*) But then what an impression it makes on you, when the doctor's finished with you, and you come out and see, there, in the waiting-room, the chair where not so long ago you sat, in ignorance, awaiting the verdict! Now you find it occupied by some other patient, he too with his own secret illness. Or you may find the chair empty, impassive, waiting for someone else to come and sit on it. (*Pause.*) But what were we saying? Ah, yes . . The pleasures of the imagination—I wonder how I came to think of a chair in one of those doctor's waiting-rooms where patients are waiting to be seen?

THE TRAVELLER: Yes . . . actually . . .

THE MAN WITH THE FLOWER: You don't see the connection? Neither do I. (*Pause.*) The thing is this: we all have our own private, apparently unconnected, images and memories; images created by such deeply personal experiences, that if we allowed ourselves to expose them in everyday conversation, we just wouldn't understand one another. There's nothing more illogical, often, than analogies based on such private images. (*Pause.*) But perhaps the connection here is this, look: do you think those chairs get any pleasure fantasising about the patients sitting on them in the waiting-room? About what illnesses they may be hatching, where they'll go, what they'll get up to after the consultation? No pleasure at all. It's the same with me: none at all. So many patients come, and go, and the chairs, poor things, just stay there waiting to be sat upon. And that's exactly the way I spend my life. One moment I'm taken up by this, another by that. At this moment I'm taken up by you, and believe you me, I get no pleasure from the fact that you missed your train, from your family waiting for you on holiday, from all the worries I suppose you must have too.

THE TRAVELLER: If only you knew!

THE MAN WITH THE FLOWER: Thank God, if they're only worries. (*Pause.*) There're those who are worse off, my dear sir. (*Pause.*) I was saying how I need to use my imagination to cling to other people's lives, but that's all it is, there's no pleasure in it, it's not because I'm interested, on the contrary . . . It's that I need to share everyone else's problems, so I can judge life as futile and vain, so much so that nobody should really mind if it comes to an   end. (*with dark rage.*) But you have to go on proving it to yourself, you know, on and on, without mercy. Because, my dear sir, we all feel this unquenchable thirst for life, we feel it here, like an ache in our throat, but we don't know what it's made of, we can never satisfy it. Because in the very act of living, life is always so full of **itself, we** can never taste it to the full. All we can really savour is the past, which remains alive inside us. That's where the thirst for life comes from, from the memories that bind us. But bind us to what? Why, to all this nonsense here . . . to these petty worries . . . to so many stupid illusions . . . fatuous occupations . . . Yes, yes, what now seems nonsense to us . . . what now seems a bore—and I'd go as far as to say, what now seems to us a misfortune, a real misfortune—yes, sir, I wonder what flavour all that will acquire in four, five years' time. What taste these tears will have . . . And life, by God, the mere thought of losing it . . . especially when you know it's a matter of days . . . (*At this point the head of* A WOMAN *dressed in black peers around the right-hand corner of the street.*) There you are . . . Can you see? There, look, on that corner . . . Can you see the shadow of a woman? There, she's hiding herself!

THE TRAVELLER: What? Who . . . who was that?

THE MAN WITH THE FLOWER: Didn't you see her? She's hiding.

THE TRAVELLER: A woman?

THE MAN WITH THE FLOWER: Yes, my wife.

THE TRAVELLER: Ah! your wife?

THE MAN WITH THE FLOWER (*after a pause*): Keeps an
eye on me from a distance. Sometimes I feel like going over
and kicking her, believe you me. But what's the point? She's
like one of those stray, obstinate bitches: the more you kick
them, the closer they stick to your heels. (*Pause.*) You have
no idea how that woman is suffering on my account. Doesn't
eat, doesn't sleep. Follows me around day and night. Like
that, from a distance. If only she took the trouble to dust that
slipper of a hat she wears on her head, those rags . . . —She
doesn't even look like a woman any more, more like an old
rag. Even her hair has turned dusty forever, here, at the
temples. And she's barely thirty-four years old. (*Pause.*) You
can't imagine how angry she makes me sometimes. I jump at
her, and scream in her face—Idiot!—shaking her at the same
time. She takes it all. Stands there, looking at me with such
eyes . . . eyes that make me feel, I swear to you, here, in my
fingers, a wild urge to strangle her. But it's no good. She just
waits for me to move away, and starts following me again,
from a distance. (*At this point* THE WOMAN *peers around
the corner again.*) There, look . . . that's her peering round the
corner again.

THE TRAVELLER: Poor woman!

THE MAN WITH THE FLOWER: Poor woman my foot!
You know what she'd like? She'd like me to stay at home!
Calmly, quietly, so she can cuddle me with all her most
ardent love and care. So that I could wallow in the perfect
order of all the rooms, in the cleanliness of all the furniture,
in that mirrored silence which there used to be in my home,
measured out by the tick-tock of the dining-room clock.
That's what she'd like! Now I ask you, so that you may
understand the absurdity—but no, what do I mean,
absurdity, the macabre ferocity of this pretence . . . I ask you,
whether you think it possible that the houses of Avezzano,
the houses of Messina, knowing that an earthquake was
about to shatter them, would have been quite happy to stay
there calmly in the moonlight, standing in an orderly line
along the streets and squares, obeying the planning orders of
the town Council. No, by God, those houses of stone and

beams would've run for their lives! Imagine the citizens of Avezzano, the citizens of Messina, calmly undressing themselves to go to bed, folding up their clothes, placing their shoes outside the door, and tucking themselves underneath the bedclothes, to enjoy the freshly-laundered sheets in the full knowledge that in a few hours they would be dead. Does it seem feasible to you?

THE TRAVELLER: But perhaps your wife . . .

THE MAN WITH THE FLOWER: Let me finish! If only, my dear sir, death were like one of those strange, disgusting insects which someone unexpectedly finds on you . . . You're walking down the street; suddenly some passer-by stops you and, extending two fingers of one hand, cautiously, says to you—'Excuse me, may I? You, my dear sir, have death on you.' Wouldn't it be wonderful? But death isn't like one of those disgusting insects. I wonder how many people walking around, casually, unawares, have it on them? No one sees it. They go around making quiet plans for tomorrow, and the day after. Now I . . . (*Gets up.*) Look my dear sir . . . Come over here . . . (*Makes* THE TRAVELLER *get up, and leads him over to the street lamp.*) Here, under the light . . . Come on . . . I want to show you something . . . Look here, under the moustache, here, you see that pretty, violet nodule? You know what it's called? Ah, such a sweet name, sweeter than a caramel: epithelioma, it's called. Say it, hear the sweetness: epithelioma . . . Death, you understand? passed by. Stuck this flower in my mouth and said to me—'Keep it, my friend: I'll be back in eight or ten months!' (*Pause.*) How can you tell me: with the flower in my mouth, could I possible stay at home, calmly and quietly, as that poor wretch would like me to? (*Pause.*) I scream at her—'Oh yes, you want me to kiss you?'—'Yes, kiss me!'—Do you know what she did? The other week, with a pin. She scratched herself here, on the lip and took hold of my head and tried to kiss me . . . Kiss me on the mouth. Because she says she wants to die with me. (*Pause.*) She's crazy . . . (*Pause.*) I will not stay at home. At the shop window is where I need to be, so I can admire the skills of the shop assistants. Because, you see, if I found myself faced for one moment by the void inside me . . . well, you understand, I could easily take the life of a perfect stranger just like that . . . take out a gun and kill someone, someone like you, who just happens to have missed his train . . . . (*Laughs.*) No, no, have no fear, my dear sir, I was only joking! (*Pause.*) I'm going now. (*Pause.*) I'd kill myself if ever . . . (*Pause.*) But there's such beautiful apricots in season just now . . . How do **you** eat them? With the skin on, I bet, is that right? You break them in two, you squeeze them open with your fingers, like two succulent lips . . . Ah, how delicious! (*Laughs. Pauses.*) My best wishes to your dear wife and daughters on holiday. (*Pause.*) I can just picture them all dressed in white and blue, in a beautiful green meadow in the shade . . . (*Pause.*) Please, do me a favour, in the morning, when you arrive. I imagine the village is some little way from the station. At dawn, you might easily feel like walking there. The first little tuft of grass you see by the roadside, count the blades for me. However many blades there are, that's how many days I have left to live. (*Pause.*) Make sure you pick a nice thick one. (*Laughs, then:*) Good night, my dear sir.

He strolls off, humming to the sound of the distant mandolin, in the direction of the right-hand corner; but at a certain point, thinking his wife might be waiting for him, he turns and scurries off, in the opposite direction, followed by the stupified gaze of the carefree traveller

CURTAIN

RIGHT YOU ARE
(IF YOU THINK YOU ARE)

Cosi è, se ui pare

1917

Translated by
Bruce Penman

CHARACTERS

LAMBERTO LAUDISI
SIGNORA FROLA
SIGNOR PONZA, her son-in-law
SIGNORA PONZA
COUNSELLOR AGAZZI
SIGNORA AMALIA AGAZZI, his wife
DINA AGAZZI, their daughter
SIGNORA SIRELLI
SIGNOR SIRELLI
THE PREFECT
COMMISSARY CENTURI
SIGNORA CINI
SIGNORA NENNI
Other LADIES and GENTLEMEN
The AGAZZI family's FOOTMAN

The action takes place in an Italian city which is the administrative centre of a province. (The PREFECT is the head of the provincial administration, and COUNSELLOR AGAZZI is his second in command; COMMISSARY CENTURI is a subordinate official.) Time: 1917.

ACT ONE

The drawing-room in COUNSELLOR AGAZZI's *house. Side-doors to left and right, main door at back of room.* SIGNORA AMALIA AGAZZI *and her daughter* DINA *are in conversation with her brother* LAMBERTO LAUDISI, *who is pacing angrily up and down. A man of quiet elegance, about forty years old, he is wearing a violet-coloured jacket with black lapels and frogs.*

LAUDISI: So he's gone off to refer the matter to the Prefect, has he?

AMALIA (*about forty-five, with grey hair; her manner shows a marked consciousness of the importance she derives from her husband's position in society; though she also lets it be understood that if occasion arose she could play his part herself, and would often play it quite differently from him*): Good heavens, Lamberto! It **is** about one of his own subordinates, you know!

LAUDISI: His subordinate at the Prefecture, maybe, but not outside! Not at home!

DINA (*nineteen years old, she has an air of understanding everything better than Mama or even Papa; but this air is mitigated by her lively, youthful charm*): But he came home and installed his mother-in-law in the flat next door to us, on the same landing!

LAUDISI: And wasn't he fully within his rights? There was a small, suitable flat to let, and he took it for his mother-in-law. Is it the duty of a mother-in-law (*slowly, with deliberate, ironic emphasis*) to visit the wife and daughter of her son-in-law's superior officer and pay her humble respects to them?

AMALIA: No one said anything about duty. It was myself and

Dina who made the first move. We went to call on the lady in question, and we weren't allowed into the flat! We weren't asked in!

LAUDISI: And what is the object of your husband's visit to the Prefect? To use official authority to exact a simple act of courtesy?

AMALIA: Not an act of courtesy . . . more an act of reparation. You **can't** just leave two ladies standing outside your door like stuffed dummies!

LAUDISI: You're being very arrogant. Can't people keep themselves to themselves in their own homes, if they want to?

AMALIA: You're deliberately ignoring the fact that the original act of courtesy came from us—we were making a friendly gesture towards a newcomer to our city.

DINA: Don't get so excited, Uncle Tino! Let's be honest, if that's what you want. Let's admit that our act of courtesy was based on curiosity. But doesn't that strike you as quite natural?

LAUDISI: It's natural, all right, because you've nothing else to occupy your time.

DINA: No, no . . . look here, Uncle Tino. Suppose you're standing over there, minding your own business. All right? Suddenly I arrive. Looking as cool as can be—or, better still, wearing the gallows look we associate with the gentleman in question—I dump something on the little table right in front of you. Something like . . . let's say . . . a pair of shoes belonging to the cook!

LAUDISI (*with an indignant start*): What have the cook's shoes got to do with all this?

DINA (*quickly*): There you are! You're surprised, aren't you? It all strikes you as very odd—and so you promptly ask me to explain.

LAUDISI (*speechless for a few seconds, smiling coldly; then he recovers his aplomb*): My sweet Dina! You're a very clever girl; but I'm no fool either, you know. So you come in and dump the cook's shoes on the table in front of me, with the deliberate intention of arousing my curiosity. And because you did it on purpose, with that object, you certainly can't reproach me if I ask you about it, and say: 'Why, my dear, are the cook's shoes here on the table? But now you've got to prove to me that this Signor Ponza (described by your father as a boor and a blackguard) had a similar object when he installed his mother-in-law in the next-door flat.

DINA: Oh, very well, then! He didn't do it on purpose. But you can't deny that his way of life is strange enough to arouse the natural curiosity of the whole town. May I tell you about it? When he arrived here, he rented a small flat on the top floor of that big, gloomy block out at the edge of the town, overlooking the market gardens. Have you seen it? Inside, I mean?

LAUDISI: Have you been to see it yourself, by any chance?

DINA: Yes, Uncle Tino, I have! With Mama. And we aren't the only ones, you know. Everyone has been to have a look. There's a dark courtyard—like a mine-shaft. And on the top floor there's a balcony going right round the inner wall, with a flimsy iron railing and lots of baskets hanging there with long strings attached to them.

LAUDISI: And so . . . ?

DINA (*with indignation and amazement*): That's where he's chosen to dump his wife!

AMALIA: And he's put his mother-in-law here, next door to us!

LAUDISI: So the mother-in-law is installed in a nice little flat in the middle of town?

AMALIA: You see? And he makes her live apart from her daughter.

LAUDISI: How do you know that? It may be the old lady's own choice—she may want the extra freedom.

DINA: No, no! What nonsense, Uncle Tino! Everybody knows he did it!

AMALIA: When a daughter gets married, it's natural enough for her to leave her mother's house and go and live with her husband, even if that means living in another city. But when a poor mother finds she can't face existence without her daughter and follows her to a town where both of them are strangers, you must admit that it's hard to understand why she should be compelled to live apart from her.

LAUDISI: You're not showing much imagination! Is it really so difficult to see that there might be such incompatibility of temperament between them—it could be her fault, or his fault, or nobody's fault—such incompatibility, that even in those circumstances . . .

DINA (*interrupting in amazement*): What incompatibility do you mean, Uncle Tino? Between mother and daughter?

LAUDISI: Why should the daughter come into it?

AMALIA: Because the other two certainly aren't incompatible. They're always in each others' pockets. . .

DINA: . . . although they are mother-in-law and son-in-law! That's what amazes everybody.

AMALIA: He comes here every evening, to keep her company.

DINA: And once or twice in the daytime too!

LAUDISI: Do you by any chance suspect them of being lovers?

DINA: No, no! What a thing to say! A poor old lady like that!

AMALIA: But he never takes her daughter to see her! He never, never brings his wife here to see her mother!

LAUDISI: Perhaps she's ill, poor soul; perhaps she can't go out.

DINA: No, that's not it at all. Her mother goes to see her . . .

AMALIA: She goes to see her, all right; but only from a distance! We know as a matter of definite fact that the poor mother isn't allowed to go upstairs to her daughter's flat!

DINA: She can only speak to her from the courtyard!

AMALIA: Just imagine it! From the courtyard!

DINA: And her daughter peers down at her from that high balcony, right up in the heavens! The poor lady goes into the courtyard, and pulls the string attached to her daughter's basket; a bell rings up above, and the daughter comes to the balcony. She stands in the courtyard, at the bottom of that mine-shaft, craning her neck back like this, and calls up to her. And she can't even see her properly against the glare of the light coming from above!

There is a knock at the door and the FOOTMAN *comes in.*

FOOTMAN: We have some visitors, Signora.
AMALIA: Who are they?
FOOTMAN: Signor Sirelli, his wife and another lady.
AMALIA: Oh, show them in.

Exit FOOTMAN *with a bow. Enter* SIGNOR AND SIGNORA SIRELLI *and* SIGNORA CINI.

AMALIA: My dear Signora Sirelli!
SIGNORA SIRELLI (*a plump, red-haired lady, still young; dressed with excessive provincial elegance; burning with insatiable curiosity; harsh in her manner towards her husband*): I've taken the liberty of bringing along my good friend Signora Cini, who has been longing to make your acquaintance.
AMALIA: Delighted . . . But please sit down. (*Completing the introductions.*) This is my daughter, Dina . . . and this is my brother, Lamberto Laudisi.
SIRELLI (*about forty, fat, balding, pomaded, with pretensions to elegance and creaking, well-polished shoes; he bows in turn to* AMALIA *and* DINA): How d'you do? . . . How d'you do? (*Finally, he shakes hands with* LAUDISI.)
SIGNORA SIRELLI: Oh, Signora Agazzi, we've come to your house as to the fountain of all knowledge—two poor pilgrims hungry and thirsty for information.
AMALIA: And what do you two ladies want to be informed about?
SIGNORA SIRELLI: Why, about this infuriating new Secretary at the Prefecture! The whole town is talking of nothing else.
SIGNORA CINI (*a foolish old lady, full of eager, sly malice masked by an air of artless spontaneity*): Yes, we're all so curious about him—as curious as . . . as . . . as I don't know what!
AMALIA: But I assure you that we don't know any more about it than everyone else does.
SIRELLI (*triumphantly, to his wife*): What did I tell you? They

know no more than I do—perhaps less! (*Turning to the others.*) For example, do you know the **real** reason why that poor mother can't visit her daughter's flat?

AMALIA: I was just discussing that with my brother.

LAUDISI: You all seem to me to be out of your minds!

DINA (*going on quickly to ensure that no one takes any notice of her uncle*): They say it's because her son-in-law forbids it.

SIGNORA CINI (*in wailing tones*): But that's not all!

SIGNORA SIRELLI (*emphatically*): That's not all! It's worse than that!

SIRELLI (*spreading out his hands to focus attention upon himself*): This is a brand-new piece of freshly-revealed information! (*Very slowly and clearly.*) He keeps her locked up!

AMALIA: His mother-in-law, you mean?

SIRELLI: No, not his mother-in-law—his wife!

SIGNORA SIRELLI: Yes, his wife! His wife!

SIGNORA CINI (*wailing as before*): Locked up! Locked up!

DINA: You see, Uncle Tino? Although you want to make excuses . . .

SIRELLI (*astonished*): What was that? Do you really want to make excuses for that monster?

LAUDISI: I don't want to make excuses for him at all! I'm just saying that (with due respect to the ladies) the curiosity you are all showing is quite intolerable. If there were no other objection to it, it would be intolerable because it's futile!

SIRELLI: Futile, did you say?

LAUDISI: Yes, futile! . . . That's right, dear ladies, I said futile!

SIGNORA CINI: But surely, just wanting to **know** . . .

LAUDISI: To know what, Signora? What can we really know about other people? Can we know who they are . . . or what they are . . . or what they do . . . or why they do it?

SIGNORA SIRELLI: You can pick up bits of news; you can gather information . . .

LAUDISI: But if there's anyone who ought to be fully in the picture from the start, it's yourself, Signora Sirelli, since your husband is always so well informed about everything.

SIRELLI: Here! I say! . . .

SIGNORA SIRELLI: He's quite right, you know, my dear! . . . (*She turns towards her hostess.*) The truth is, Signora Agazzi, that my husband always claims to know everything, and yet what do *I* know? Nothing!

SIRELLI: Naturally! She doesn't accept anything I say! She always doubts that things are really as I tell her! In fact she maintains that they can't be as I tell her! And she sometimes even assumes the opposite to be true!

SIGNORA SIRELLI: But really, some of the stories you come along with . . .

LAUDISI (*laughing heartily*): Ha! ha! ha! With your permission, Signora Sirelli, I will answer your husband. (*To* SIRELLI.) Listen, my dear fellow! How can you expect your wife to accept the things you tell her, when you describe them—naturally enough—as they are for you?

SIGNORA SIRELLI: He describes them as they can't possibly be!

LAUDISI: No, no, my dear lady; allow me to say that **you** are wrong there. You can be quite sure that your husband describes things as they are . . . as they are for him.

SIRELLI: As they are in reality! As they are in reality!

SIGNORA SIRELLI: Nothing of the sort! You always get things wrong!

SIRELLI: It's you that gets things wrong! I never do!

LAUDISI: No, no, my friend! Neither of you is wrong. Let me prove it to you. (*Getting up from his chair, he goes and stands in the middle of the room.*) Now look at me, both of you! . . . you can see me, can't you?

SIRELLI: Naturally!

LAUDISI: Don't speak too soon, my dear fellow . . . And now, come here!

SIRELLI (*with a puzzled smile; a little disconcerted, as if unwilling to take part in a joke he doesn't understand*): What for?

SIGNORA SIRELLI (*giving him a push; in angry tones*): Go on! Do what he says!

LAUDISI (*to* SIRELLI, *as he hesitantly approaches*): Can you see me? Look more closely at me. Touch me.

SIGNORA SIRELLI (*to her husband, who is still exhibiting the same hesitation as before*): Go on! Touch him!

LAUDISI (*to* SIRELLI, *who lifts one hand and touches him lightly on the shoulder*): Good . . . well done! You're sure you're touching me as well as seeing me?

SIRELLI: I should say so!

LAUDISI: No uncertainty about you, obviously! You can sit down now.

SIGNORA SIRELLI (*to her husband, who has not moved but is still standing stupidly in front of* LAUDISI): It's no good standing there blinking like that! Come and sit down at once!

LAUDISI (*addressing* SIGNORA SIRELLI, *after her bewildered husband has made his way back to his seat*): And now, Signora, pardon me if I invite **you** to come over here . . . or rather (*quickly correcting himself*) if I come over to you. (*He stands in front of her, and goes down on one knee.*) You can see me all right, can't you? Now lift up one little hand and touch me! (SIGNORA SIRELLI *still sitting in her chair, puts one hand on his shoulder;* LAUDISI *stoops quickly to kiss it, murmuring.*): What a dear little hand!

SIRELLI: Here, I say! Steady on!

LAUDISI: Don't take any notice of him! You're sure you're touching me as well as seeing me? No uncertainty about you, either, I can see! But whatever you do, don't tell your husband, or my sister, or my niece, or Signora . . .

SIGNORA CINI (*helpfully*): Cini!

LAUDISI: . . . Signora Cini here—don't tell them anything about the way you see me. They'd only tell you that you're wrong. But in fact you're not wrong at all. I really am just as you see me. But that doesn't alter the fact that I am also really just as your husband sees me, **and** my sister, **and** my niece, **and** Signora . . .

SIGNORA CINI (*as before*): Cini!

LAUDISI: . . . Signora Cini here. Every one of them is right too!

SIGNORA SIRELLI: What happens, then? Do you keep on

changing according to who's looking at you?

LAUDISI: But of course I do, my dear lady! And isn't the same true of yourself? Don't you change in the same way?

SIGNORA SIRELLI (*very quickly and urgently*): Oh, no, no, no! For myself, I don't change at all, I swear it!

LAUDISI: And, believe me, I don't change **for myself**, either! And I'm quite capable of maintaining that all of you are wrong if you see me otherwise than as I see myself. But I'd be very presumptuous to do so—just as you, dear lady, are very presumptuous to make the same claim for yourself.

SIRELLI: But what exactly is the point of all this rigmarole?

LAUDISI: Can't you see the point? . . . And yet you are all so eager to find out if people are like this or if things are like that, as though things and people were really like this or like that in themselves.

SIGNORA SIRELLI: Are you saying that no one can ever know the truth?

SIGNORA CINI: Aren't we to be allowed to believe even in things we can see and touch?

LAUDISI: Yes, of course you can believe in them, Signora! But you should also show due respect for the things other people touch and see, even if they are contrary to what you touch and see yourself!

SIGNORA SIRELLI: Now look here, Signor Laudisi! I don't want to know about all this! I'm not talking to you any more—you'll drive me out of my mind!

LAUDISI: Very well! Go on talking about Signora Frola and her son-in-law, all of you; I promise not to interrupt again.

AMALIA: Well, thank heaven for that! . . . but really, Lamberto, it would be better still if you left us together!

DINA: Yes, yes, Uncle Tino! Why don't you leave us altogether?

LAUDISI: No, what's the point of that? I enjoy hearing you talk. I'll keep quiet, believe me! At the very worst, I may laugh to myself a couple of times; and if I laugh too loudly, I'm sure you will all forgive me.

SIGNORA SIRELLI: And to think that we came here simply to enquire about that . . . but, excuse me, Signora Agazzi, isn't your husband Signor Ponza's superior officer in the service?

AMALIA: Office life is one thing, Signora Sirelli, and home life is another.

SIGNORA SIRELLI: Yes, of course! But haven't you even tried to see the mother-in-law, now she's in the next-door flat?

DINA: We certainly have! We've been to see her twice!

SIGNORA CINI (*with a little jump; all agog*): Aha! So you **have** spoken to her!

AMALIA: We weren't allowed into the flat! We weren't asked in!

SIRELLI: ⎫ Good heavens! . . . How extra-
SIGNORA SIRELLI: ⎬ ordinary! . . . Why ever was that? . . .
SIGNORA CINI: ⎭ etc.

DINA: This very morning . . .

AMALIA: The first time we stood in front of the door for more than a quarter of an hour. No one opened it, and we couldn't even leave a visiting-card. Then we tried again this morning.

DINA (*with a horrified gesture*): And **he** came and opened the door!

SIGNORA SIRELLI: And what a face he's got, hasn't he? Really evil! He's upset the whole town with that face! And always dressed in black like that! All three of them are dressed in black, aren't they, including the younger lady—the daughter?

SIRELLI (*crossly*): No one's ever **seen** the daughter, as I've told you dozens of times! . . . She probably does wear black too. They come from a little village in Marsica . . .

AMALIA: . . . which was apparently totally destroyed . . .

SIRELLI: . . . wiped right out, razed to the ground, by the last earthquake.

DINA: They've lost all their relations, so people say.

SIGNORA CINI (*who can't wait for the rest of the interrupted story*): Yes? What happened next? He opened the door, you were saying . . .

AMALIA: When I saw him standing there in front of me, with

that face, I could hardly get the words out to tell him that we'd come to visit his mother-in-law. And there was no response—not even a word of thanks!

DINA: Just a little bow!

AMALIA: A very little one—only his head moved.

DINA: Only his eyes, I'd say! And what eyes! They're the eyes of a wild beast, not of a man!

SIGNORA CINI (*still impatient for the sequel*): Yes? Then what happened? What did he say?

DINA: Embarrassed as anything, he . . .

AMALIA: Bristling like anything, he told us that his mother-in-law wasn't very well, and that our kindness was much appreciated. And then he just stood there in the doorway, waiting for us to go away!

DINA: You can imagine how humiliated we felt!

SIRELLI: What boorish manners! You can be sure that it's all his fault. Maybe he keeps his mother-in-law locked up as well!

SIGNORA SIRELLI: And what a nerve! To behave like that to a lady . . . a lady who's the wife of his superior officer!

AMALIA: Yes, my husband got really angry this time. He regards it as a serious lack of respect, and he's gone to lodge a strong complaint with the Prefect. He's asking for a definite act of reparation.

DINA: And here he is! Here's Papa!

Enter COUNSELLOR AGAZZI, *a man of fifty, with bristly red hair, beard and gold-rimmed spectacles; ill-natured and over-bearing.*

AGAZZI: Oh, hallo, Sirelli. (*He comes over to the sofa, bows and shakes hands with* SIGNORA SIRELLI.) Good afternoon, Signora Sirelli!

AMALIA (*doing the introductions*): Signora Cini . . . this is my husband.

AGAZZI (*bowing and shaking hands with* SIGNORA CINI): Delighted. (*He turns and addresses his wife and daughter with some solemnity.*) I must tell you that Signora Frola will be here any minute now.

SIGNORA SIRELLI (*clapping her hands exultantly*): So she's coming, is she?

AGAZZI: Naturally! Could I be expected to allow my house, my wife and daughter to be so blatantly insulted?

SIRELLI: Exactly! That's just what we were saying.

SIGNORA SIRELLI: And it might have been just as well to take the opportunity . . .

AGAZZI (*anticipating what she is going to say*): . . . to draw the Prefect's attention to all the other things that people in town are saying about that gentleman? That's all right—I've done it!

SIRELLI: Good! Splendid!

SIGNORA CINI: Such inexplicable behaviour! Really inconceivable!

AMALIA: Barbarous, I call it! (*To her husband.*) Do you realise that he keeps both those poor women locked up?

DINA: No, no, Mama; we still don't know about his mother-in-law!

SIGNORA SIRELLI: Well, there's no doubt about his wife being locked up, anyway.

SIRELLI: What did the Prefect say?

AGAZZI: Well . . . he was very . . . very **disturbed** . . .

SIRELLI: Quite right too!

AGAZZI: He had in fact already heard something about it, and . . . he agrees that steps should now be taken to clear up this mystery, to discover the truth.

LAUDISI (*laughing loudly*): Ha! ha! ha! ha!

AMALIA: That was just about the one thing missing—your silly laugh!

AGAZZI: And why is he laughing?

AMALIA: Because he thinks it's impossible to get at the truth.

Enter FOOTMAN.

FOOTMAN (*in doorway*): Excuse me . . . Signora Frola is here!

SIRELLI: Ah! She's arrived!

AGAZZI: And now, my dear Lamberto, we shall see if it's really impossible to discover the truth!

SIGNORA SIRELLI: Oh, good! I'm so pleased this has

happened!

AMALIA (*standing up*): Shall we have her shown in now?

AGAZZI: Not like that ... Please sit down again, my dear, and wait for her to come in. Everyone must remain seated ... (*To the* FOOTMAN, *after a brief pause*.) Show her in.

Exit FOOTMAN. *A few moments later* SIGNORA FROLA *comes in, and everyone stands up.* SIGNORA FROLA *is an extremely neat-looking little old lady, modest and agreeable in her manner. There is much sadness in her eyes, but this is alleviated by the constant gentle smile on her lips.* AMALIA *steps forward and holds out her hand.*

AMALIA: Come in, Signora Frola! (*Keeping* SIGNORA FROLA'*s hand in hers,* AMALIA *proceeds with the introductions*.) My old friend Signora Sirelli ... Signora Cini ... my husband ... Signor Sirelli ... my daughter Dina ... my brother Lamberto Laudisi . . . and now do sit down, Signora Frola!

SIGNORA FROLA: I'm so sorry ... I do apologise for having failed in my duty, right up to the present moment. You, Signora, were so very kind and generous as to honour me with a visit, when I ought to have been the first to call on you.

AMALIA: Oh, no one bothers about things like that between neighbours, Signora Frola! Especially when you were all alone here, and a stranger in our town; you might really have needed . . .

SIGNORA FROLA: Oh, thank you, thank you! Really **too** kind . . .

SIGNORA SIRELLI: And are you alone here in our town, Signora Frola?

SIGNORA FROLA: No, I have a married daughter, who also moved into town not long ago.

SIRELLI: And your son-in-law's the new Secretary at the Prefecture, isn't he? Signor Ponza?

SIGNORA FROLA: Yes, that's right. And I do hope that Counsellor Agazzi will forgive me, and forgive my son-in-law, too . . . .

AGAZZI: To tell you the truth, I **was** a little upset . . .

SIGNORA FROLA (*interrupting him*): And quite rightly so! Quite rightly! But I do hope you'll forgive him all the same. You see, we've been so confused by our misfortune . . .

AMALIA: Yes, of course! You were in that terrible disaster!

SIGNORA SIRELLI: You lost some relations, I expect?

SIGNORA FROLA: We lost everybody . . . everybody! There's hardly a trace of our little village left. It's just a small heap of ruins in the middle of the countryside, totally abandoned.

SIRELLI: Just as I thought!

SIGNORA FROLA: I had just the one sister and her daughter, who wasn't married. My poor son-in-law was much more cruelly afflicted. He lost his mother, two brothers and their wives, one sister and her husband, and two small nephews.

SIRELLI: A real holocaust!

SIGNORA FROLA: These things affect your whole life! They leave you stunned!

AMALIA: Yes, of course!

SIGNORA SIRELLI: And so quickly! From one moment to the next! It must be enough to drive you out of your mind!

SIGNORA FROLA: It makes you forgetful. You fail in your duty without meaning to, Counsellor . . .

AGAZZI: Oh, there's no need to say any more about that, Signora Frola.

AMALIA: It was partly because we knew about your misfortune that my daughter and I made the first move on calling on you.

SIGNORA SIRELLI (*excitedly*): Exactly! They knew how lonely you must be! But forgive me, Signora Frola, if I enquire how it is that, when you've had this terrible disaster, and when your daughter is living in the same town . . . (*She loses the thread for a moment, and then goes on a little less confidently.*) I'd have thought . . . the ones that are left would all want to be together . . .

SIGNORA FROLA (*intervening to spare* SIGNORA SIRELLI's *embarrassment*): You're wondering why I live on my own, aren't you?

SIRELLI: Yes . . . it does seem rather strange, to be perfectly frank.

SIGNORA FROLA (*sadly*): Yes, I can understand that. (*After a pause, she goes on, as if seeking an escape route.*) It seems to me that when a son or daughter gets married, one ought to leave them to themselves, to make their own life.

LAUDISI: Quite right! Exactly so! And their new life, with their marriage partner, is bound to be different from their previous existence.

SIGNORA SIRELLI: But not to this point, Signor Laudisi! A daughter doesn't have to shut her mother right out of her life!

LAUDISI: Who said anything about shutting out? As I understand it, this is a case of a mother who realises that her daughter cannot and should not remain tied to her by the same links as before, now that she has a life of her own to lead.

SIGNORA FROLA (*very grateful*): Oh, thank you, thank you, Signor Laudisi! That's just what I was trying to say.

SIGNORA CINI: But I expect your daughter will often be coming here to keep you company?

SIGNORA FROLA (*uneasily*): Well . . . yes . . . we do see each other, of course . . .

SIRELLI (*quickly*): But your daughter never goes out of doors! Or at least no one's ever seen her out of doors!

SIGNORA CINI: Perhaps she has to look after her children.

SIGNORA FROLA (*quickly*): No, there aren't any children so far. And there probably won't be, now; she's been married for seven years. She has plenty to do at home, of course—but that's not the point. (*She smiles sadly and then adds, as if seeking another escape route.*) In the country, you know, in small villages, we women hardly ever go out.

AGAZZI: Not even to visit your mother, if she doesn't live with you any more?

AMALIA: But I expect Signora Frola goes to see her daughter?

SIGNORA FROLA (*quickly*): Why, yes, of course. I go every day—sometimes twice a day.

SIRELLI: And do you go up all those stairs to the top floor of that block once or twice a day?

SIGNORA FROLA (*very pale, but still trying to treat this agonising interrogation as humorous conversational exchange*): Well, no; I don't actually go upstairs. You're quite right; it would be too much for me. I don't go up. My daughter comes to the balcony. We see each other and talk to each other like that.

SIGNORA SIRELLI: And is that all? Don't you ever see her close to?

DINA (*putting her arm round her mother's neck*): Speaking as a daughter, I would never expect my mother to climb up a hundred stairs for me; but I'd never be contented just to see her and talk to her from a distance without ever being able to put my arms round her and feel her close to me.

SIGNORA FROLA (*very upset and embarrassed*): You're quite right! I can see that I'll have to explain. I don't want you ladies and gentlemen to get a wrong impression of my daughter, and think she's lacking in consideration or affection towards me. And I don't want you to think anything like that about me, either. A hundred stairs would be no obstacle to a mother, however old and tired and weak she might be, if the reward for climbing them were a chance of pressing her daughter to her heart.

SIGNORA SIRELLI (*triumphantly*): So there it is! Just what we'd been saying! There must be a reason!

AMALIA (*significantly*): You see, Lamberto? There **is** a reason!

SIRELLI (*quickly*): It's your son-in-law, isn't it?

SIGNORA FROLA: Oh, for heavens' sake, don't think badly of him! He's such a good young fellow! You can't imagine how kind he is, or the tender affection and delicate consideration he has for me—not to speak of the loving care he shows towards my daughter. Believe me, I couldn't have wished her a better husband!

SIGNORA SIRELLI: Oh . . . Well, in that case . . .

SIGNORA CINI: In that case, Signor Ponza can't be the reason!

AGAZZI: Certainly not! I can't imagine, after what has been

said, that he would forbid his wife to visit her mother, or forbid his mother-in-law to go upstairs to his flat and spend a little time with her daughter.

SIGNORA FROLA: No, no; it isn't a matter of forbidding. I didn't say he'd forbidden us to do anything. The decision is mine and my daughter's,

SIGNOR AGAZZI: We deny ourselves that pleasure—quite voluntarily, believe me—out of respect for his feelings.

AGAZZI: I don't quite understand, Signora Frola. What could he be offended at?

SIGNORA FROLA: It isn't a matter of being offended, Signor Agazzi. It's more a feeling that he has—a feeling which is perhaps rather hard to understand. Once you do understand, it becomes easy to sympathise—as I've found myself, although it involves a considerable sacrifice for me and for my daughter.

AGAZZI: I think you must agree that there's something rather strange about everything that you've told us.

SIRELLI: Yes, indeed—strange enough to arouse, and justify, a certain degree of curiosity.

AGAZZI: And a certain degree of suspicion.

SIGNORA FROLA: Suspicion? Against my son-in-law? Oh, please don't say that! What sort of suspicion is there, Signor Agazzi?

AGAZZI: I'm not saying there is any suspicion. Don't be alarmed, Signora Frola. I'm merely indicating that there might be.

SIGNORA FROLA: No, no! Suspicion of what? We're in perfect agreement! Both I and my daughter are perfectly happy!

SIGNORA SIRELLI: Is it a question of jealousy on his part, perhaps?

SIGNORA FROLA: I don't **think** you can call it jealousy, where a mother's involved. I'm not sure, though . . . Anyway, it's like this: he wants to have his wife's heart all to himself. Even the right and natural love that my daughter feels for me—and he admits that it's right and natural, admits it wholeheartedly—even that has to be channelled through him, has to reach me through him. That's how it is.

AGAZZI: Oh! Really! That seems to me to be a case of outright cruelty, if you'll pardon my saying so.

SIGNORA FROLA: No, no, not cruelty! Don't say cruelty, Signor Agazzi! It's something quite different, believe me. I don't know how to put it. A matter of nature, perhaps? No, not nature . . . Perhaps it's more like a kind of illness, do you think? It's like an excess of love, shut in on itself—exclusive, that's the word for it. His wife has to live inside that closed space, and isn't allowed to go out, and no one else is allowed to go in.

DINA: Not even her mother?

SIRELLI: Utter selfishness, *I* call it!

SIGNORA FROLA: Maybe it is. But it's a kind of selfishness that gives itself and everything it has—a whole world—to its partner in life. I'd really be the selfish one myself, if I wanted to force my way into the closed garden of love where I know my daughter is living so happily, amid such adoration. Don't you think, dear ladies, that that should be enough for any mother? And then, I do see my daughter, I do talk to her . . . (*She pauses, and then goes on with a graceful, confidential little gesture.*) My daughter has a little basket in the courtyard, hanging from a string; I tug it when I get there to let her know I've arrived. And every day we use it to exchange a couple of short letters—just a few words, about the day's event. That's enough for me. I'm used to it now—resigned, perhaps—and I don't mind any more.

AMALIA: Well, if you and your daughter are happy . . .

SIGNORA FROLA (*getting up*): Oh! Yes, we are—as I've said already. My son in law's so kind—believe me. He couldn't be kinder. We all have our own little weaknesses, and we must treat each other's weaknesses with sympathy.

SIGNORA FROLA *says goodbye to* AMALIA, SIGNORA SIRELLI, SIGNORA CINI *and* DINA; *then she turns to* COUNSELLOR AGAZZI.

SIGNORA FROLA: I hope I have been forgiven . . .

AGAZZI: What nonsense, Signora Frola! We're most grateful

to you for your visit.

SIGNORA FROLA (*bows to* SIRELLI *and* LAUDISI; *then turns to* AMALIA): No, no; please don't get up, Signora Agazzi!

AMALIA: But of course, Signora Frola! I'll just see you out.

SIGNORA FROLA *goes out, accompanied by* AMALIA, *who returns a few moments later.*

SIRELLI: Well! well! Well! Did you all think that was a satisfactory explanation?

AGAZZI: It wasn't an explanation at all. There's some mystery behind all this.

SIGNORA SIRELLI: We shall never know what pain there is in that poor mother's heart.

DINA: Or in the heart of the daughter!

There is a short pause.

SIGNORA CINI (*speaking from a corner of the room, where she has taken refuge to hide her tears*): Her voice! You could hear the tears in her voice!

AMALIA: You certainly could! Especially when she said that she'd gladly climb more than a hundred stairs, if the reward were the chance of pressing her daughter to her heart.

LAUDISI: The thing that struck me most of all was her anxiety, not to say her determination, to protect her son-in-law from any kind of suspicion.

SIGNORA SIRELLI: No, no! Why, she couldn't find any excuses for him.

LAUDISI: Excuses for what? Is there any suggestion of violence? Or of brutality?

Enter FOOTMAN.

FOOTMAN (*standing in doorway*): Signor Ponza is here, Signor, and asks if he can have a word.

SIGNORA SIRELLI: Signor Ponza? Good heavens!

Everyone is very surprised and shows signs of anxious curiosity, bordering on dismay.

AGAZZI: He wants a word with me, does he?

FOOTMAN: Yes, sir; that's what the gentleman said.

SIGNORA SIRELLI: Oh, Signor Agazzi, do please see him in here! Though I'm a little bit frightened, I'm very curious to see him close to, the monster!

AMALIA: But what can he want?

AGAZZI: We'll see. But please sit down. Everyone must remain seated. (*Turning to the* FOOTMAN.) Show him in!

The FOOTMAN *bows and goes out. A couple of moments later* SIGNOR PONZA *comes in. He is dark and thickset, with a grim, almost threatening look. He is dressed all in black. His hair is thick and black, his forehead is low, and he has a large black moustache. He continually clenches and unclenches his fists. He speaks forcibly—with barely-contained violence, in fact. From time to time he wipes the sweat from his face with a black-edged handkerchief. When he speaks, his eyes remain fixed, hard and gloomy.*

AGAZZI: Come on in, Signor Ponza! (*Introduces him.*) Signor Ponza, our new Secretary: this is my wife . . . and Signora Sirelli . . . and Signora Cini . . . and my daughter . . . and Signor Sirelli . . . and my brother-in-law Signor Laudisi. Please sit down, Signor Ponza.

PONZA: Thank you. I will only disturb you for a couple of minutes.

AGAZZI: Would you like to speak to me privately?

PONZA: No, what I have to say can be said in front of everybody. In fact I felt it to be my duty to offer an explanation.

AGAZZI: Are you referring to the question of your mother-in-law visiting us? If so, there's no need for you to go on, because . . .

PONZA: No, it isn't that. In fact I must make it plain that my mother-in-law, Signora Frola, would undoubtedly have paid you a visit before Signora Agazzi and the Signorina Agazzi so kindly went to see her, if I hadn't done everything in my power to stop her, since I cannot allow her to make visits or to receive them.

AGAZZI (*very angry*): And why not, may I ask?

PONZA (*with rising agitation, despite his efforts to control himself*): My mother-in-law has presumably spoken about her daughter to you ladies and gentlemen, and told you that I have forbidden her to see my wife, or to come upstairs to my flat?

AMALIA: No, no! Signora Frola spoke of you with the utmost respect and kindness!

DINA: She never said a word against you.

AGAZZI: She said that she refrains from going up to her daughter's flat out of consideration for your feelings—though what those feelings can be is frankly more than we can understand.

SIGNORA SIRELLI: But if we were to say what we really think . . .

AGAZZI: . . . we'd have to call it a case of cruelty! Yes, downright cruelty!

PONZA: That's just what I've come here to explain, Signor Agazzi. Signora Frola is in a most pitiable situation. But my own situation is equally tragic—and it puts me under obligation to make excuses for myself, to give you chapter and verse of a misfortune which I would never have revealed except in response to this violent pressure! (*He pauses for a moment and looks round at all of them in turn; then he goes on in a slow, staccato voice.*) Signora Frola is mad.

ALL (*with a start of amazement*): Mad?

PONZA: Yes—for the last four years.

SIGNORA SIRELLI (*loudly*): Well, she doesn't look it!

AGAZZI (*bewildered*): Mad? How can she be mad?

PONZA: She doesn't look it, but she is mad, all the same. And her madness consists in her belief that I am stopping her seeing her daughter. (*In a spasm of fierce, agonising emotion.*) But she has no daughter! Her daughter has been dead for four years.

ALL (*astonished*): Dead? . . . Good Heavens! . . . What was that? . . . Dead? . . . etc

PONZA: Yes, she died four years ago. That was what sent her mother mad.

SIRELLI: But . . . your present wife?

PONZA: My **second** wife—I married her two years ago.

AMALIA: And Signora Frola thinks that **she's** her daughter?

PONZA: Yes. It's been her salvation, in a way. She was sitting one day by her window in . . . in the place where they were looking after her, and she looked out and saw me walking down the street with my second wife. It seemed to her that she'd found her daughter again, brought back to life. She began to laugh, and to tremble all over; she roused herself from the state of black despair into which she had fallen, and awoke to this other form of insanity. At first her mood was exultant and carefree; then she gradually became calmer. She showed some signs of distress, but managed to find a way of resigning herself to it. She is, in fact, quite happy, as you may have noticed yourselves. She persists in believing that her daughter is still alive, but that I want to keep her all to myself and not let her see her any more. You could say that she's cured, in a way. So much so, that she doesn't seem to be mad at all, when you talk to her.

AMALIA: It's true! She doesn't!

SIGNORA SIRELLI: In fact she says that she's happy with things as they are . . .

PONZA: She says that to everybody. And she has a genuine feeling of affection and gratitude towards me, because I try to help her in every way I can. It costs me considerable personal sacrifice. I have to maintain two households. I have to persuade my wife—fortunately she enters into the spirit of the thing in the most Christian manner, but I have to persuade her to make a continual effort to confirm Signora Frola in the delusion that she is her daughter. My wife comes to the window, speaks to her, writes her little notes . . . But Christian charity has its limits, after all! I can't ask my wife to share a home with her. And meanwhile the poor woman is a sort of prisoner, locked up indoors, for fear that Signora Frola will try to get into her flat. It's true that the old lady's quite calm, and has a very gentle disposition; but, as you can imagine, the affectionate caresses that she would lavish on my wife would be quite intolerable to her.

AMALIA (*impulsively, in a voice full of horror and pity*): Poor lady! Yes, I **can** imagine it!

SIGNORA SIRELLI (*speaking to her husband and* SIGNORA CINI): Do you hear that? Signora Ponza **prefers** to stay locked up indoors!

PONZA (*bringing the conversation to a close*): Well, Signor Agazzi, I expect you see now why I couldn't let my mother-in-law visit you—until I was compelled to, that is.

AGAZZI: Yes, I do indeed. I understand everything now.

PONZA: Anyone who has a misfortune like mine should keep himself to himself, in normal circumstances. Having been compelled to let my mother-in-law come and see you, however, I felt it my duty to give you this explanation out of respect for my own official position, so that it will not be thought among our fellow-citizens in the town that a public servant could be capable of such an enormity, or that I would let jealousy or anything else make me prevent a poor mother from seeing her daughter. (*Standing up.*) Thank you, Counsellor Agazzi! (*He bows deeply to* AGAZZI, *and then inclines his head towards* LAUDISI *and* SIRELLI, *saying.*) Thank you, gentlemen!

Exit PONZA *by the centre door.*

AMALIA (*bewildered*): Oh! So she's mad, then!

SIGNORA SIRELLI: Poor old lady! Quite mad!

DINA: Yes—because she thinks she's the mother of another lady who isn't her daughter at all! (*Burying her face in her hands in horror.*) How terrible!

SIGNORA CINI: But who would ever have guessed it, to look at her?

AGAZZI: I'm not so sure. From the way she talked . . .

LAUDISI: You'd already spotted that she was mad, from the way she talked?

AGAZZI: I don't say that. But there was certainly something. She couldn't find the words for what she was thinking.

SIGNORA SIRELLI: Naturally, poor woman! She wasn't thinking rationally.

SIRELLI: There's one thing that strikes me as very odd, if

she's mad. She wasn't thinking rationally, I agree. But her way of working out reasons why her son-in-law won't let her see her daughter, and making excuses for him, and adapting herself to those excuses . . .

AGAZZI: But that's just what proves that she is mad! All those efforts to find excuses for her son-in-law, without ever being able to produce an acceptable one!

AMALIA: Yes—she kept on saying things and then taking them back.

AGAZZI (*to* SIRELLI): And if she weren't mad, do you think she could possibly accept those conditions—not seeing her daughter except through a window and so on—for the reasons that she gave us: that is to say, because of the man's excessive, morbid affection for his wife and his determination to keep her all to himself?

SIRELLI: Exactly. But then could she accept those conditions if she **were** mad? And resign herself to them so calmly? That's what I find so strange. (*Turning to* LAUDISI.) What do **you** think?

LAUDISI: Oh, I don't think anything at all!

There is a knock at the door and the FOOTMAN *comes in, looking rather worried.*

FOOTMAN: Excuse me, Signora. Signora Frola is here again . . .

AMALIA (*horrified*): Good heavens, what can it be this time? Are we never going to be rid of Signora Frola?

SIGNORA SIRELLI: Yes, I can see how you must feel! Now that you know she's mad!

SIGNORA CINI: My word! I wonder what new story she's brought with her this time! I'd love to hear what she has to say . . .

SIRELLI: I'd be interested, too. I'm not at all convinced that she really is mad.

DINA: Yes, do let her come in, Mama! There's nothing to be afraid of. She's so calm and gentle!

AGAZZI: We must let her come in, there's no doubt about that. Let's see what she wants. If necessary, steps can be

taken. But please sit down. Everyone must remain seated.
(*To the* FOOTMAN.) Show her in!

Exit FOOTMAN.

AMALIA: Help me, everybody, for heavens' sake! What I am
to say to her, now!

Enter SIGNORA FROLA. AMALIA *gets up and timidly goes
to meet her; the others look at her in dismay.*

SIGNORA FROLA: May I come in?
AMALIA: Yes, of course, Signora Frola! As you can see, my
friends are still here . . .
SIGNORA FROLA (*with a pleasant but very sad smile*): And I
can see they all regard me as a poor madwoman—and you
too, dear Signora Agazzi!
AMALIA: No, no, Signora Frola; what are you saying?
SIGNORA FROLA (*very sorrowfully*): Oh, Signora Agazzi,
better the discourtesy of letting you stand outside my door,
as I did the first time you called on me! I could never have
guessed that you'd come back again and force me to make a
visit, the consequences of which I could all too clearly
foresee.
AMALIA: No, no—believe me, we're delighted to have you
with us again.
SIRELLI: Signora Frola is clearly very distressed, and we
don't know why. Let's give her a chance to tell us.
SIGNORA FROLA: Haven't you just had a visit from my son-
in-law?
AGAZZI: Why, yes, Signora Frola. He came to see me about
. . . about something to do with the office. That's what it was.
SIGNORA FROLA (*wounded and alarmed*): You're saying
that out of kindness, to calm me down, but . . .
AGAZZI: No, no! It's the truth—you can be sure of that.
SIGNORA FROLA (*as before*): Did he keep calm, at least?
Did he speak calmly?
AGAZZI: Yes, indeed. He was as calm as he could be, wasn't
he?

The others all nod in agreement.

SIGNORA FROLA: Oh dear. You ladies and gentlemen think you're reassuring me, while I'm trying to reassure you! About my son-in-law!

SIGNORA SIRELLI: But why should that be necessary, Signora Frola? We've told you and we tell you again . . .

AGAZZI: . . . that he came to see me about office matters.

SIGNORA FROLA: But I can see the expression in your eyes as you look at me! Please be patient—it isn't my fault. From the way you look at me, I can tell that he must have come here and provided you with evidence of something I wouldn't have revealed for the whole world . . . During my first visit, when you asked me all those questions—and very painful questions they were from my point of view, I can assure you—you can all bear witness to the fact that I didn't know what to say in reply. I gave you an account of our life together that couldn't have satisfied anybody—I admit it! But what was I to do? I couldn't tell you the truth! Nor could I tell you the same story that my son-in-law tells people—that my daughter's been dead for four years and that I'm a poor madwoman who thinks she's still alive and he won't let me see her!

AGAZZI (*bewildered by the evident sincerity of* SIGNORA FROLA's *manner*): Well . . . what is the position, then? Your daughter . . .

SIGNORA FROLA (*quickly and anxiously*): So it's true—he did tell you that story! Why are you trying to conceal the fact from me?

SIRELLI (*hesitantly, watching her closely*): Yes . . . in point of fact . . . he did say . . .

SIGNORA FROLA: I knew he had! And I know all too well how deeply it distresses him to have to tell people that story about me! This is a terrible misfortune, Signora Agazzi. With much effort and suffering, we've found a way of overcoming it; but only if we go on living exactly as we are at present. I do realise that people are getting to notice, that there's bound to be gossip and suspicion. But then he's so good in the office—so zealous, so meticulous. I'm sure you'll have noticed this yourself by now, Signor Agazzi!

AGAZZI: No, to tell you the truth, I haven't yet had the opportunity to do so.

SIGNORA FROLA: But please, please don't judge him by appearances! He's a splendid worker; his superiors have always said so. And what's the point of torturing him with this enquiry into his private life—into a family misfortune which has been overcome, as I said just now, but which could still harm him in his career if it became public knowledge?

AGAZZI: No, no, Signora Frola; don't distress yourself like that! No one's going to torture him.

SIGNORA FROLA: But how can you expect me not to be distressed when I see him compelled to tell people this absurd, horrible story? As if you could really believe that my daughter's dead, that I'm mad, and that this is his second wife! He **has** to tell people that story—it's an absolute necessity for him. It's the only way that he's been able to recover his peace of mind and his self-confidence. But he's aware of the monstrous nature of what he's saying! When he's compelled to tell his story, he gets excited and confused. You must have noticed that!

AGAZZI: Yes, he certainly was a bit excited.

SIGNORA SIRELLI: But what does this mean? It must be he that's mad!

SIRELLI: Of course it must be he! (*Looking round triumphantly at the others.*) Didn't I say so?

AGAZZI: But . . . is that really possible?

General agitation amongst the others.

SIGNORA FROLA (*quickly—clasping her hands together*): No, no, no gentlemen! What can you be thinking! There's just this one subject that must never be mentioned to him. Just think: would I leave my daughter alone with him, if he were really mad? He isn't! And you can see the proof of that at the office, Counsellor Agazzi, where he fulfils all his duties in such an exemplary way!

AGAZZI: Ah, but now you'll have to give us an explanation, Signora Frola, a clear explanation of what's going on. Can it really be true that your son-in-law came here and made up the whole story for our benefit?

SIGNORA FROLA: Yes, I will explain everything, I will! But he deserves your sympathy, Signor Agazzi!

AGAZZI: But look here! You're telling us that your daughter isn't dead?

SIGNORA FROLA (*horrified*): No, no! She isn't dead! Heaven forbid!

AGAZZI (*shouting angrily*): Then it must be your son-in-law that's mad!

SIGNORA FROLA (*beseechingly*): No, no—please listen . . .

SIRELLI (*triumphantly*): Yes, of course it must be he!

SIGNORA FROLA: No, listen to me, gentlemen! Please listen! He isn't mad! He's not mad! Let me speak! You've seen him yourselves—he's so robust, so physically strong! So . . . passionate! When he got married, he was seized by an absolute frenzy of love. My daughter was rather delicate, and there seemed to be a risk that he'd . . . well, almost destroy her. In the end, it was agreed by the doctors and everyone else (including his relations, who all died in the earthquake) that the only thing to do was to take her away, without warning him in advance, and put her in a . . . in a nursing-home. He was already in rather a state, of course, because of his . . . over-passionate feelings; and when he found she'd gone he fell into a state of furious despair. He really began to believe that his wife had died. He wouldn't listen to anything we said; he insisted on wearing black, and did all sorts of other crazy things. There was no way of getting that idea out of his head. Just about a year later, my daughter had recovered and was quite her old self again; and when we took her back to him, he said, 'No, that's not my wife!' He looked straight at her and said, 'No, it isn't she!' What agony it was! He'd go right up to her, he'd seem to recognise her for a moment, and then it'd be gone again . . . The only way we could persuade him to take her back was to arrange, with the help of some friends, for them to go through a second form of marriage.

SIGNORA SIRELLI: Ah! So that's why he says that she's his second wife!

SIGNORA FROLA: Yes, but he doesn't believe it himself—he hasn't believed it for quite some time. He has to persuade other people that it's true. Otherwise, you see, he wouldn't feel safe; because he still probably has moments when he's afraid that his wife will be taken away from him again. (*Softly, with a confidential smile.*) That's why he keeps her locked up—why he keeps her all to himself. But he worships her. I'm not worried; and my daughter is happy. (*Standing up.*) I must be going now, in case he comes back to see me again, since he's so excited. (*With a gentle sigh, waving her clasped hands from side to side.*) What we need is patience! My poor daughter has to pretend to be someone else; and I, dear ladies, have to pretend to be mad. But what can we do? As long as his peace isn't disturbed . . . But please don't get up; I know the way out. Thank you, thank you!

Exit SIGNORA FROLA *hurriedly, bowing and saying goodbye as she leaves by the centre door. The others remain standing, looking at each other in stunned amazement. There is a silence. Then* LAUDISI *makes his way to the centre of the stage.*

LAUDISI: There you are, staring at each other with nothing to say! What price the truth now? (*Laughing loudly.*) Ha! ha! ha! ha!

CURTAIN

ACT TWO

The study in COUNSELLOR AGAZZI's *house. The furniture is old, and old pictures hang on the walls. The main door, covered by a curtain, is at the back of the room. A side door, left, also curtained, leads into the drawing-room. There is a large fireplace, right, with a big mirror over the mantlepiece. A telephone stands*

on the writing-desk. There are also a small sofa, an armchair,
various other chairs, etc. AGAZZI *is standing by the desk, with*
the telephone receiver to his ear. LAUDISI *and* SIRELLI,
seated, look expectantly at him.

AGAZZI: Hallo! . . . Yes . . . Is that Centuri? . . . Well? . . .
Good, that's fine! . . . (*A long pause, during which he listens*
intently.) But how can that be possible? . . . (*Another long*
pause.) Yes, I see that; but surely, with a bit of effort . . .
(*Another long pause.*) It does seem very strange that you can't
. . . (*Another pause.*) Yes, yes; I understand (*Another pause.*). .
Well, just see what you can do . . . Goodbye! (*He hangs up.*)
SIRELLI (*anxiously*): What's the news?
AGAZZI: Nothing—nothing at all.
SIRELLI: So they didn't find anything . . . ?
AGAZZI: Everything has been lost or destroyed—town hall,
archives, registers, the lot!
SIRELLI: Are there no survivors who could help?
AGAZZI: There's no record of any survivors; and if there are
any, it would be very difficult to trace them now.
SIRELLI: So all we can do is to make up our minds to believe
one story or to believe the other, without any proof?
AGAZZI: I'm afraid so.
LAUDISI (*standing up*): Why not take my advice, and believe
both of them?
AGAZZI: But how can we do that, when . . .
SIRELLI: . . . when they completely contradict each other?
LAUDISI: Then don't believe either of them!
SIRELLI: You can't be serious! The proofs are missing, and
the recorded facts are missing; but truth must be either on
one side or the other.
LAUDISI: The recorded facts, indeed! What would you try to
deduce from them?
AGAZZI: Well, really! Take the registration of the daughter's
death, for example—assuming for the moment that Signora
Frola is mad. Unfortunately that document is missing,
because everything is missing; but it must have existed, and it

might turn up tomorrow. If it does, it'll be clear that the son-in-law is right and the mother-in-law is wrong.

SIRELLI: If that document were put into your hands tomorrow, could you deny the evidence of your own eyes?

LAUDISI: I don't deny anything! I'm very careful not to! It's you, not I, that have to have recorded facts and documents to help you affirm things or deny them, I've no use for your documents. For me, reality is to be found not in pieces of paper, but in the minds of those two people—minds to which I have no access, apart from the little they choose to tell me.

SIRELLI: Exactly! And don't they both tell you that one of the two is mad? Either she's mad or he is! But which?

AGAZZI: That's the question!

LAUDISI: But, in the first place, it isn't true that both of them say that one of them's mad. Signor Ponza says that Signora Frola is mad; but she denies the assertion, not only for herself, but for him, too. He was formerly a bit disturbed mentally, she says, because of his over-passionate feelings; but he's all right now—as sane as can be.

SIRELLI: Ah! So you agree with me—you're inclined to believe what the mother-in-law says?

AGAZZI: If one accepts what she says, the whole situation can be explained perfectly well.

LAUDISI: But it can be explained equally well if one accepts what **he** says.

SIRELLI: You mean . . . neither of them is mad? But one of them must be, dammit!

LAUDISI: But which? You can't tell, and nor can anyone else. And that's not because of the obliteration of the recorded facts you're so anxious to find, not because they've been destroyed or lost in some physical disaster, some fire or earthquake; no, it's because these two people have obliterated those facts from their own consciousness, destroyed them in their own minds, if you follow me. And now she had created for him—or he has created for her—a fantasy world which has the same consistency as the world of reality, in which they are now living in perfect peace and harmony. And this private reality of theirs can never be destroyed by the production of any written records whatever, because the two of them see it, hear it, touch it and take it in with the air they breathe. If such a document had turned up, it could only have served to enable you to satisfy a foolish curiosity. But it hasn't turned up—and now you're condemned to the extraordinary torture of having reality and fantasy standing in front of you side by side, and not being able to tell which is which!

AGAZZI: That's all metaphysics, my dear fellow! Pure metaphysics! We'll soon see if it's really impossible to tell which is which!

SIRELLI: We've heard first his story and then hers. But suppose we put them together, face to face in the same room—do you really think it'll still be impossible to tell reality from fantasy?

LAUDISI: All I ask is permission to go on laughing.

AGAZZI: All right! All right! We'll see who has the last laugh! But don't lets waste any more time now! (*He goes to the left-hand door and calls.*) Amalia! Signora Sirelli! Come on in!

Enter AMALIA, SIGNORA SIRELLI *and* DINA.

SIGNORA SIRELLI (*wagging a playfully threatening finger at* LAUDISI): Still at it, Signor Laudisi? Still talking nonsense? Laudisi? Still talking nonsense?

SIRELLI: Oh, he's incorrigible.

SIGNORA SIRELLI: But however can he avoid being affected by the passion that's seized the rest of us—the uncontrollable itch to find a solution to this mystery, which threatens to send us all mad? I didn't sleep a wink last night!

AGAZZI. Please, Signora Sirelli—just don't take any notice of him.

LAUDISI: Yes, my brother-in-law's the man to listen to. He'll make sure you sleep well tonight.

AGAZZI: Very well then. Let's make our arrangements. You ladies will go to Signora Frola's flat . . .

AMALIA: And will we be allowed in?

AGAZZI: Good heavens, I should think so!

DINA: It's our duty to return her visit.

AMALIA: But if Signor Ponza won't let her visit people or be visited . . .

AGAZZI: That was earlier on, when no one knew anything. But now that Signora Frola has been forced to speak, and has given us her account of the reasons which led her to be so unforthcoming . . .

SIRELLI: . . . she may be quite glad of the opportunity to talk to us about her daughter.

DINA: She's such an agreeable old lady! To my mind, there's no doubt about it at all. It's Signor Ponza that's mad!

AGAZZI: Don't lets jump to conclusions . . . Now then, please listen to me! (*He glances at the clock.*) Don't stay there too long—just a quarter of an hour and no more!

SIRELLI (*To* SIGNORA SIRELLI): Yes—do be careful about that!

SIGNORA SIRELLI (*getting very angry*): And why are you saying that to **me**, may I ask?

SIRELLI: Well, you know, once you start talking . . .

DINA (*to prevent a quarrel developing between the two of them*): A quarter of an hour, then, a quarter of an hour! I'll keep an eye on the time.

AGAZZI: I shall go to the Prefecture, and I shall be back here at eleven o'clock—in about twenty minutes.

SIRELLI (*anxiously*): And what about me?

AGAZZI (*to* SIRELLI): Just a minute. (*To the ladies.*) You will make some excuse to Signora Frola and bring her back here, shortly before my return.

AMALIA: But . . . what excuse shall we make?

AGAZZI: Any excuse you like! You'll think of something while you're talking. Women aren't usually short of an excuse—and you've got Dina and Signora Sirelli to help you. You'll take Signora Frola into the drawing-room, of course. (*He goes to the left-hand door and opens it wide, pulling back its curtain.*) The door must be left open—wide open, like that—so that your voices can be heard in this room. On my desk, here, I'm leaving some documents which I ought to be taking with me to the Prefecture. It's a file of office papers specially prepared for Signor Ponza's attention. I shall pretend that I've forgotten them, and make that the excuse for bringing him here. And then . . .

SIRELLI (*anxiously*): But excuse me, when do you want me to come in?

AGAZZI: You come in a minute or two after eleven—when the ladies are already in the drawing-room, and I'm already here in the study with Signor Ponza. You come here to fetch Signora Sirelli. You make sure that the servant shows you in here. Then I invite all the ladies to join us . . .

LAUDISI (*quickly and ironically*): . . . and the truth will immediately become apparent!

DINA: But seriously, Uncle Tino, once the two of them are face to face . . .

AGAZZI: Oh, don't listen to him, for heavens' sake! And now, please go! There's no time to lose!

SIGNORA SIRELLI: Yes, lets go at once! I'm not even stopping to say goodbye properly!

LAUDISI: Well, I'll say goodbye to myself for you, then. (*He shakes hands with himself.*) And good luck!

Exeunt AMALIA, DINA *and* SIGNORA SIRELLI.

AGAZZI (*to* SIRELLI): We'd better go, too. Straight away, I think.

SIRELLI: Yes, of course. Goodbye, Lamberto.

LAUDISI: Goodbye to you both!

Exeunt AGAZZI *and* SIRELLI. *Left on his own,* LAUDISI *strolls round the room, smiling ironically to himself and shaking his head. Finally he stops in front of the big mirror over the mantlepiece, looks at his reflection and begins to talk to it.*

LAUDISI (*looking into the mirror*): Ah, here you are! (*He waves a hand in salute, winks knowingly, and laughs sarcastically.*) Tell me, my dear fellow—which of us two is mad? (He raises his hand again, pointing his finger at his reflection, which points back at him. With another sarcastic laugh, he goes on.) Just as I thought—I say it's you, and you point your finger at me! Well, well! Between the two of us, we should know each other pretty well by now, eh? The trouble is that other people won't see you as I see you. So what's to become of you, my poor friend? For my part, when I stand in front of you and see you and touch you, I see and touch myself; but what's to become of you for the others? For them, you're a ghost, my dear fellow—nothing but a ghost! But see what fools they are! They ignore their own ghost—the ghost they carry with them all the time—and dash about, fully of curiosity, in pursuit of someone else's ghost—in the firm belief that it's something quite different from their own.

The FOOTMAN *comes in in time to hear the end of* LAUDISI's *speech to the mirror, to which he listens in amazement before addressing him.*

FOOTMAN: Signor Lamberto . . .

LAUDISI: What is it?

FOOTMAN: Two ladies are at the door. Signora Cini and another lady.

LAUDISI: Do they want to see me?

FOOTMAN: They asked for the mistress. I told them she was next door, visiting Signora Frola; and then . . .

LAUDISI: And then . . . ?

FOOTMAN: They looked at each other; they smacked their hands with their gloves, exclaiming 'Is she? Is she?' and finally they asked me, very excited, if there was anyone at home at all.

LAUDISI: And you said there wasn't?

FOOTMAN: I said **you** were here, Signore.

LAUDISI: Me? The real me? Certainly not! The me they think they know? Perhaps!

FOOTMAN (*more astonished than ever*): What was that, Signore?

LAUDISI: But can't you see the difference?

FOOTMAN (*as before; with a dismal attempt at a slack-jawed smile*): I don't understand you, Signore!

LAUDISI: Tell me—who are you talking to?

FOOTMAN (*dumbfounded*): What was that? Who am I talking to? Why, to you, Signore.

LAUDISI: But are you really sure that I'm the same person that these ladies want to see?

FOOTMAN: I don't know, Signore. They said the mistress's brother . . .

LAUDISI: My dear fellow! In that case, it must be me. Yes, it's me all right; so you can show them in. Go on.

Exit FOOTMAN, *looking back at* LAUDISI *several times as if he can't believe his ears. After a short pause, enter* SIGNORA CINI *and* SIGNORA NENNI.

SIGNORA CINI (*in the doorway*): May we come in?

LAUDISI: Of course, Signora—come along!

SIGNORA CINI: I gather that Signora Agazzi isn't at home .. I've brought my friend Signora Nenni (*Introducing her*; Signora Nenni *is an even more foolish and affected old lady than* SIGNORA CINI *herself. Like her, she is full of eager curiosity; but she is wary and timid at the same time*), who is so anxious to meet Signora . . .

LAUDISI (*quickly*): Signora Frola?

SIGNORA CINI: No, no! Signora Agazzi—your sister!

LAUDISI: Well, she's coming, she'll be here before long. Signora Frola's coming too. But do please sit down. (*He steers them both to the sofa, and then politely sits down between them, saying.*) With your permission . . . There's plenty of room for three. Signora Sirelli has gone with my sister.

SIGNORA CINI: Yes—we gathered that from the footman.

LAUDISI: All the preparations are complete now, you know! Oh, it'll be a memorable scene, a really memorable one! At eleven o'clock—in just a few minutes time! In this room!

SIGNORA CINI (*puzzled*): Preparations? Preparations for what?

With an air of mystery, LAUDISI *raises both hands and slowly brings the tips of his index fingers together; then he repeats the message verbally.*

LAUDISI: For the confrontation! (*With an admiring gesture.*) What a master-stroke!

SIGNORA CINI: W-what confrontation?

LAUDISI: The confrontation of the two parties! **He** will be the first to arrive. He'll come into this room.

SIGNORA CINI: Signor Ponza, do you mean . . . ?

LAUDISI: Yes, that's right. And **she** will be taken in there. (*Pointing to the drawing-room.*)

SIGNORA CINI: Signora Frola, you mean?

LAUDISI: Yes, Signora. (*Once again, he expresses his meaning initially with an eloquent movement of the hands and then repeats it verbally.*) To get the pair of them here face to face, while the rest of us watch and listen! What a master-stroke!

SIGNORA CINI: And that will reveal . . . ?

LAUDISI: It'll reveal the truth. Not that we don't know the truth already! It's just a matter of making it plain for all to see.

SIGNORA CINI (*surprised and very excited*): Ah! So the truth is already known? Which of them is it, then? Which of them is mad? Which?

LAUDISI: Let's think it over. See if you can guess. Which of them do you say it is?

SIGNORA CINI (*giggling uncertainly*): Why . . . really . . . I . . .

LAUDISI: Is she mad, or is he? Think it over! Guess! Don't be afraid!

SIGNORA CINI: Well, I'd say it was he!

LAUDISI (*looks at her for a moment before replying*): Yes, it's he.

SIGNORA CINI (*giggling contentedly*): It is? Just as I thought! Yes, of course! It had to be he!

SIGNORA NENNI (*also giggling contentedly*): He's the one! That's what we all said, we women!

SIGNORA CINI: And how did it all come out? Proofs have been found, I suppose? Documents?

SIGNORA NENNI: Police records, no doubt? Just what we said! With the authority of the Prefecture, something definite was bound to be discovered.

LAUDISI (*motions the two old ladies to come closer and then addresses them in soft, mysterious tones, weighing every syllable*): It's the marriage certificate—for the second marriage.

SIGNORA CINI (*looking as if she has received a blow in the face*): The *second* one?

SIGNORA NENNI (*very perturbed*): What was that? The *second* marriage?

SIGNORA CINI (*recovering her aplomb; crossly*): So he's right after all!

LAUDISI: It's a question of the recorded facts, dear ladies. The record of the second marriage seems clear enough.

SIGNORA NENNI (*almost weeping*): Then it must be she that's mad!

LAUDISI: It certainly seems like it!

SIGNORA CINI: But what does all this mean? First you said it was he and now you say it's Signora Frola?

LAUDISI: That's right. But you see, Signora Cini, it's quite possible that the certificate of the second marriage is a fake, as Signora Frola assures us it is—a forgery concocted with the help of some friends to support Signor Ponza in his delusion that his present wife is not her daughter, but someone else.

SIGNORA CINI: So it's a question of a document . . . a document without any value?

LAUDISI: That depends . . . It has a value, dear ladies—the value that anyone cares to give it! Let's think about the letters that Signora Frola says her daughter sends down to her by the basket in the courtyard every day. We admit these letters exist, don't we?

SIGNORA CINI: And suppose we do . . . what then?

LAUDISI: Then here's another set of documents, Signora! These letters, or rather notes, are documents too! But their value is the value you care to give them. Signor Ponza will come and tell you **they** are fakes—forgeries concocted to support Signora Frola in **her** delusion.

SIGNORA CINI: But in that case there's nothing we can know for certain—nothing at all!

LAUDISI: Don't say 'nothing at all', Signora Cini; we mustn't exaggerate! Excuse me—how many days are there in the week?

SIGNORA CINI: Why, seven, of course.

LAUDISI: Monday, Tuesday, Wednesday . . .

SIGNORA CINI (*continuing the series*): Thursday, Friday, Saturday . . .

LAUDISI: . . . and Sunday! And now, Signora Nenni, how many months are there in the year?

SIGNORA NENNI: Twelve!

LAUDISI: January, February, March . . .

SIGNORA CINI: That'll do, Signor Laudisi! You're just making fun of us!

Enter DINA, *running in through the main door.*

DINA: Oh, Uncle Tino, would you please help . . . (*She stops short on catching sight of* SIGNORA CINI.) Why, Signora Cini, I didn't know you were here!

SIGNORA CINI: Yes, I came along with my friend Signora Nenni . . .

LAUDISI: . . . who is so anxious to meet Signora Frola.

SIGNORA NENNI: No, no; that's not it at all!

SIGNORA CINI: Still trying to tease us, Signor Laudisi? Oh, Signora Agazzi, he **has** gone on at us! It's been like sitting in a train as it approaches a station through an unending series of points; clatter-clatter, clatter-clatter, clatter-clatter! We're quite dazed!

DINA: He's been very naughty lately—with us, too! Please be patient with him. (*To* LAUDISI.) Well, Uncle Tino, I don't need any help now. All I can do is to go and tell Mama who's here . . . But what a dear old lady Signora Frola is, Uncle! If you could just hear her talk! She's so kind . . . If you could see her little flat, with everything so clean, so orderly, so elegant, and such spotless little white covers on the furniture. And she showed us all her daughter's letters.

SIGNORA CINI: Really? Though, as Signor Laudisi was saying, those letters may . . .

DINA: But he doesn't know anything about them! He hasn't read them!

SIGNORA CINI: But couldn't they be fakes?

DINA: Fakes, indeed! Don't listen to him! How could a mother be wrong about the expressions used by her own daughter? Why, the most recent letter, written only yesterday . . . (*She stops short, hearing a murmur of voices in the drawing-room, through the open door.*) But here they are—they've arrived!

DINA *crosses left to look through the door into the drawing-room.* SIGNORA CINI *hurries after her.*

SIGNORA CINI: Is **she** there too? Signora Frola?
DINA: Yes, she is! But come on in! We've all got to be in the drawing-room! Is it eleven o'clock yet, Uncle?

Enter AMALIA *from the drawing room, very agitated.*

AMALIA: All this is quite unnecessary now! There's no need for any further proof!
DINA: I agree with you. There's no point in it now!
AMALIA (*upset and anxious, she hastily greets* SIGNORA CINI): So nice to see you, Signora Cini!
SIGNORA CINI: And this is Signora Nenni, who came with me to . . .
AMALIA (*another hasty greeting*): Delighted, Signora Nenni! (*A moment's pause; then, emphatically.*) **He's** the one that's mad! There's no doubt about it!
SIGNORA CINI: That's right! It must be!
DINA: If only we could get a message to Papa, and stop this trick being played on the poor old lady!
AMALIA: I know! We've brought her in here, and now . . . ! It seems so treacherous!
LAUDISI: It is! It's a most unworthy trick! You're right! Especially when it's becoming obvious to me that **she's** the one that's mad! She must be!
AMALIA: What? how can it be her? What do you mean?
LAUDISI: Of course it's she. It must be!
AMALIA: You can't be serious!
DINA: We're fully convinced that it isn't!
SIGNORA NENNI (*giggling*): Yes, you are, aren't you? You are!
LAUDISI: I'm sure that it is she because you're so certain that it isn't!

DINA: Oh, let's go into the drawing-room and leave him here! Can't you see he's doing this on purpose?

AMALIA: Yes, let's go into the drawing-room. (*Standing by the left-hand door.*) This way, please, ladies!

Exeunt SIGNORA CINI, SIGNORA NENNI *and* AMALIA. DINA *is about to follow them, when* LAUDISI *calls her back.*

LAUDISI: Dina!

DINA: I won't listen to you! I won't! I won't!

LAUDISI: If you really don't need any further proof, shut that door!

DINA: And what about Papa? He left the door open like that. He'll be here in a minute with . . . with that man. If he finds it shut . . . !
You know what he's like!

LAUDISI: You and your mother (but especially you yourself) will persuade him that there was no point in keeping it open. Aren't you convinced that you're right?

DINA: Yes—absolutely convinced!

LAUDISI (*with a challenging smile*): Then shut the door!

DINA: You want me to provide you with a spectacle of indecision . . . No, I won't shut it—but only because of Papa.

LAUDISI (*as before*): Would you like **me** to shut it?

DINA: On your own responsibility, yes!

LAUDISI: But I don't share your certainty that the son-in-law is the one that's mad.

DINA: Well, come into the drawing-room and listen to the old lady talking, as we have done. You'll soon find that **you** have no doubts on the subject either! Will you come?

LAUDISI: Yes, I'll come. And I'm ready to shut the door now—on my own responsibility.

DINA: Really? Even before you've heard her speak?

LAUDISI: The point is, I'm quite sure that by now your father has come to the same conclusion that you have—that no further proof is needed.

DINA: You're sure of that?

LAUDISI: Of course! Your father's talking to Signor Ponza.
By now he'll be quite sure that it's Signora Frola that's mad.
So . . . (*Approches the door in a determined manner.*) I'll shut
it!

DINA (*impulsively holding him back*): No, no! (*Regaining her
poise.*) I'm sorry, Uncle Tino! But . . . if you don't mind . .
we'll leave it open.

LAUDISI (*laughing in his usual manner*): Ha! ha! ha!

DINA: I'm only saying that because of Papa!

LAUDISI: And Papa might have something to say to
you!—We'll leave it open.

*The sound of piano music comes through the door from the
drawing-room—a melancholy, graceful old tune from Paisiello's
'Nina, pazza per amore.'*

DINA: Ah! D'you hear that? How well she plays!

LAUDISI: Is that the old lady?

DINA: Yes, she was telling us how, in the old days, her
daughter often used to play that old tune for her. Doesn't she
play it beautifully! Let's go in and listen to her!

Exeunt LAUDISI *and* DINA *through the left-hand door. The
stage remains empty for a while, during which the piano can still
be heard from the drawing-room. During the following scene,*
PONZA *is deeply disturbed as soon as he hears that music, and
his discomposure increases progressively as the action develops.*
AGAZZI *is the first to appear, on the far side of the centre door.*

AGAZZI (*ushering* PONZA *into the room in front of him*): Go
on in, Signor Ponza! (*Going over to the desk to pick up the
papers he has planted there.*) Ah, there they are—that's where
I must have left them! Take a seat, Signor Ponza!

PONZA *remains standing, gazing with horror towards the door
through which the music is coming.*

AGAZZI: Yes, here they are! (*He picks up the file and walks
over to* PONZO, *turning over the pages.*) As I was saying, it's a
tangled dispute that's been going on for years. (*Disturbed by
the music, he too turns round and glares towards the drawing-*

room.) That music! What a time to choose! (*With a gesture that seems to say 'Stupid women!' he turns back to* PONZA.) But who can be playing? (*Looking through the doorway into the drawing-room, he sees* SIGNORA FROLA *at the piano, and makes a surprised gesture.*) Good lord!

PONZA (*very agitated, coming right up to* AGAZZI): In heavens' name. Is that she, playing the piano?

AGAZZI: Yes, it's your mother-in-law. Doesn't she play well!

PONZA: But what's happening? You've brought her back in here again? And you're making her play the piano?

AGAZZI: I don't see what harm there can be in that!

PONZA: But not **that** piece of music, for goodness sake! It's what her daughter used to play!

AGAZZI: Perhaps it upsets you to hear it for that reason?

PONZA: It doesn't upset me—it upsets her! It does her incalculable harm! I've already explained to you, Signore, and to the ladies of your family, how that poor, unfortunate woman is situated . . .

AGAZZI (*trying to calm him down as he grows more and more agitated*): Yes . . . quite so . . . but listen!

PONZA (*ploughing remorselessly on*): I've explained that she needs to be left in peace—that she can't receive visits, and can't visit anyone else! I'm the only one who understands how she must be treated! You people are ruining her, destroying her!

AGAZZI: No, I don't see that at all. My wife and daughter are perfectly capable . . . (*He breaks off for a moment as the music in the drawing-room comes to an end; a round of applause follows.*) There you are! Listen to that!

The following exchange of remarks can be clearly heard in the study:

DINA: But you still play beautifully, Signora Frola!

SIGNORA FROLA: Ah, but my Lina's the one you ought to hear! My Lina really does play beautifully!

PONZA (*frantic, wringing his hands*): 'Her Lina'! Did you hear that? 'Her Lina', she says!

AGAZZI: Why, yes. Wasn't that her daughter's name?

PONZA: But she said she **plays** beautifully! **Plays**! In the present tense!

Once again, SIGNORA FROLA's *words can be clearly heard in the study.*

SIGNORA FROLA: No, no, she hasn't been able to play the piano, ever since it happened . . . That's probably what she misses most, poor girl!

AGAZZI: It seems pretty natural to me. She thinks her daughter's still alive . . .

PONZA: But she shouldn't be made to say these things. That's something she mustn't say! You heard it yourself: 'ever since it happened', she said! She's talking about **that** piano! You don't know about it, of course—the piano that belonged to the poor girl that's dead!

Enter SIRELLI. *Hearing* PONZA's *last few words and observing his state of extreme exasperation, he stands just inside the door as if thunderstruck.* AGAZZI, *also somewhat dismayed, beckons him forward.*

AGAZZI (*to* SIRELLI): Please ask the ladies to come in here.

Keeping as far away from PONZA *as possible,* SIRELLI *makes his way across to the left-hand door and delivers his message.*

PONZA: The ladies? in here? No, no! It'd be better to . . .

Enter SIGNORA FROLA, AMALIA, SIGNORA SIRELLI, DINA, SIGNORA CINI, SIGNORA NENNI *and* LAUDISI. *Ushered in by the horror-struck* SIRELLI, *the ladies also show signs of dismay. When* SIGNORA FROLA *catches sight of her son-in-law in that state of extreme excitement, quivering with almost animal fury, she is terrified. During the following scene, he addresses her in a very violent manner; while he does so, she periodically glances knowingly at the other ladies. This scene should be given a rapid and lively tempo.*

PONZA: So you are here! Here again in this house! And what have you come here for?

SIGNORA FROLA: I came here because . . . because . . . but

don't be angry . . .

PONZA: You came here to tell some more of your . . . But what **have** you been telling these ladies?

SIGNORA FROLA: Nothing, I swear it! Nothing!

PONZA: 'Nothing', indeed! I heard you! This gentleman (*Indicating* AGAZZI.) was with me and heard you too! 'She plays beautifully', you said! Who does? Is it Lina that plays beautifully? You know very well that your daughter's been dead for four years!

SIGNORA FROLA: Of course she has! Don't get so excited, my dear boy! Of course, of course!

PONZA: And then you said: 'She hasn't been able to play the piano ever since it happened.' Of course she hasn't! How could she play the piano, when she's dead?

SIGNORA FROLA: Exactly! And isn't that what I said to you ladies? She hasn't been able to play the piano since it happened. Not when she's dead!

PONZA: Why are you still worrying about that old piano, then?

SIGNORA FROLA: I'm not! I'm not! I never think about it!

PONZA: I smashed it up myself, as you know very well! When your daughter died, I smashed it up, to prevent it coming into the hands of . . . of the other one, who can't play a note anyway. You know she can't!

SIGNORA FROLA: That's right! She can't play a note!

PONZA: And what was your daughter's name? It was Lina, wasn't it? And my second wife's name? Tell them all that; you know the answer very well. What's her name?

SIGNORA FROLA: Giulia! Her name's Giulia. It's perfectly true, ladies and gentlemen; her name's Giulia!

PONZA: So she's Giulia, not Lina! And not so much of your winking at people when you say that her name's Giulia!

SIGNORA FROLA: No, no! I didn't wink!

PONZA: I saw you! You did wink! I saw it quite plainly! You're trying to ruin me! You're trying to make these people think that I want to keep your daughter all to myself—as if she wasn't dead! (*Breaking into terrible sobs.*) As if she wasn't dead!

SIGNORA FROLA (*running across to* PONZA, *and speaking with great humility and tenderness*): No, no, my dear son! For heavens' sake, try to calm down! I never did that! I never said she was still alive! Did I, dear ladies? Did I?

AMALIA:} No!
DINA: } No ... No! ...

SIGNORA SIRELLI: Never! Never! She never said that! She always said her daughter was dead!

SIGNORA FROLA: That's right! I said she was dead! Of course! And I said how good you are to me! (*To the ladies.*) It's the truth, isn't it? (*To* PONZA.) I wouldn't ruin you! I wouldn't harm your career!

PONZA (*a terrible, bristling figure*): But you go around looking for pianos in other people's houses so you can play your daughter's favourite pieces and say 'Lina plays like this, only better!'

SIGNORA FROLA: No, no! It was just that ... I only did it to show ...

PONZA: But you mustn't **do** that! You can't **do** that! Whatever can possess you to make you go on playing the things your daughter used to play?

SIGNORA FROLA: You're right! You're quite right, my poor, poor boy! (*Overcome by a tender emotion, she begins to weep.*) I'll never do it again! Never!

PONZA (*standing very close to* SIGNORA FROLA, *in a terrible voice*): And now go! Get out of here! Go!

SIGNORA FROLA: Yes ... yes ... I'll go ... I'm going ... Merciful heavens!

Exit SIGNORA FROLA *in tears, looking back at everybody with little beseeching gestures as if urging them to be kind to her son-in-law.*

The others are left staring at PONZA *with a mixture of pity and horror. As soon as his mother-in-law has left, however, he seems to undergo a complete change, becoming perfectly calm and resuming his normal manner.*

PONZA (*very matter-of-fact*): I owe you ladies and gentlemen an apology for this deplorable spectacle; but there was no

other way in which I could undo the harm you have done—unintentionally, unknowingly, and out of feelings of the purest sympathy—to that most unfortunate woman.
I had no alternative! Don't you see that this is the only way to keep her delusion intact—for me to yell the truth in her face as if it were a mad fancy of my own? I hope you will forgive me—and also that you will excuse me if I leave you now. I must go to her at once.

Exit PONZA *hurriedly, by the centre door. The others are left looking at each other in silent bewilderment.*

LAUDISI (*coming forward*): And so, ladies and gentlemen, now we know the truth! The truth! (**laughing**) Ha! ha! ha! ha!

CURTAIN

ACT THREE

Scene–as for Act Two. LAUDISI *is sprawled in an armchair, reading. A confused sound of many voices can be heard through the left-hand door, which leads to the drawing-room. The* FOOTMAN *appears at the centre door, ushering in* COMMISSARY CENTURI.

FOOTMAN: This way, if you please. I'll inform the Counsellor.
LAUDISI (*turning round and catching sight of* CENTURI): Ah! the Commissary! (*Jumping up and calling back the* FOOTMAN *as he prepares to go through into the drawing-room.*) Pst! Wait a moment! (*Turning to* CENTURI.) Any news?
CENTURI (*a tall, stiff, gloomy official, aged about forty*): Yes,

there is some news.

LAUDISI: Splendid! (*He turns to the* FOOTMAN.) Don't bother! I'll go in there (*nodding towards the left-hand door*) and fetch my brother-in-law, in a couple of minutes.

The FOOTMAN *bows and goes out by the centre door.*

LAUDISI (*to* CENTURI): You've certainly done wonders! The whole town is in your debt! D'you hear the noise they're making? Well, what news is there? What definite news?

CENTURI: Well, we've finally been able to trace someone . . .

LAUDISI: Someone from Signor Ponza's village? Someone from the neighbourhood who knows what happened?

CENTURI: Yes, Signore. We have some facts—not many, but quite definite facts.

LAUDISI: Good! Splendid! Can you give me an example?

CENTURI: All the data that I have received in this connection is here. (*He takes an envelope out of his inside jacket pocket—an unsealed, yellow envelope containing a single sheet—and hands it to* LAUDISI.)

LAUDISI: Aha! Let's see! (*He takes the sheet of paper out of the envelope and reads it through—silently, except for a series of little exclamations of 'oh!' and 'ah!' in various tones, starting with satisfaction, going on with doubt and something very like pity, and ending with complete disillusionment.*)

LAUDISI: But there's nothing here—no definite facts at all, Commissary!

CENTURI: All that we have been able to find is there.

LAUDISI: But all the doubts are still there, as strong as ever! (*He looks at* CENTURI *for a moment and then comes to a sudden decision.*) Commissary! Do you want to do a really good deed? Do you want to do your fellow-citizens a memorable service, for which God will undoubtedly reward you?

CENTURI (*staring at him in perplexity*): What service d'you mean? I . . . I'm not sure!

LAUDISI: I'll tell you. Sit down at that desk. Tear this sheet of paper in two, and throw away the half that contains this useless material; then take the other half-sheet, and write

something precise and definite on it—some real information!

CENTURI (*astonished*): You want me to do what? . . . What
information d'you mean?

LAUDISI: **Any** information! Any information you please!
(But attribute it to those two people from Signor Ponza's
village.) It's for the good of everybody—it'll restore
tranquillity to the whole district! Truth is all they want;
which truth it is doesn't matter, as long as it's positive and
categorical. So give them what they want!

CENTURI (*loudly; with growing indignation; controlling his
temper with difficulty*): But how can I give them something I
haven't got? Do you want me to commit a forgery? I'm
amazed that you should dare to make such a suggestion to
me! And I could put it much more strongly than that! And
now, will you kindly announce me to Counsellor Agazzi at
once.

LAUDISI (*spreading his arms in a gesture of defeat*): Yes, of
course! Immediately! (*Crosses to left-hand door and opens it.
The murmur of voices from the crowd in the drawing-room
abruptly swells to a roar. When* LAUDISI *goes in, however,
there is a sudden silence, and his voice can be heard from the
drawing-room making the following announcement.*) Gentlemen, Commissary Centuri is here. He's brought some
definite news—information from people who really know
the facts!

Cheering and clapping follow this speech. CENTURI *is visibly
disturbed, as he knows very well that the news he has brought will
not satisfy the expectations that have just been aroused.*

Enter AGAZZI, SIRELLI, LAUDISI, AMALIA, DINA,
SIGNORA SIRELLI, SIGNORA CINI, SIGNORA NENNI,
*and many other ladies and gentlemen. All crowd into the study
through the left-hand door, led by* AGAZZI. *Excited and
exultant, they clap their hands and shout 'Well done, Centuri!'*

AGAZZI (*holding out both hands*): Good old Centuri! Didn't
I say so! I knew you'd get to the bottom of it!

ALL: Well done! Well done! Let's hear the news! Let's see the proofs! Which of them is it? Which? Which?

CENTURI (*stunned, bewildered and dismayed*): No, no, really! The fact is, Counsellor Agazzi, that I . . .

AGAZZI: Please, gentlemen, please! Give him a chance!

CENTURI: It's true that I've done whatever was possible; but really, when Signor Laudisi says that I . . .

AGAZZI: . . . that you've brought us some definite news!

SIRELLI: Some positive facts!

LAUDISI (*loudly, with determination, getting his word in first*): Not very many facts, it's true, but definite as far as they go! Some genuine informants have been traced! People from Signor Ponza's village! People who know what happened!

ALL: At last! At last! At last!

CENTURI (*with a shrug, handing the sheet of paper to AGAZZI*): I'd better give you this, Signore.

Everyone crowds around AGAZZI as he unfolds the paper.

AGAZZI: Let's see . . . Let's see . . .

CENTURI (*angrily going up to LAUDISI*): But **your** behaviour, Signor Laudisi . . .

LAUDISI (*quickly, in a loud voice*): Really, Commissary! Please give the Counsellor a chance to read this document!

AGAZZI: Please be patient for a moment, gentlemen! Give me some room. I'll read it as quickly as I can!

A moment's silence follows, broken by the clear voice of LAUDISI.

LAUDISI: I know what's in it! I've read it!

Everyone leaves AGAZZI and crowds noisily round LAUDISI.

ALL: You have? Well, what does it say? What's the news?

LAUDISI (*slowly and emphatically*): It is now quite certain— quite indisputable, on the authority of someone from Signor Ponza's village—that Signora Frola has been in a nursing-home!

ALL (*bitterly disappointed*): Oh!

SIGNORA SIRELLI: Signora Frola!

DINA: So it must be she that's mad?

AGAZZI *has now finished reading the document.*

AGAZZI (*waving the paper in the air and shouting*): No, no, no! It doesn't say anything like that in here!

ALL (*leaving* LAUDISI *and crowding back to* AGAZZI *again*): What was that? What does it say, then? What does it say?

LAUDISI (*loudly, to* AGAZZI): But it does say so! It says 'the lady'! It specifically says 'the lady'!

AGAZZI (*answering even more loudly*): Nothing of the sort! This gentleman says he **thinks** so and so to be the case—he doesn't even pretend to be sure! And he doesn't know whether it was the mother or the daughter who was sent to the nursing-home.

ALL (*welcoming this piece of information*): Ah!

LAUDISI (*obstinately*): But it must be the mother, there's no doubt of that!

SIRELLI: No, no! It's the daughter, gentlemen—it can only be the daughter!

SIGNORA SIRELLI: Signora Frola told us so herself, anyway!

AMALIA: Quite right! So she did! They took her daughter away, without warning the husband in advance . . .

DINA: . . . and put her in a nursing-home! That's what she said!

AGAZZI: But in any case, this informant doesn't even come from the right district! He says that he used to go there a lot . . . . that he doesn't remember very well, but . . . that he thinks he heard someone say . . . and so on.

SIRELLI: All in the air, in fact!

LAUDISI: Forgive me for asking this, but if you're all so convinced that Signora Frola's right, what's the point of searching for further proof? Why not make an end of it? It's the son-in-law that's mad, and let's talk about something else!

SIRELLI: That's fine, my dear fellow, just fine—apart from the fact that the Prefect is of the opposite opinion, and takes every opportunity of showing his complete confidence in Signor Ponza!

CENTURI: Yes, gentlemen, that's perfectly correct! The Prefect believes Signor Ponza's story—he's told me so himself.

AGAZZI: But the Prefect hasn't spoken to Signora Frola yet!

SIGNORA SIRELLI: I'm sure he hasn't! He's only heard the husband's story!

SIRELLI: And there are others in this room who agree with the Prefect.

A GENTLEMAN: Yes, I do, for one! Because I know of a similar case—one where a mother was driven mad by her daughter's death, and now she believes that her son-in-law is preventing her from seeing her. Just like this one!

SECOND GENTLEMAN: No, there is a difference. In that other case, the son-in-law hasn't remarried and is living alone. Signor Ponza, on the other hand, has a wife living with him . . .

LAUDISI (*struck by a sudden thought*): Good heavens, gentlemen! Did you hear that? There's the clue we've been waiting for! The egg of Columbus! (*Patting* SECOND GENTLEMAN *on the back*.) Congratulations, sir! Did you hear that, everybody?

ALL (*perplexed, not getting the point*): What d'you mean? What is it? What?

SECOND GENTLEMAN (*dazed*): What did I say? I don't understand . . .

LAUDISI: 'What did I say?', indeed! You solved the whole problem! Just be patient for a moment, gentlemen! (*To* AGAZZI.) Is the Prefect coming here?

AGAZZI: Yes, we're expecting him. But why do you ask? What's in your mind?

LAUDISI: There's no point in his coming here to talk to Signora Frola. At present he believes the son-in-law's story; if he speaks to the mother-in-law, he won't know what to believe, any more than we do. No, no! There's something quite different for the Prefect to do in this instance—something that only he **can** do!

ALL: What d'you mean? What? What d'you mean?

LAUDISI (*beaming*): But didn't you hear what this gentleman said?

Signor Ponza has a wife living with him! A wife!

SIRELLI: You mean . . . get the wife to talk? Why not? Why not?

DINA: But the poor woman's kept shut up, like a prisoner . . .

SIRELLI: The Prefect will have to assert his authority and make her talk!

AMALIA: She's certainly the one person who could give us the truth!

SIGNORA SIRELLI: But she'll just say what her husband tells her to say!

LAUDISI: She will—if she has to speak in his presence! Undoubtedly!

SIRELLI: She'll have to have a personal interview with the Prefect!

AGAZZI: And on that basis the Prefect will certainly be able to use his authority to make her tell him what the situation really is! That's it! that's it! Don't you agree, Centuri?

CENTURI: Why, yes, of course—provided the Prefect likes the idea!

AGAZZI: It really is the only way! We ought to tell the Prefect about this, and save him the trouble of coming here for the moment. **You** go and tell him, my dear Centuri!

CENTURI: Yes, sir. I'll take my leave of you, Signor Agazzi, and of these ladies and gentlemen.

Exit CENTURI, *bowing.*

SIGNORA SIRELLI (*clapping her hands*): Good! Good! Well done, Signor Laudisi!

DINA: Well done, Uncle Tino! What a brilliant idea!

ALL: Well done! Well done! It's the only way! Yes, the only way!

AGAZZI: Well, well! How was it we didn't think of that before?

SIRELLI: After all, no one's ever seen her! It's as if she wasn't really there, poor woman!

LAUDISI (*as if thunderstruck by another new idea*): Aha! But are you sure she **is** really there?

AMALIA: Good heavens, Lamberto! **What** did you say?

SIRELLI (*pretending to laugh*): You surely can't want to shed doubt on her existence!

LAUDISI: Don't let's jump to conclusions! You say yourselves that no one's ever seen her!

DINA: What nonsense! Signora Frola sees her and talks to her every day!

SIGNORA SIRELLI: And the son-in-law says so, too.

LAUDISI: True enough. But just think about it for a moment! Logically speaking, there ought to be nothing in that flat but a ghost.

ALL: A ghost!

AGAZZI (*to* LAUDISI): Oh, do stop it, my dear fellow!

LAUDISI: Let me finish, please. Yes, a ghost! The ghost of a second wife, if Signora Frola is right; the ghost of Signora Frola's daughter, if we believe Signor Ponza. The ghost exists for Signor Ponza or Signora Frola; but what we don't know is whether there's a real woman behind the ghost, a woman who exists for herself. At the present state of our knowledge, I consider that we have grounds to doubt it!

AMALIA: Rubbish! You won't be happy until we're all as mad as you are!

SIGNORA NENNI: I'm trembling all over!

SIGNORA CINI: What pleasure can be get out of frightening us all like that?

ALL: But he's not serious! He can't be serious!

SIRELLI: She's a woman of flesh and blood, there's no doubt about that! And we'll make her talk! We'll hear her story!

AGAZZI (*to* LAUDISI): **You** suggested the Prefect should talk to her, remember?

LAUDISI: Yes, indeed; provided that there really is a woman up there in that flat—an ordinary woman! But consider the matter carefully, gentlemen! There can't be an **ordinary** woman in that flat—there can't be! I, at least, now have the gravest doubts about it.

SIGNORA SIRELLI: He really does want to drive us all mad!

LAUDISI: Well, well! We shall see!

ALL (*confused uproar*): But other people have seen her, too! . . .

She looks down from the balcony! . . . She writes those letters! . . . He's doing it on purpose, to make fun of us!

Amid the confusion, CENTURI *returns, very hot and bothered.*

CENTURI: The Prefect is coming! The Prefect!

AGAZZI: Coming here? Didn't you give him my message?

CENTURI: He'd already started. He was on the way here, with Signor Ponza, when I met him.

SIRELLI: With Signor Ponza, eh?

AGAZZI: But if he's got Ponza with him, he'll probably go straight to Signora Frola's flat! Centuri, will you please go and wait outside the door and ask the Prefect to be kind enough to come in here for a moment first, as he said he would?

CENTURI: Yes, of course, Signor Agazzi. I'll go at once.

Exit CENTURI *hurriedly by the centre door.*

AGAZZI: And now, ladies and gentlemen, please be so kind as to go into the drawing-room for a minute.

SIGNORA SIRELLI: But you'll put it to him squarely, won't you, and tell him she's the only one who can give us the truth!

AMALIA (*standing by the left-hand door*): This way, ladies, please!

AGAZZI: You stay here, Sirelli. And you too, Lamberto . . . (*Waiting until all the others have left the room.*) But please leave the talking to me!

LAUDISI: Yes, of course! Naturally! But if you'd rather I joined the others . . .

AGAZZI: No, it's better for you to be here . . . But here he is!

Enter the PREFECT—*a man of about sixty, tall, fat, with an air of easy good nature. He is followed by* CENTURI.

PREFECT: My dear Agazzi!—you here, too, Sirelli?—my dear Laudisi! (*He shakes hands with all three of them.*)

AGAZZI (*offering him a chair*): Excuse me for asking you to come in here first.

PREFECT: I was meaning to—as I'd said I would. I'd have come to see you afterwards, anyway.

AGAZZI *notices* CENTURI *standing in the background.*

AGAZZI: Come on, Centuri! Come and sit here!

PREFECT: Well, Sirelli, I hear that you are one of the people most passionately concerned and most deeply perturbed by all this gossip about our new Secretary!

SIRELLI: Oh no, Signore! Believe me, everyone in town is just as perturbed as I am!

AGAZZI: It's perfectly true—everybody is extremely excited.

PREFECT: I must confess that I can't understand why!

AGAZZI: That's because you haven't seen the things we've seen, living next to the mother-in-law as we do.

SIRELLI: You see, Signore, you haven't yet heard what that poor lady has to say.

PREFECT: Well, I was on my way to see her just now! (*Turning towards* AGAZZI.) I originally promised to see her here, in your flat, as you wanted me to; but then the son-in-law came and begged me—as a very great favour and to put a stop to all this chatter—to go to her place. But I hope no one thinks I would ever have done so if I hadn't been absolutely certain that the visit would provide proof that his story is true!

AGAZZI: Yes, it would, in a way! With her son-in-law there, that poor old lady . . .

SIRELLI (*quickly completing the sentence*): . . . would say whatever he wanted her to say! And that proves she isn't the one that's mad!

AGAZZI: We had a practical demonstration of that yesterday!

PREFECT: Yes, I know, my dear fellow! That's because he deliberately makes **her** think that **he's** mad! He warned me about that in advance. And in fact, how else could the poor, unhappy woman retain faith in her delusion? It's a real torment for him, believe me—a perpetual martyrdom!

SIRELLI: Yes, it must be! Unless of course you assume that the delusion is on his side—that he believes that her daughter is dead to give himself confidence that his wife won't be taken away from him again! In that case, Signore, as you can see for yourself, the perpetual martyrdom is on Signora Frola's side, not on Signor Ponza's!

AGAZZI: That's where the doubt arises—a doubt must surely be present in your own mind . . .

SIRELLI: . . . just as it is in everyone else's!

PREFECT: **Doubt**, do you say? To begin with, I can't see the faintest signs of doubt in yourselves! And I confess that there's no doubt in my mind either—though my opinion is the opposite of yours. How about you, Laudisi?

LAUDISI: You'll have to excuse me, Signore—I've promised my brother-in-law not to say anything.

AGAZZI (*impatiently*): What nonsense! If the Prefect asks you something, tell him! (*To the* PREFECT.) I did ask him to keep quiet; and I'll tell you why. For the past couple of days he's been amusing himself by stirring things up and adding to the general confusion.

LAUDISI: Please don't think that, Signore! I've been doing the very opposite—making every effort to clarify the situation.

SIRELLI: And just how has he set about clarifying the situation? First of all, by maintaining that it's impossible to discover the truth—and then, more recently, by suggesting that Signor Ponza's flat is inhabited, not by a woman of flesh and blood, but by a ghost!

PREFECT (*with cheerful amusement*): Not really? What an extraordinary idea!

AGAZZI: Well, you see how it is! It's a waste of time to listen to him!

LAUDISI: And yet . . . and yet it was **my** idea to ask the Prefect to come here!

PREFECT: Does that mean you agree with the view that I would be well advised to have a word with the lady in the neighbouring flat here?

LAUDISI: Heaven forbid! I think you're quite right to go on believing Signor Ponza's story!

PREFECT: Good! Good! So in fact you agree that Signor Ponza is right?

LAUDISI (*quickly*): No, no! I also think that the people here should go on believing Signora Frola's story, and let that be the end of it!

AGAZZI (*to the* PREFECT): See what I mean? Not much logic there!

PREFECT (*to* AGAZZI): Shall I continue? (*To* LAUDISI.) In your view, then, the mother-in-law's story is also worthy of credence?

LAUDISI: Undoubtedly! One hundred per cent! Just like Signor Ponza's story!

PREFECT: But in that case, excuse me, what follows?

SIRELLI: They do contradict each other, after all!

AGAZZI (*impatient and determined*): Now please listen to me! I'm not taking either side—I **refuse** to take either side for the moment! He may be right, and so may she! But the matter must be decided—and there's only one way of deciding it!

SIRELLI: The way suggested by Laudisi here!

PREFECT: Indeed? Well, well! Let's hear it!

AGAZZI: In the absence of any other kind of factual proof, we can only suggest that you should use your authority to obtain a statement from the wife.

PREFECT: From Signora Ponza?

SIRELLI: Her husband mustn't be there, of course!

AGAZZI: In that way, she'll be able to tell the truth.

SIRELLI: She'll say if she's Signora Frola's daughter, as we all think she must be . . .

AGAZZI: . . . or if she's Signor Ponza's second wife obligingly playing the part of the daughter, as he maintains . . .

PREFECT: . . . and as I wholeheartedly believe!—But I agree that there's only one way of deciding the matter. I know that poor Signor Ponza asks nothing better than a chance to show everyone that he's right. He spoke to me in such a docile, submissive manner! He'll be better pleased than anybody; and you good people will be able to set your minds at rest.—Would you do something for me, Centuri? (CENTURI *stands up.*) Go and fetch Signor Ponza from next door! Ask him in my name to come in here for a moment!

CENTURI: Certainly, Signore. (CENTURI *bows and goes out by the centre door.*)

AGAZZI: I only hope he'll agree to the plan!

PREFECT: He'll agree straight away! You'll see! We'll get the whole thing sorted out in a quarter of an hour—here, before your very eyes!

AGAZZI: Here? In my house?

SIRELLI: Do you think he'll be prepared to bring his wife here?

PREFECT: Just leave it to me!—Yes, I will see her here, because I know very well that otherwise you people would still think that I'd somehow managed to . . .

AGAZZI: No, no! What an idea!

SIRELLI: Never! We'd never think that!

PREFECT: Go along with you! Knowing that I'm convinced that Signor Ponza's right, you'd be bound to suspect that, since he is a public servant, I might want to hush the whole thing up and . . . no, no, I want you to hear what's said yourselves! (*To* AGAZZI.) Where's your wife?

AGAZZI: In there . . . with some other ladies.

PREFECT: This place seems to have been turned into a real conspirators' den!

Enter CENTURI.

CENTURI: Excuse me, Signore—Signor Ponza is here.

PREFECT: Thank you, Centuri.

PONZA *appears in the doorway.*

PREFECT: Come in, Ponza, my dear fellow—come in!

PONZA *bows.*

AGAZZI: And please sit down!

PONZA *bows again and takes a chair.*

PREFECT: You know these gentlemen, I think . . . Signor Sirelli . . .

PONZA *stands up and bows.*

AGAZZI: Yes, I have introduced him . . . and this is my brother-in-law, Signor Laudisi.

PONZA *bows again.*

PREFECT: I sent for you, my dear Ponza, to tell you that I
and these friends of mine . . . (*Pausing as he notices that*
PONZA *seems to be greatly perturbed and agitated by what he
is saying.*) Is there something you want to say?

PONZA: Yes, Signore. I wish to make an immediate
application for transfer!

PREFECT: But why do you want to do that? You were talking
to me in such a patient, dutiful way just now!

PONZA: But I have been made the target, Signore, of an
unprecedented degree of harassment!

PREFECT: Oh, come, come now! No exaggeration, please!

AGAZZI (*to* PONZA): **Harassment**, did you say? Are you by
any chance complaining of harassment by **me**?

PONZA: I'm complaining of harassment by everyone! And
that's why I'm going! (*To* PREFECT.) I'm going, Signore,
because I cannot endure this heartless, ferocious inquisition
into my private life, which is going to damage and ultimately
destroy the work of Christian charity to which I have
devoted so much effort and so many sacrifices. I revere and
respect that poor old lady as if she were my own mother; and
yesterday, in this very room, I was placed in a position where I
had to speak words of violent, aggressive cruelty to her. And
when I went to her flat just now, I found her so humiliated,
so agitated . . .

AGAZZI (*interrupting him—speaking very calmly*): That's
very strange. Every time Signora Frola has spoken to us,
she's done so in the calmest possible manner. The only
agitation we've noticed, Signor Ponza, has been exhibited by
yourself—up to and including the present moment!

PONZA: That's because you . . . you don't realise what you're
making me suffer!

PREFECT: My dear Ponza, try to calm yourself! What's
wrong? I'm here, you know! And you also know with what
deep sympathy and with what complete belief I've listened to
all you have to say. Isn't that true?

PONZA: Forgive me, Signore. It is true, as far as you yourself are concerned; and I'm deeply grateful.

PREFECT: Good! Now listen—you say you revere and respect poor Signora Frola as if she were your own mother. Very well, then—try to realise this. The reason my friends here are showing so much interest in the matter is precisely because they too are fond of the old lady!

PONZA: But they're killing her, Signore! I've told them so—I've explained it all to them more than once!

PREFECT: Show a little patience, please! All that will stop as soon as the matter is cleared up. And we'll clear it up here and now. All the materials for a solution are here. You have in your own hands the simplest and surest method of removing all doubts from the minds of these gentlemen! Not from my mind, because I have no doubts!

PONZA: But they've made up their minds not to believe a word I say!

AGAZZI: No, that isn't true. When you came here after Signora Frola's first visit and told us that she was mad, we were all very surprised, but we did believe you. (*To the* PREFECT.) But then, you see, the next thing was that the old lady came back again, and . . .

PREFECT: Yes, I know; you told me about that. (*To* PONZA.) She came back and told them the very story that you are trying to keep alive in her mind. Now you must realise how natural it is that anyone who listens to her after listening to you should be afflicted by a certain distressing doubt. And so these gentlemen, who have heard what she had to say, no longer feel able to place complete confidence in what you tell them, my dear Ponza. So it's clear enough what we have to do. We won't trouble your mother-in-law or yourself for any more information at present. You are certain that your story is true, and so am I; and I don't see how you can object to the idea of getting it confirmed, here and now, by the one person in the world who knows the facts—the one person, that is, apart from yourself and your mother-in-law!

PONZA: Who do you mean?

PREFECT: I mean your wife, Signor Ponza!

PONZA (*loudly and indignantly*): No, Signore! Never!

PREFECT: And why not, may I ask?

PONZA: Am I to bring my wife here to convince those who doubt my word?

PREFECT (*quickly*): No—to make a statement to **me**! Is there any difficulty about that?

PONZA: But I implore you, not my wife! No, no! Please leave her out of it! You have my word for what has happened; you can believe me!

PREFECT: In point of fact, Signor Ponza, I'm beginning to come round to the view that you're doing all you can to **stop** people believing you!

AGAZZI: Yes; especially when one remembers how he did everything he could—including a repeated act of gross discourtesy to my wife and daughter—to prevent Signora Frola from coming here and talking to us.

PONZA (*in a furious outburst*): But what do you want from me? In heavens' name! It seems my poor, unfortunate mother-in-law isn't enough for you; you want to get my wife here too! This is an outrage that I can't endure! My wife is going to stay where she is—at home! I'm not going to drag her into anyone's presence! (*To* PREFECT.) It's enough for me, Signore, that **you** believe me. And I'll go and write out my application for transfer! (PONZA *stands up.*)

PREFECT (*banging his fist on the desk*): Just a moment! In the first place, Signor Ponza, I cannot permit you to take this tone with your superior officer here—or with myself, after all the courtesy and understanding that I've shown to you. In the second place, I must again warn you that I'm beginning to have second thoughts about what you've told me, in view of your violent opposition to a suggested process of confirmation which has been requested, in your own interest, by myself and by no one else—a process which, moreover, seems to me to be wholly unobjectionable. There is no reason why my colleague Signor Agazzi and I should not receive a visit from a lady—or go and visit her, if you prefer it.

PONZA: So you're going to force me to agree?

PREFECT: As I said before, I'm making this request for your own good. As your superior officer, I could convert the request into an order!

PONZA: Very well then. Very well. If that's how it is, I'll bring my wife here, just to get it over!—But how can I be sure that the poor old lady won't see her?

PREFECT: Yes, that's a point . . . as she's in the neighbouring flat . . .

AGAZZI (*quickly*): We could visit Signora Frola while the Prefect talks to Signora Ponza.

PONZA: No, no! That's what I'm afraid of! I don't want any more of your surprises and tricks, with their catastrophic consequences!

AGAZZI: You needn't worry about us!

PREFECT (*to* PONZA): Or if you'd rather, you could bring her along to the Prefecture at some convenient time.

PONZA: No, no; I'd rather it was here and now—straight away! I'll go to the other flat myself and stand guard over my mother-in-law when I get back. And now I'll go and fetch my wife! And that'll be the end of it!... the end of it! (*Exit* PONZA *hurriedly, by the centre door.*)

PREFECT: I must admit that I wasn't expecting this opposition from him.

AGAZZI: See if he doesn't go and tell his wife what he wants her to say!

PREFECT: No, no! You needn't worry about that! I shall be interrogating the lady!

SIRELLI (*to the* PREFECT): Did you notice his agitation,— his continual state of fury?

PREFECT: Yes—I've seen him like that before. Perhaps it was the idea of bringing his wife here . . .

SIRELLI: . . . of releasing her from custody, one might say!

PREFECT: Ah, but the fact that he keeps his wife shut up like a prisoner can be explained without assuming him to be mad!

SIRELLI (*to the* PREFECT): If you'll excuse my mentioning it, Signore, you haven't yet heard what the poor lady has to say.

AGAZZI: Exactly! And Ponza says that he keeps her shut up for fear of what Signora Frola might do.

PREFECT: But even if that didn't arise . . . he could, quite simply, be a jealous husband!

SIRELLI: But that wouldn't explain why he doesn't even have a housemaid in his flat! He makes his wife do all the housework herself!

AGAZZI: And **he** does all the shopping, every morning!

CENTURI (*to the* PREFECT): It's true; I've seen him myself! He comes back from the shops with a boy to carry the things . . .

SIRELLI: . . . and the boy isn't allowed inside the door!

PREFECT: Good heavens, gentlemen! He told me all this and said what a nuisance it was, while I was talking to him earlier on!

LAUDISI: He certainly provides an irreproachable information service!

PREFECT: He does these things to save money, Laudisi! He has the expense of maintaining two households.

SIRELLI: But that's not the point we're trying to make! Does it seem credible to you that a second wife would take on such a burden . . .

AGAZZI (*emphatically*): . . . the burden of the humblest household duties! . . .

SIRELLI (*continuing his speech*): . . . for the sake of a woman who is her husband's mother-in-law but is nothing to her personally?

AGAZZI: Isn't that a bit too much to believe?

PREFECT: It **is** a lot to believe . . .

LAUDISI (*interrupting*): . . . a lot to believe of an **ordinary** second wife!

PREFECT (*quickly*): Yes, I must agree, it's a lot to believe. But this, too can be explained—not, admittedly, in terms of the wife's generosity, but in terms of the husband's jealousy. And though Signor Ponza may or may not be mad, I don't think there's any doubt that he's jealous.

A confused clamour of many voices is heard from the drawing-room.

AGAZZI: What's going on in there?

Enter AMALIA, *hurriedly, by the left-hand door, in great consternation.*

AMALIA (*addressing the company at large*): It's Signora Frola! She's here!

AGAZZI: No! Good God! Who sent for her?

AMALIA: Nobody! She came of her own accord!

PREFECT: No! For heavens' sake! Not now! Send her away, Signora Agazzi!

AGAZZI: Yes, send her away at once! Don't let her in here! Whatever happens, she mustn't come in! If he finds her here again, it'll really look like a trap!

Enter SIGNORA FROLA, *trembling and weeping, in a supplicating attitude, holding a handkerchief in her hand. She is accompanied by a crowd of people from the drawing-room, all very agitated.*

SIGNORA FROLA: Gentlemen, gentlemen, for pity's sake! Oh, Signor Agazzi, won't you tell them?

AGAZZI (*stepping forward, very angry*): I tell you, Signora, that you must leave this room immediately! You can't stay here!

SIGNORA FROLA (*bewildered*): Why do you say that? Why? (*To* AMALIA.) Dear, kind Signora Agazzi, I appeal to you!

AMALIA: But, you see, Signora Frola ... Look! The Prefect is here ...

SIGNORA FROLA: The Prefect? Oh, Signore, for pity's sake! I was going to come and see you ...

PREFECT: No, Signora, you must be patient! I can't listen to you now! You must go! You must go at once!

SIGNORA FROLA: Yes, I'll go! I'll leave today. I'll go right away, and you'll never see me again!

AGAZZI: No, no, Signora Frola! Just be so good as to go back to your own little flat for a moment! Please do me this personal favour! You can have a word with the Prefect afterwards.

SIGNORA FROLA: But why? What's happening? What is it?

AGAZZI (*losing his patience*): Your son-in-law will be back here in a minute. That's what's happening! Do you understand!

SIGNORA FROLA: I see. Well, then, of course, I must go—I'll go at once! All I wanted to say was this: for pity's sake, please stop what you're doing! You think you're helping me and you're doing me so much harm. I shall have to go right away, if you go on like this; I shall have to pack up and move out today, so that he can be left in peace!—But what do you want from him now? Why has he got to come here and see the Prefect? Why?

PREFECT: It's nothing, Signora, nothing at all! Don't worry—but please, please, do go!

AMALIA: Yes, Signora Frola—please do what we ask!

SIGNORA FROLA: Oh, Signora Agazzi! You people are taking away my one remaining consolation—the pleasure of seeing my daughter sometimes, even if it was from a distance! (*She begins to weep.*)

PREFECT: But no one has said anything like that! You've no reason to pack up and move out. We're only asking you to go back to your own flat for a moment. Don't worry!

SIGNORA FROLA: But I do worry! I worry about him! I came here to intercede with you all for him—not for myself, but for him!

PREFECT: Very well, then! You needn't worry about him, either. I give you my personal assurance of that. You'll see that the whole matter will soon be cleared up and everything will be all right.

SIGNORA FROLA: But how can I believe that, when I can see that everyone here is so bitterly hostile to him?

PREFECT: That isn't true, Signora Frola! I'm on his side! **Don't worry!**

SIGNORA FROLA: Oh, thank you, thank you! That means that you understand . . .

PREFECT: Yes, indeed, Signora; I do understand.

SIGNORA FROLA: I've explained it all so many times to all these ladies and gentlemen—it's a misfortune in the past: a misfortune that we've got over, and there's no point in returning to it now.

PREFECT: Yes, yes, of course! I assure you that I do understand!

SIGNORA FROLA: My daughter and I are quite content to live like this—yes, my daughter too! And so . . . (*To the* PREFECT.) Please, **please** make them stop what they're doing. Because if you don't, there's nothing left for me to do but go right away and never see her again, even from a distance! So for pity's sake leave in peace!

A movement becomes noticeable in the crowd; everyone gesticulates as if trying to convey a message. Some members of the crowd gaze towards the door. Two or three voices, speaking in undertones, can be heard.

VOICES: Oh dear! . . . Here she is! . . . Here she is!

SIGNORA FROLA *notices the general dismay and confusion and begins to tremble.*

SIGNORA FROLA (*in a puzzled, moaning voice*): What is it? What's happening?

Everyone draws back to make way for SIGNORA PONZA, *who enters and walks stiffly forward. She is in deep mourning and her face is covered by an impenetrable, thick, black veil.*

SIGNORA FROLA (*with a rending cry of frantic joy*): Oh! Lina! Lina! Lina! (*She rushes forward and clings to the veiled figure with all the passion of a mother who has not embraced her daughter for years. At the same moment,* PONZA's *voice can be heard calling outside.*)

PONZA (*outside*): Giulia! Giulia! Giulia!

At the sound of PONZA's *voice,* SIGNOR PONZA's *body visibly goes rigid in the old lady's embrace. A moment later* PONZA *dashes in. The first thing he sees is* SIGNORA FROLA *clinging passionately to his wife.*

PONZA (*furiously*): I knew it! What a base, cowardly way to take advantage of my trust in your good faith!

SIGNORA PONZA (*turning her veiled face towards him with*

solemn dignity): Don't be afraid! There's nothing to be afraid of! And now both of you can go!

PONZA (*softly, lovingly, to* SIGNORA FROLA): Yes . . . let's go! . . . let's go!

SIGNORA FROLA *has relinquished her grip of* SIGNORA PONZA *with trembling humility, and now hastens to echo* PONZA's *words.*

SIGNORA FROLA: Yes, yes . . . Let's go, my dear boy! Let's go!

With their arms round each other's waist, weeping in two different keys, PONZA *and* SIGNORA FROLA *make their way towards the door, exchanging affectionate caresses and whispered endearments. They go out together. There is a moment's silence. Having watched them out of sight, all present, bewildered and touched at the same time, turn their attention to the veiled figure of* SIGNORA PONZA. *She looks round at them through her veil with sad dignity.*

SIGNORA PONZA: What more can you gentlemen want from me now? This, as you can see, is a misfortune that must remain a secret, because there is only one remedy for it; and that is the remedy that has already been provided by family love and duty.

PREFECT (*touched by her words*): And we earnestly desire to respect that family love and duty, Signora! . . . And what we want to hear from you is . . .

SIGNORA PONZA (*speaking slowly and very clearly*): What do you want from me? The truth? The truth is this, and this alone: I am the daughter, yes, the daughter of Signora Frola . . .

ALL (*welcoming the news*): Ah!

SIGNORA PONZA (*as before*): . . . and I'm the second wife of Signor Ponza . . .

ALL (*murmurs of astonishment and disappointment*): No! . . . Impossible! . . . How can that be so?

SIGNORA PONZA (*as before*): It is so! . . . and for myself, I am neither one nor the other.

PREFECT: Impossible, Signora! You must be one or the other, for yourself!

SIGNORA PONZA: Not at all. For myself, I am what others believe me to be. (*She looks round at everyone through her veil for a moment and then goes out. A silence follows.*)

LAUDISI: Well, ladies and gentlemen, you've heard the voice of truth! (*Looking round the company in mocking defiance.*) Are you all happy now. (*He bursts out laughing.*) Ha! ha! ha! ha!

CURTAIN

LAZARUS

Lazzaro

1927

Translated by
Frederick May

CHARACTERS

DIEGO SPINA
SARA, his wife, but now no longer living with him
LUCIO and LIA, their children
ARCADIPANE, a farm-bailiff
DEODATA, Lia's governess
GIONNI, a doctor of medicine engaged in research
MONSIGNOR LELLI
CICO, God's rent-collector
MARRA, a notary
THE TWO NATURAL CHILDREN of Sara and Arcadipane
  (they do not speak)
A DOCTOR
A POLICEMAN
PEOPLE WHO COME IN FROM THE STREET
TWO PEASANTS

The time is the present (i.e. 1929)

ACT I   The hanging garden of Diego Spina's house
ACT II The rustic porch of Diego Spina's farmhouse
ACT III The same as Act II, a few minutes later

ACT ONE

The scene is the hanging garden at the house of DIEGO SPINA.
*The house, an old and unpretentious building, is on the Left (the
actor's Left, that is.) The front wall is seen in profile; there is a
small drooping rustic porch, supported by pillars, beneath which
one can see the doors that lead into the rooms on the ground floor.
Along the back of the stage there runs a wall between three and
four feet high, roughly constructed, whitewashed and topped off
with a crest of broken glass. Half-way along this wall, and sharply
outlined against the background of the strange blue sky—it's
almost as if it were enamelled—there is a huge black cross bearing
a depressing, painted, bleeding figure of Christ. Beside the cross
there rises the trunk of a very tall cypress tree, which grows up
from the road that lies below the wall. This wall, which bounds the
house, continues round the right-hand side of the stage; it is broken
into mid-way along by the upper landing of the flight of steps
leading down to the road. At ground-level there are one of two
flower-beds, with flowering plants here and there, intersected by
gravel paths on which stand some seats painted green.*

When the curtain rises DEODATA *and* LIA *are on stage.* LIA
*is fifteen, but looks a mere child. Her hair falls loosely over her
shoulders, and is set off by a lovely bow of sky-blue ribbon. Her
legs are paralysed, and she is confined to an invalid-chair which
she wheels about herself with a speed and dexterity that have
become second nature to her. Her legs are covered by a shawl.*
DEODATA *is about forty. Tall and strongly-built, she is dressed
in black and is wearing a black cap on her head. She is seated on
an iron stool and is making lace on a pillow. It is an April
afternoon.*

LIA (*absorbedly*): He hasn't written for more than a month.

DEODATA (*after a pause*): Lucio?

LIA: And his last letter . . . Well, Daddy couldn't make head or tail of it. He wouldn't let me read it.

DEODATA: He's probably all worked up about his exams. Your father, is always getting such ideas into his head.

LIA: Maybe, But I'm just as bad, you know. I get ideas like that too.

DEODATA: Good girl! You're just as bad. You've infected me too with this **disease** of yours . . .

LIA: Ugh! No, you mustn't call it a disease . . .

DEODATA: Yes, it's a **disease**! A disease! Because . . . Oh, time and time again you . . . Look! You start imagining that somebody's thinking something. You make that person aware of what you're imagining. And the thought that didn't in the first place exist at all, now really does come into his head. And who has made that thought come into his head? **You** . . . By imagining what you did.

LIA: Forgive me for asking, but aren't **you** busy doing a little imagining at the moment? Suggesting that Lucio doesn't write because he's worried about his exams?

DEODATA: I'm just trying to find some sort of an explanation for his silence. Like many another explanation, it might quite well be the probable one. And it's got the virtue too of being one that, while I'm busy imagining it, doesn't harm him and doesn't cause me to grieve . . . At least, not till I have to. (*There is a pause*).

LIA: Oh, if only he hadn't been so obstinate about going up to the university!

DEODATA: Ah, as for that . . . You see, I didn't approve of him going there either. When he came out of the seminary he could have settled down quietly and contentedly and followed his sacred calling as a priest, without going off to learn all that devilry they teach you up there at the university!

LIA: But if he'd done that he'd have had to go off immediately and do his military service . . .

LIA: Oh yes, I know that! That was his excuse for doing what he did. As if he wasn't going to have to do it just the same when he was twenty-six! If you want my opinion, he'd have found it much less of a burden at twenty-one! But there, what's the use of talking about it? Your father too . . . The thought of seeing him turn up at any minute without his cassock, and in a soldier's uniform . . . Well, for **him**, it would have been like seeing the Devil himself!

LIA: It was because Lucio was so run-down. He couldn't bear the thought of his having to face all the rough and tumble of life in the army . . .

DEODATA: It's no use! In this house I shall just have to keep my mouth shut quite tight! I reason things out. I've got into the nasty, vicious habit of reasoning things out, living here among you people . . .

LIA: Who don't reason anything out at all . . .

DEODATA: There you go! There's no happy medium about this family! Either you're mad or you're saints. Your father's probably a saint . . . No, he certainly *is* a saint! But sometimes, you know, if I forget myself and really start paying attention to what he's doing and saying, well . . . God forgive me! . . . But . . . With those glaring eyes of his . . . He really and truly seems to me to be stark staring mad!

LIA (*she smiles her amusement*): Why don't you tell him so?

DEODATA: I shall, don't you worry! I'll tell him all right! I've been bottling it up inside me for a long time now! I'll tell him this very day, in front of everybody! It'll help to get it off my conscience too! You make me laugh, you and your 'run-down'! Why is he run-down? Because of the life he led in the seminary! Too shut up! Too much hard studying! If you want my opinion, the remedy for all his troubles was a complete change. A life in the open-air! But, oh no! Not on your life! On with his studies! Heaven only knows how long he's going to go on cramming things into that head of his! He'll end up by ruining his health completely! But when you've told him all this and **shown** him what it all adds up to . . . It means absolutely nothing as far as he's concerned. He bothers about people's health as little as he bothers about anything else! He spreads out his hands and raises his eyes to

Heaven. Or if you do think that he's been listening to what you've been saying, and that he's picked up some suggestion that you've let fall, quite suddenly you're brought up against the realization that what you suggested . . . Well, he's simply made use of it to commit some fresh piece of lunacy. Like what he's up to now . . .

LIA: You mean handing over the farm?

DEODATA: Yes. A fine way of giving you country air! Which is what Dr Gionni next door suggested to him!

LIA: But what does he mean to do?

DEODATA: With the farm? D'you mean to say you still haven't realized? He's turning it into a hospice for the indigent poor.

LIA: And what does that mean?

DEODATA: It means that all the beggars in town, and for miles around, will get their board and lodging, here on the farm, at his expense! And that the two of you, he and you, will be living there with them! **Yes!** You'll thrive on the country air! You mark my words! After it's been thoroughly polluted by all their wretched filthy rags and tatters!

CICO's voice is heard coming from the foot of the steps Right.

CICO'S VOICE: May I come up? Any objections?

DEODATA: Oh, it's you, Cico? Come on up! Come on!

CICO comes up the steps. He is a queer little wisp of an old man. His eyes are small and blue—almost glassy—sharp, merry, eloquent. On his scalp, which gleams with a high polish, he is wearing a small red convict's cap. Twisted round his neck is a long blue scarf, which hungs down before and behind. He speaks in spasmodic outbursts: every now and again he breaks off short, and looks at you with those small, merry, eloquent eyes of his, accompanying his gaze with a mute smile. He is both shrewd and cunning.

CICO: Ruined, Deodata, ruined. (He sees LIA and immediately whips off his cap.) Ah, so you're here too, dear little lady? Your humble servant! (Then once more to DEODATA.) Ruined.

DEODATA: Who's ruined you, you stupid old donkey?

LIA: Daddy, I'll bet!

CICO: **And the Devil!** Daddy and the Devil! The pair of them. That's how things happen, little lady. The more a man's a saint, the closer the Devil creeps up to his elbow. (*Sneezes.*) Do you mind? (*He puts his cap on again.*) Once I start sneezing . . . I'm quite capable of letting rip with a hundred blasts, one straight after the other! And it's good-bye to what I was saying! I can't get another word out!

LIA: What have Daddy and the Devil done to you?

CICO: I've told you . . . **Ruined me!** I'd got a wonderful idea! Oh, it was a wonderful idea! I was raking the money in in sackfulls. I'd discovered a profession for myself. I'd taken out my licence.

DEODATA: You mean you'd given up begging?

CICO: Begging my foot! *I* am a rent collector. Licensed.

DEODATA: You, a rent collector?

LIA: For whom?

CICO: For God, little lady. God's rent-collector. I'd composed a bit of patter, and as soon as I began to recite it . . . Oh, you can't imagine the huge crowds I had gathering all round me!

Men and women, of every class, age
and profession—
sailors, countryfolk, townsfolk—
we are all tenants
of The Lord.
Tenants of the Lord,
Who is the owner of the two houses.
Two houses . . .
Yes . . .
Two houses.
One of them . . . Look, we can see it . . . Look, look at it
. . . All around us.
And The Lord would be a good and kindly Landlord
to all of us alike,
if it weren't for the fact that so many, so many of us,

avid in greed and haughty in their pride,
had taken it as their own private property,
when it
ought instead to be a house common to us all.
There's some that've got granaries, barns, and storelofts;
and there's some that haven't got a yard of rope
nor enough wall to stick a nail in,
so as to be able to hang themselves;
and it's most of us that're like this, and that're like me.
But meanwhile the others had better be thinking
that God's the Landlord
of the other house as well . . . The one up there,
the one He makes us pay the rent for
. . . Each and every one of us . . .
In advance, whilst we're still down here.
The poor, like me,
we pay it every day with the suffering
and the toil we know, punctually, at every hour of the
    night and day
as far as the rich are concerned, on the other hand, all
    that's asked of them by way of payment
is to do the odd good turn every now and again.
And so it comes about,
ladies and gentlemen, that I'm really and truly
here in The Lord's Name
to claim, (*He holds out his hand.*)
the little something that's due
from you.
God's rent-collector—that's me!

The money came raining in, little lady. Like hailstones. But
now, with all this devilry of a hospice that your father's
thinking of founding . . . Well, you can imagine just how
much rent in advance for the house up there I'm likely to
collect from now on! They'll say to me, 'You've now got a
house yourself down here . . . Go and live in it!'
DEODATA: Good for you, Cico! So you too think this idea of
the hospice is the suggestion of the Devil? Eh?

CICO: Of course it is! And I've got the proof of it tucked away inside me! D'you know what I've got inside me?

LIA: Yes, I do. Yes. It's the Devil that says 'No'.

CICO: You're right . . . I swear he does too! He's always doing it! Without me wanting him to! I say 'Yes', and he says 'No'. And he says it in my own voice. In a whisper . . . Right down low . . . While I'm speaking. Look, here's what I mean . . . Yesterday, I was standing in front of a mirror stuck in a shop-window. I said to myself, 'Why, God, why? You've given us teeth, and one by one You take them away from us. You've given us sight, and You take it away from us. You've given us strength, and You take it away from us. Now look at me, Lord, look at the state You've left me in! Just look at me! So, of all the lovely things You've given us, we aren't supposed to bring any of them back to You when we come? I must say You'll enjoy Yourself a hundred years from now, when You see a bunch of scarecrows like me popping up in front of You!'

DEODATA: That was the Devil talking! It couldn't possibly have been you!

CICO: Oh, it wasn't! **Possibly** it wasn't! It was the Devil. And I was ever so glad that Monsignor Lelli, who happened to be passing at the time, gave him the reply he was asking for! 'Oh, you stupid stupid donkey, God has brought you to this condition that it shall not trouble you greatly to die!'

DEODATA: And quite right too! Good for Monsignor Lelli!

CICO: As you say! But do you know what that stinking Devil actually dared to fling back at him in a whisper? Right down low he whispered it! 'Then when He takes away our teeth He ought to take away our desire to chew as well . . . And He **doesn't**!' Oh, they all burst out laughing—Monsignor Lelli along with the rest of them. And I was left there, looking a proper muggins, I can tell you! It wasn't right . . . It wasn't fair of them to laugh! Leaving me like that, without a word to say for myself by way of reply! It's not the sort of thing people **ought** to find funny! This what-I've-said about the hospice . . . This charity home . . . That was one of the things he's been telling me . . . Deep down inside me.

DEODATA: The Devil, you mean?

CICO: The Devil. Every time I got to the end of my bit of patter he'd say, 'But, in the meantime, what about if the poor had a house of their own down here as well?' D'you understand? And now the Master's really and truly gone and given them one! (*The voice of* DR GIONNI *is heard as he climbs the steps.*)

DR GIONNI'S VOICE: She's alive again! She's alive again!

DR GIONNI *comes into sight. He is carrying a small white doe-rabbit in his hands. He hurries over to* LIA's *chair. He's a handsome, yet unattractive man, with a full fair beard, gold-rimmed spectacles . . . About forty years of age. He is wearing a long white linen operating-theatre gown, belted in the middle.*

GIONNI: Here you are! Here's your dear little rabbit for you again! She's come back to life.

LIA (*quivering all over with a joy which is almost dismay, she takes the rabbit*): Alive? Oh, dear! Yes! Yes! Look!

DEODATA: Is it possible?

GIONNI: Since last night, as a matter of fact. Yes, soon after I took her home with me . . .

LIA: Oh, so very soon?

GIONNI: I didn't say a word to you about it this morning, because I wanted to be quite sure first . . .

LIA: But what have you done to her? How did you do it?

GIONNI: Nothing. Just a little prick with a needle.

LIA: Oh, my poor little Riri! Where?

GIONNI: In her heart.

LIA (*utterly astonished*): In her heart? And she came back to life again?

GIONNI: She's not the first case.

DEODATA: Get along with you! Who are you trying to fool? It's a different rabbit!

GIONNI (*to* LIA): Do **you** think it's a different rabbit?

LIA: Why, of course I don't! It's Riri! (*To* DEODATA.) Do you really think I don't know her? Look, she knows me too!

CICO: Oh, no! No! This just can't be! She was dead . . . And you've brought her back to life?

DEODATA: It's a different rabbit, I tell you! Or if it's the same one . . . Well, that means it wasn't dead in the first place!

LIA: She was as dead as could be!

GIONNI: Adrenalin.

LIA: And now she's alive!

CICO: Oh, I'm going barmy!

DIEGO SPINA *and* MONSIGNOR LELLI *enter from the steps.* DIEGO SPINA *is a little over forty. Tall and lean, with an intensely pale and cadaverous face, the whole force and expression of which are concentrated in the fierce glow of his hard, ever-mobile eyes. They are the eyes, you might almost say, of an infuriated madman. His beard and moustache are sparse, straggling, and unkempt. His hair is parted in the middle and piled up on either side of the parting, as a consequence of the habit he has of pushing the masses of hair up like this when he passes his hands over his head.* MONSIGNOR LELLI, *outwardly sweet and gentle, is not always successful in concealing beneath his smile and his friendly gaze all the bitterness that lurks in his heart. He is very old.*

DIEGO (*coming forward*): What's happening?

LIA (*immediately; exultant*): Oh, it's you, Daddy? Look! Look at my Riri! She's come back to life again!

DIEGO: What on earth are you talking about?

LIA: Look at her! Just look at her! Here she is . . . Alive!

DIEGO: It's not possible!

CICO (*to* MONSIGNOR LELLI): Dead, and he's brought her back to life again!

MONSIGNOR LELLI (*with the smile of a man who doesn't believe what he's saying*): A miracle?

CICO (*quivering with rage*): Tell him at once that it's nothing of the sort! Don't laugh! It's not right, Monsignore, it's not proper!

MONSIGNOR LELLI: I'm not laughing, Cico! But, forgive me, if the rabbit has contrived to come back to life . . .

DIEGO (*promptly, harshly*): It's a sure sign that it can't possibly have been dead in the first place!

MONSIGNOR LELLI: Obviously! All quite simple!

DEODATA: There, just what I said myself!

LIA: No, Daddy! She **was** dead! She was really and truly dead! Wasn't she, Doctor?

DIEGO (*peremptory, stern, clipping his words incisively, without giving the* DOCTOR *a chance to reply*): It cannot possibly be true! (*Then, turning once more to the* DOCTOR, *with an air of nervous irritation.*) Really, Doctor, you oughtn't to . . . You ought not to . . .

CICO (*as though unable to understand why all this fuss is being made about something which, to him, is the most natural thing in the world*): What oughtn't I to do?

DIEGO: You oughtn't to tell my daughter such abominable stories!

GIONNI: Why do you call them abominable?

DIEGO: Oh, so you think it's quite normal for us to be able to . . .?

GIONNI: If you'd only taken the trouble to keep up with . . .

DIEGO: I have done so! We can read it about them in the newspapers, unfortunately, these triumphs of science—and all the other things like them! And I know all about the disgraceful way you torture those wretched little animals you keep in your laboratory! It appals me, **utterly**.

GIONNI: But I've brought this one back to life . . .

MONSIGNOR LELLI (*instantly*): . . . from what was **apparently** death.

GIONNI (*promptly and firmly*): There was no **apparently** about it at all. She **was** dead.

DIEGO: Do you mind telling me how you can be so dogmatic about it.

GIONNI: Good Lord, do you really suppose that a doctor doesn't know when . . . ?

DIEGO (*severely, cutting him off short*): I know this . . . God alone can recall the dead to life by performing one of His miracles!

CICO: There you are! Good for you!

MONSIGNOR LELLI: Precisely!

CICO: That, Monsignore, is my belief too. God alone. I do not for one moment presume to have wrought the miracle myself I can, you see, conceive of science as another instrument from the Hand of God. Everything depends upon our being able to comprehend one another.

MONSIGNOR LELLI: Are you really serious? I mean . . . About the way **you** interpret what's happened.

GIONNI: As serious as I'm convinced of the truth of our faith . . . . Yours and mine.

DIEGO (*angrily, contemptuously, he snatches the rabbit out of* LIA's *hand and gives it to* GIONNI): Here, take it! Take it back to your laboratory!

LIA (*impulsively*): No, not my Riri!

DIEGO: That will do, Lia!

GIONNI: My intention, Signor Spina, was to bring a little joy to your daughter. Is this how you thank me?

MONSIGNOR LELLI: There is one faith, and one faith only!

GIONNI: And that bids me take this rabbit back to my laboratory?

LIA: No, Daddy!

MONSIGNOR LELLI (*to* LIA): If God took her from you . . .

GIONNI: God is giving her back to her again!

DIEGO (*at the end of his tether*): Doctor, I beg you, will you please . . . ? Really!

GIONNI: Very well, then! I'll take her back with me! I'll take her! (*He goes off towards the steps. Just before he begins his descent he turns to* LIA.) Don't worry, my dear! I'll keep her alive for you!

DIEGO (*lovingly he bends over his weeping daughter*): I don't like to see you crying . . . I don't want you to cry, Lia . . . You know what it is we have to do . . . We offer up to God . . .

LIA: Yes, Daddy . . . Yes! Yes! . . . I'm going in now! I'm going in . . . (*She goes off towards the house in her wheel-chair and disappears through one of the doors under the portico. They all follow her with their eyes.*)

MONSIGNOR LELLI: You might perhaps have let her keep it.

DEODATA (*angry and upset*): I should just think you might have! An innocent pleasure like that . . . !

MONSIGNOR LELLI: Ah, no! That's the precise point at issue! **Not** innocent! Not when it was regained by such means!

DIEGO (*a touch repentant*): You heard her say, all of you, didn't you, that as far as she was concerned the creature **was** dead?

DEODATA: And to get it back again . . . Alive . . .

DIEGO (*turning upon her angrily*): Do you realize the full implications of what you're saying?

CICO: Dead and then back to life again!

DIEGO: That we should believe such a thing possible . . . Do you realize that? And that she should have the proof there on her knees? Oh, I felt so angry deep down inside me . . .

DEODATA: What? Who made you feel angry? The child?

DIEGO: No, listening to that man and what he had to say!

DEODATA: And what had that got to do with the child anyway? Snatching the rabbit out of her hands like that . . . Like a brute . . .

DIEGO: And aren't I confessing that I regret my harshness? It seems to me that I am.

DEODATA: It never entered my head for a single instant to think of any of the horrible things you saw in the affair! Now, you listen to me! I've kept it bottled up long enough! And now I'm going to tell you, here and now, in front of Monsignor Lelli. The trials that God sends us . . . Let's accept them with resignation . . . All the sacrifices, all of them . . . If He commands you to make them . . . Well, make them . . . . And be happy to do so . . . But it's got to be Him . . . Or His Vicar down here on earth! Look here, Monsignor Lelli'll do just as well . . . If it's in His Name that he orders me to do something. But not you! You, if you like, **you** can sacrifice **yourself** . . .

DIEGO: I . . .

DEODATA: Yes, you've been sacrificing yourself, your whole life long! But when you start insisting that other people ought to sacrifice themselves as well . . . Oh no, that's going too far!

DIEGO: I? I start insisting . . . ? Against their will?

DEODATA: That's how I see it anyway! Will . . . What sort of will do you think your daughter's got, when it comes to facing up to you? Yes, I tell you! Yes! You sacrifice everyone else along with yourself! Perhaps you don't even notice you're doing it. But look here . . . At this very moment . . . What you've planning to do now . . .

DIEGO: What I'm planning to do?

DEODATA: Oh, that hospice of yours!

DIEGO: Oh, so it's the hospice again, is it?

DEODATA: Forgive me for asking . . . But have you thought about me? . . . Have you ever given a thought to all the love I've always bestowed on your poor afflicted daughter? All the loving care . . . **My** loving care . . . That now she'll have to go without?

DIEGO: Why will she have to go without it?

DEODATA: You ask me that? You surely don't expect me to come and live in that hospice of yours? Along with all the retired beggars you're pensioning off? I've even heard a rumour that you're going to invite that Scoma slut to join you!

CICO: Yes, yes! That Scoma woman . . . She goes around telling everybody!

DEODATA: And, of course, we all know why! It's a reward for her virtue!

MONSIGNOR LELLI: That will do, Deodata!

DEODATA (*as though unable to rest in peace, revealing all the resentment of an ancient rivalry*): That witch! She goes about begging, with her own picture in a frame, slung round her neck like a scapula! And it's not in God's Name that she begs for alms! Oh, no! Not on your life! It's because of what she **was**. . . . It's in honour of **that**! And we all know what **she** was, don't we? Her picture tells you **that** anyway. You just try not giving her anything! She'll spit the most foul language after you! Curse you up hill and down dale!

MONSIGNOR LELLI: I've already told you, Deodata . . . **That will do!**

DEODATA: Yes, Monsignor, but you do realize, don't you . . . ?

MONSIGNOR LELLI (*his meaning clear, if subtly veiled*): It would be rather more to the point if you tried to do a little **realizing** yourself!

DEODATA: But I do realize! I do understand! And since you say that . . . Will you allow me to . . .? No, it's not really me. Will you allow my **conscience** to say a word or two? Don't worry . . . I'll keep quite calm! Calm as calm! It's the voice of conscience. Look deep down inside yourselves. I may be mistaken. But I must speak out frankly. And say all I've got to say. (*To* DIEGO.) It's an excuse . . . Nothing more or less . . . An excuse for your own weakness, this idea of yours for founding a hospice up there on the farm!

DIEGO: My **weakness**?

DEODATA: Yes! Your weakness in never having plucked up enough courage to chuck them off the farm . . .

MONSIGNOR LELLI (*with the utmost severity*): Hold your tongue, Deodata!

DIEGO: No! No! Let her say what she has to say!

DEODATA: **Your wife.** Who's been living there for years and years in mortal sin with a man . . . Your servant . . . by whom she's had two children.

DIEGO (*with a sorrowing simplicity*): Why do you call it weakness?

DEODATA: 'Why', he says! **Why**? Why, because you've never had the courage to . . .

DIEGO (*promptly, cutting her short*): I have had the courage to . . . To resist myself! The more I've been humiliated in the eyes of other people by what she's done, the greater has been the courage I have shown! You're one of those other people yourself! And you call it weakness! Just like the rest of them!

DEODATA: Forgive me for asking, but this is **your** daughter that's here, or isn't it? And tell me . . . Did the doctors prescribe country air for her, or did they not? Even if there wasn't anything else, your daughter . . . and no one else . . Your daughter ought to be able to give you the strength you need, to do what you should have done years ago. Instead of which you keep her shut up here in this house, just so that her mother . . . that worthless creature . . . Can go on enjoying all the country air herself!

DIEGO (*loudly, so as to cut short what she is saying*): You're not to talk like that! You don't know what you're saying!

DEODATA (*after a short pause in a low voice, almost as if she can't help herself, but must say what she has to say—to herself at least*): So you'll even go so far as to **defend** her!

DIEGO (*promptly, at once*): No. It's you who's defending her . . . . Yes, **you**! . . . Without knowing that you're doing it.

DEODATA: I am?

DIEGO: Yes, **you** are. Because it was she who wanted her daughter to have precisely what you have been demanding for her . . . Just now.

DEODATA: Country air?

DIEGO: Country air. (*A pause. Then he says.*) Why do you think she left me? We were never able to reach any agreement on how we were to bring up our children. That came first . . Then we disagreed about their education too.

DEODATA: Oh, so that was why she left you?

DIEGO: That was why . . . That was why she left me. (*Another short pause.*) Monsignore, she loved them with a love that was . . . I don't know . . . too . . . In my opinion, too **carnal**. The same as so many other mothers. Neither more nor less.

CICO: Oh, a mother . . . (*And immediately he claps his hand over his mouth.*)

DIEGO: And it was on her account, as a matter of fact . . . The little girl's . . . When she fell ill . . . **She** firmly believed that it was all my fault . . . Because I'd insisted on sending her away to school too young . . . I'd sent her to board with the Sisters . . . . It was on account of the little girl that she hated me . . . She couldn't bear the sight of me any longer . . . She cursed my house and went away to live on the farm . . .

DEODATA: With that man?

DIEGO (*angrily*): What do you mean, 'with that man'? That happened two years later. She went to live on the farm . . . Waiting for me to take the child out there to her . . . The child who by this time had lost the use of her legs.

DEODATA: Ah! . . . And you . . . ?

DIEGO: I refused.

DEODATA: That was wrong of you!

DIEGO (*to* MONSIGNOR LELLI): She made it a condition of our reconciliation that I fetch the other child back home as well.

DEODATA: Lucio?

DIEGO: Lucio. She wanted me to remove him from the seminary to which I'd sent him. Monsignore, I might . . . Perhaps . . . Have done even that. But to admit that it was all my fault . . .

MONSIGNOR LELLI: You mean, what happened to the little girl?

DIEGO: In all conscience I couldn't bring myself to believe that it was my fault! And if I'd withdrawn Lucio . . . Prevented him from following his career in the Church . . . As if by way of making amends for something for which I refuse to except the blame. If I'd done that it would have led to my giving way to her, to doing exactly as she wanted with my children.

MONSIGNOR LELLI: Inevitably.

DIEGO: It would have meant being false to myself, to what I felt to be true, to my principles . . .

MONSIGNOR LELLI: And you say that you might even have done all this?

DIEGO: Yes. I was on the point of doing it . . . More than once.

MONSIGNOR LELLI: It grieves me to hear you say so!

DIEGO: By the Grace of God, I was able to realize . . . Each time . . . That I should have been doing it only because I still loved and . . . **Wanted** that woman . . .

MONSIGNOR LELLI: I see.

DIEGO: And that it was only because of this vile lust of the flesh . . .

MONSIGNOR LELLI: I understand!

DIEGO: I won the battle with myself. And nobody ever knew the tears I shed as I refused to surrender! And nobody ever knew of my secret hope that **she** might give way instead . . . Out of compassion for her crippled child.

DEODATA: She certainly ought to have felt compassion!

DIEGO: The hatred she felt for me was stronger; and she didn't yield.

DEODATA (*with an outburst of diabolical glee*): You're still in love with her! You're still in love with her!

DIEGO: Of course I'm not! What on earth are you talking about?

DEODATA: It's as plain as the nose on your face! You're still in love with her! You can see it a mile off!

CICO (*trembling all over with excitement*): There you are, you see! It's the Devil again! Mine was just about to say the same thing . . . And hers got his spoke in first!

DIEGO (*with a sad smile*): Yes, Cico . . . You're quite right . . . It was the Devil. What harm do you think there can possibly be now in this love which I must feel . . . Yes, even for her? I'm right, aren't I, Monsignore? (*To* DEODATA, *after a pause.*) As you can see very clearly, it would be unjust of me . . . . It would be a double injustice on my part . . . If I were now to take advantage of the fact that Lia needs the country air on account of her health . . . That's to say, of the very remedy which she herself proposed at that time for the child . . . And on account of which . . . Since I refused to give in . . . She is now living in sin.

DEODATA: You don't mean to say, do you now, that you believe that **that's** your fault?

DIEGO: If I had only taken the children up there to her . . .

MONSIGNOR LELLI: No! No! The wrong which you committed was something quite different . . . Quite, quite different. You did wrong in not throwing her out in time . . . I mean, the moment you saw that she'd taken up with that man . . .

DIEGO: Yes, but . . .

MONSIGNOR LELLI: You ought not to have tolerated it. You ought not to have allowed her go on living her adulterous life in your house . . . If the farm was yours . . . I was under the impression that it belonged to her . . .

DIEGO: No, it's mine. It belongs to me . . .

MONSIGNOR LELLI: It really has been most shocking . . . Absolutely outrageous! But since you didn't do it at the

proper time . . . When you had every right to do it . . . Well,
you certainly can't do it now. (*To* DEODATA.) He can't
plead the excuse of his daughter's health . . . Not now. That
would put him in the wrong and her in the right.

DIEGO: No . . . You see, Monsignore, you don't know what a
terrible effect it had on me when first I heard of it! I forced
myself to keep in check. To do nothing . . . to . . . live out the
life of my torment . . . Letting it go on and on . . . Without
affording it the slightest relief . . . Quite the reverse in fact . . .
I chose rather to be the scorn of all my neighbours . . . The
button which is radiant in the fire that moulds it . . . That was
my victory . . . **Martyrdom**. A long, long martyrdom. It was
long because my wound kept opening afresh . . . And the
blood . . . Black, **bitter** blood . . . Welled out again and again.
They told me that she'd given up everything . . . That she'd
cast off all her lovely clothes . . .

DEODATA: Ah, but that's because she knows that . . . Well,
dressing the way she does now . . .

DIEGO: Like a peasant, you mean?

DEODATA: Yes . . . She's an absolute joy to look at . . . So
lovely . . . Everybody says the same thing . . . An absolute
delight . . .

CICO: Oh yes, she's lovely . . . Lovely! She still looks like a girl
of twenty! When she passes by everybody turns to look at
her. It's just as if the sun were passing by! She's a **miracle**!

DEODATA (*she is alluding to* SARA*'s bailiff lover*): I suppose
she looks so lovely, because that's how he wants her!

DIEGO (*with a sudden, violent access of rage, which dismays and
chills them all*): That is enough of that! I can't bear to stand
here and listen to . . . Not from you!

DEODATA (*dully, insensitively, after a pause*): It was you who
brought the subject up in the first place . . .

DIEGO: It wasn't out of wickedness that she gave herself to
that man. Neither is he the sort of man that you suppose.
You know, Monsignore, don't you, that he's always sent the
profits on the farm to the hospital? And always in my name.
Ever since I first refused to accept them. And those profits
have gone on steadily increasing, year by year. That farm has

become the richest and best cultivated in the whole neighbourhood.

CICO: Oh, it's Paradise itself! An Earthly Paradise! I go out there, so I know! And those two little boys . . . They're more handsome even than their mother! And they're already working on the land. Oh, you should just see them! Hoeing away, with two little hoes . . . So big! . . . Working away beside their father . . . And simply bursting with health!

DIEGO: It would certainly be a very great pity to turn them out . . . A pity for the hospital, I mean.

DEODATA: Well, I'm . . . ! He's thinking of the hospital now!

DIEGO: What I'm thinking is that they live there as poor people . . . Doing good to others. If I turn them out now, they'll have to provide for themselves . . .

DEODATA: It'll be their punishment!

DIEGO: That's as may be! But the good that they've been doing all this time mustn't just be allowed to go to waste. I shall have to carry on the good work they've been doing myself . . .

DEODATA: By setting up your hospice on the farm? You'll ruin the farm! And as for the amount of good you'll be able to do . . . ! That'll be precious little! And, what's more, you've done as much good as you need to already! It's high time you stopped! You've stripped yourself of everything! As a matter of fact, it was about this point that I wanted to talk to you, Monsignore . . . Has he got the right to carry on the way he does? When he's got a daughter who's a cripple?

DIEGO: My daughter wants for nothing . . . Save only to attain in Heaven . . . When it shall please God to call her unto Him . . . all that she could not have here on earth. It's not enough to **talk** about poverty . . . We must **experience** it. And, since that's the case, we must strip outselves of all that we possess. My daughter will live in the country, but she will see there . . . A poor man among other poor men . . . Her own father. And she will be happy, because she will see that I am happy! Yes, when all's said and done, that is the only way! Otherwise I couldn't possibly bear to think of those two, driven off the land, wanderers on the face of the earth, in search of work. (*Turning abruptly to* DEODATA.) Don't stand there staring at me like that! I pray every night to God that He will call me back to Himself! Not that I may have relief from the trials which He has been pleased to visit upon me, but that I may raise **them** up from that life of sin which is now theirs. Because I know that she has found a man . . . She has found a man.

During his speech the sun has been setting, and now the sky is all aflame with the full splendour of sunset. A bell is heard ringing at the foot of the steps.

DEODATA: Somebody's ringing. Wonder who it can be? The gate ought to be open, unless **you** shut it when you came in. (*To* CICO.) Go and see who it is, will you? Go on! (CICO *goes over to the steps. He starts back in utter astonishment, almost in dismay. He comes back over.*)

CICO: Ooooh! It's **her**! **Her!** The Missis!

DIEGO: She's . . . **Here?**

CICO: Yes . . . All dressed in red . . . With a black cloak.

DEODATA: She must have got to hear about the . . . And perhaps she's come to . . .

MONSIGNOR LELLI: About the farm?

DIEGO: But how does she dare to . . . ?

MONSIGNOR LELLI (*catches sight of her as she appears on the steps and halts on the landing*): Here she is!

DIEGO (*in a low voice*): Go indoors, all of you! Leave me alone with her. (*To* DEODATA.) Mind that Lia doesn't find out she's here.

MONSIGNOR LELLI, DEODATA *and* CICO *withdraw. They go out through one of the doors under the portico. Set against the background of the blazing sky* SARA, *dressed all in red under a black cloak, seems like an unreal apparition of ineffable beauty: she radiates freshness, health, and power.*

SARA (*absorbed by what she sees, she looks around her, comparing her memory of things with how they appear to her now—less ample, meaner, shabbier*): The garden . . . The house . . .

DIEGO: You actually dare to come and see me again? In front of the whole world?

SARA (*the same absorbed, appraising look*): And you too . . . My God, what a face!

DIEGO: Leave my face out of this! Tell me why you've come!

SARA: Oh, don't worry! As soon as people get to know why I've come, they'll realize that I **had** to come . . . And they won't be at all surprised. There will be a great deal more for them to be surprised about . . . But not my coming here.

DIEGO: Have you come because you heard . . . ?

SARA: About the hospice? No. (*She laughs.*) Oh, you were afraid that I'd come to intercede, to beg you to leave us on the farm?

DIEGO: **Isn't** that what you've come for?

SARA: No, no, of course not! It's not your farm that's keeping us alive . . .

DIEGO (*swiftly, trying to cut her short*): I know! I know!

SARA: Well, then? We live by the work that we do upon it. If necessary we can do that somewhere else. It's something that, so far as we're concerned, isn't of the slightest importance. It might, at most . . . Yes, at most . . . It might be of some importance to the poor, sick people at the hospital.

DIEGO: That's the very thing I was saying myself, only a moment or so ago . . .

SARA: There you are, you see? And since you've brought up the subject . . .

DIEGO: No! Tell me first the reason why you've come . . .

SARA: Wait a minute . . . If you're trying to find some excuse for turning us out . . .

DIEGO: It's not an excuse!

SARA: What on earth do you think they want with a farm? . . . These old town beggars, who are used to spending their lives in wandering from door to door. Used to being with lots of people. If you shut them up there, they'll feel as if they were in prison . . . It would be like punishing them—not doing them a kindness. In a year's time the farm will have died on their hands.

DIEGO: I shall be up there myself, living among them.

SARA: You? And what could you possibly do with those arms of yours? You make me laugh! You've not seen the farm . . . Not since . . . And you've got no idea what it's like now, no conception of what we've done to it. There's not one square foot of land that not's growing something . . .

DIEGO: I know that . . .

SARA: The kitchen garden . . . The vineyard . . . The orchard . . . Oh, we've got every kind of fruit you could possibly want! And, you know, we've found water! That spring which you said . . . Do you remember? . . . Said you could sometimes hear running under the bank alongside the path that leads down into the valley . . . Well, that's the one . . . We've found it! There's masses and masses of water! It's brought new life and freshness to everything! Three great cisterns always full. . . . And it flows along the ditches . . . Everywhere . . . Joyously! And it makes you heave a deep sigh of contentment when you hear its noisy rush on those hot summer evenings. . . . So . . . if this hospice of yours is only an excuse . . . Don't give it another thought.

DIEGO: I've already told you . . . It's not an excuse.

SARA: We'll leave the farm. We'll go away of our own accord. Tomorrow, if you like. We won't even put you to the trouble of turning us out. Put in another bailiff, though . . . Choose an honest one. And a man who knows the meaning of work. That's what you must do. And do it . . . Now, listen to me . . . Do it for the sake of your own flesh and blood! Have you given a thought to how you're going to provide for these children of yours?

DIEGO: The children . . . Do you mean to tell me that you're interested in them . . . . **Still?**

SARA: 'Still', you say **Still?** To **me? You?** Who was it that denied me the right to think of them **always? Always!** Of them and of them alone?

DIEGO (*his face darkening*): Let's drop the subject!

SARA: You no longer wanted me to be a mother to my children, even though it meant that you would lose me as a wife!

DIEGO: Yes, because I intended my wife to be the mother of my children, bringing them up according to my principles.

SARA: Oh, no! No! Not that! Never!

DIEGO: Yes!

SARA: Do you know what? The fact that things are as they are now proves to me . . . More decisively than ever . . . That I was in the right! Not you!

DIEGO: Let's change the subject! Let's change the subject!

SARA (*pointing to the Crucifix*): You never see anything but **That** . . . And even That you see only in the way **you** want to see it.

DIEGO: Don't blaspheme!

SARA: I, **blaspheme?** I'm the first to go down on my knees before it! But, you know, that Cross is there to give people life . . . Not death!

DIEGO: Will you be silent? What right have **you** to talk of life and death? You have forgotten that the true life is the one which lies in the world beyond. When we have cast off this flesh.

SARA: I know that God gave us this life as well as that other . . . In order that we might live it out, here below, in health and happiness! And no one can know this better than a mother! I wanted joy . . . Yes, I wanted joy and health for my children! And I looked for wealth too . . . Yes! For their sakes . . . Not for my own! I've lived as a peasant myself. I still live as a peasant. And if you leave the farm to your children, then let me tell you . . . I shall be glad I've toiled with these arms . . . Yes, you know, really and truly **toiled!** . . . To make it as prosperous as it now is . . . For their sakes!

DIEGO: They've done without it so far, with the help of God, and they can go on doing without it.

SARA: How can you possibly know that?

DIEGO: I **do** know.

SARA: So many things may happen which are far beyond your dreams.

DIEGO: Well anyway, I've provided for one of the children. And as for Lucio . . .

SARA (*as if she had been expecting this*): As for Lucio . . . ?

DIEGO: He has his vocation.

SARA: And if that is no longer sufficient for him?

DIEGO: What do you mean . . . 'If that is no longer sufficient for him'? It must be sufficient for him!

SARA: Lucio came to see me yesterday.

DIEGO (*utterly taken aback*): Lucio? What on earth are you saying? He's come back . . . ?

SARA: Yes, he's come back. And he came to **me**. That's why I said that the fact that things are as they are proves . . . Now more decisively than ever . . . that I was right.

DIEGO (*still almost incredulous*): Lucio came to **you**?

SARA: That is why you see me here. Your son came to me.

DIEGO: But . . . What do you mean . . . **Came?** Did you write to him? You sent for him, didn't you?

SARA: How on earth could I possibly have sent for him? No. And why should I have done? (*Scornfully.*) Oh, you're still thinking about the farm! I told you, I'm ready to hand it over to you tomorrow!

DIEGO: Then . . . It was of his own accord? But . . . Why? (*In dismay and bewilderment.*) He came without showing his face here . . . He's stopped writing . . . What's happened to him?

SARA: I don't know. I was in the vegetable garden. I saw him standing before me. I didn't recognize him at first. How on earth **should** I have recognized him?

DIEGO: But . . . He came out to you? With what object? What did he say?

SARA: I couldn't repeat it . . . Not the way he put it . . . You must hear him yourself! What he had to say was not for me alone. . . . For the whole wide world!

DIEGO: He must have gone mad!

SARA: He's a changed man!

DIEGO: **A changed man?** What do you mean? He must at least have given you some reason for coming.

SARA: Yes, he did. It was to recognize me.

DIEGO (*in bewildered astonishment*): To **recognize** you?

SARA: Yes. And to be born again. **He**, to be born again of me. To be born again of me, his mother. He said so! I looked at him, in dismay. How white his face has grown, just like wax! And his eyes! I saw him stretch out his arms ... Tears welled up within those terrible eyes of his ... "Mamma" he said ... I felt myself ... I felt myself purified by it ... A blessèd mother once again! He took me in his arms ... He wept on my breast ... For a long time ... A very long time ... In my arms ... Trembling all over. I've never felt anyone tremble the way he did then!

DIEGO (*almost to himself*): Oh, God! O God, help me! O God! God, God, what is it You want of me? (*To* SARA.) But ... How? ... Without giving a moment's thought to the fact that ... Up there, where he went to look for you ... You were living with a man who's not his father ... And that he .. (*Suddenly, as though a doubt has entered his mind, leaving him thunderstruck.*) But perhaps ... Oh, God! ... Perhaps he's no longer wearing his cassock?

SARA: No.

DIEGO (*as if in terror*): He's taken off his cassock? He's thrown away his cassock?

SARA: But you should hear how lovingly he still speaks of God!

DIEGO (*frantic*): Where is he? Where is he? Tell me where he is! Is he up at the farm?

SARA: No, he came with me. To talk to you.

DIEGO: He wants to talk to me?

SARA: He wants to explain things to you ...

DIEGO: Where is he?

SARA: He stayed at my sister's ... Down by Town Gate ...

DIEGO: I'm going to see him! I'm going to see him! I'm going to see him ...

And, as if quite insane, he hurls himself down the stairs. SARA *remains perplexed and a touch dismayed by his flight. She looks around her and perceives* CICO, *who is standing peering at her from behind one of the little columns, red cap on head. She waves him over. Quite suddenly the sky, which up till now has been red, becomes violet, and the stage is as if chilled all at once by this livid, sinister light.*

SARA: Come over here! You must run after him! I can't.
Lucio's come home . . . Without his cassock!

CICO: Oh, has he . . . ?

SARA: Yes! He dashed off like a madman. Go and tell them in
the house. Go and tell them in the house. **I'm going now. You
must look after him!**

And she hurries away down the steps. DEODATA *comes out of
one of the doors of the portico to see what's going on.* CICO
immediately calls out to her. DEODATA *hastens over.*

DEODATA: What did she say to you? And why did he run
away?

CICO: It's Lucio . . . Lucio . . . It's all the Devil's fault . . . He's
thrown away his cassock!

DEODATA: Lucio? Did she tell you that?

CICO: She did! She did! It's all the Devil's fault!

DEODATA: O God, help us!

CICO: He tore off, dashed down the stairs! I'm going after
him! (*Exit furiously down the stairs.*)

DEODATA: Yes, you go! Run after him! But where will he
have gone? Oh, Lord God in Heaven! All dressed in scarlet
she was! Like a flame from Hell! And to bring such news too!
(*She goes over to the porch.*) Oh, Monsignore! Monsignore!

MONSIGNOR LELLI (*coming out, in consternation*): What's
the matter? What's happened?

DEODATA: Lucio's stopped being a priest! He's thrown
away his cassock!

MONSIGNOR LELLI: No! What on earth are you saying?

DEODATA: **She** came here . . . To break the news to him! And
he's gone tearing off!

MONSIGNOR LELLI: Where to?

DEODATA: I don't know! He just dashed off! (*A confused
sound of shouting, anxious voices is heard near at hand, and
coming even nearer.*)

MONSIGNOR LELLI: Do you hear that? What can have
happened? Why are they shouting?

SHOUTS: Gently, now, gently! . . . Up there! . . . Up those
steps!
But how did it happen?

Oh, it's Signor Spina!
Not so loud! Not so loud! Remember his daughter!
But is he . . . **Dead?** How did it happen? Oh, poor soul!
Careful now! Careful as you go up the steps!
Turn round now! Head first! The steps are pretty steep!
DEODATA (*rushing over to the steps*): Oh, my God! It's the
Master! What's happened?
CICO (*coming back up the steps*): He's been run over! Run
over!
MONSIGNOR LELLI: Run along, Deodata! Don't let the
child come out!
DEODATA: But he can't be dead!
MONSIGNOR LELLI: No, no! Let's hope not! Now run
along! Run along!

*A group of men comes up the steps, panting. They were men who
were passing along the street when the accident occurred. They
are supporting the limp body of* DIEGO SPINA, *some at the
head, others at the feet. Some people are carrying small lighted
lanterns. Laboriously the men carry the body over and set it down
on one of the benches, so that it is in full view of the audience.*
DEODATA *rushes over towards the house. When the knot of
bearers has passed the head of the steps . . . That's to say, before
they've got to the point of putting the body down . . . Another
group of curious, anxious people comes into sight. Their way is
barred by* CICO.

VOICES OF THE BEARERS: Up a bit! Gently—gently! Over
here! Over here!
Put him down on that seat there!
That's it! Gently now! Over here!
MONSIGNOR LELLI: But there's no sign of any injury!
ONE OF THE BEARERS: No, not a sign!
MONSIGNOR LELLI: How did it happen?
ANOTHER OF THE BEARERS: He threw himself under a
motorcar!
MONSIGNOR LELLI: What . . . **Deliberately?** Impossible!
FIRST BEARER: Well, it certainly seemed like it!
THIRD BEARER: He was running like somebody who'd gone
stark staring mad!

FOURTH BEARER: Everybody thought the same thing . . . That he'd . . .

MONSIGNOR LELLI: Impossible! Impossible!

FIRST BEARER: The car swerved . . .

SECOND BEARER: Didn't even go over him . . .

THIRD BEARER: But it flung him against the wall so violently that he dropped down at once . . . Just like a lump of lead!

MONSIGNOR LELLI: He doesn't seem to show any sign of life!

FOURTH BEARER: Doesn't he? He was breathing up till a moment or so ago.

MONSIGNOR LELLI: He's quite cold!

CICO (*from the head of the steps, intent upon clearing a path through the curious bystanders*): Here's the Doctor! Here comes the Doctor! Mind out of the way there! Mind out of the way!

The DOCTOR *hurries up the steps and across the stage. He has been summoned in haste from the nearest surgery.*

DOCTOR (*as he hurries over, to* CICO, *who is trying to tell him all about it*): Yes, I know . . . I'd realized that . . . Run over! Let me through! . . . Let me have a look at him! (*He bends over* SPINA, *studies his appearance for a moment or so, unbuttons his collar, waistcoat, shirt . . . Listens to his heart. Meantime there is a low murmur of comment from the bystanders.*)

BYSTANDERS: Looks as if he's dead!

H'm! Yes!

What a terrible thing to happen!

Hush! Ssssh!

DOCTOR (*raising his head*): He's dead.

BYSTANDERS (*in various tones of voice*): Dead?

DOCTOR (*once more he bends down to listen to the injured man's heart. Then he gets up again, and, amidst the bewilderment and anguish, the dismay and the compassion felt by all about him, he repeats*): Dead.

CURTAIN

ACT TWO

The scene is the rustic porch of DIEGO SPINA's *farmhouse in the country. The tiles of the lean-to-style roof, which slopes away towards the back of the stage, are visible from underneath. The roof itself is supported by two pillars which are set in a low outer wall, that is broken into midway along so as to allow access—effected by means of a short flight of steps—to the porch. A stone bench runs along this wall. In the background you can see the farm: a dazzling, exultant expanse of verdure, resplendent in the sunshine—an earthly paradise. In the right-hand wall of the porch there is the opening for the staircase which leads to the upper floor of the villa. On either side of this opening there is a stone seat set against the wall. Towards the back of the stage, and beyond the stage seat, there is a small door let into the wall. In the wall Left there is the door which opens into the bailiff's quarters. It is up one step. In the middle of the stage there are an old rustic table, some old chairs, and a stool or two.*

When the curtain rises ARCADIPANE *and an old peasant are on stage. The peasant is already laden with one or two bundles, and another bundle is lying on the ground. In addition there's a large saddlebag on the table.* ARCADIPANE *is a tall, powerfully-built man, with a curly black beard; his eyes are large, smiling and as innocent as a child's. He is wearing a shaggy black cap which he has made for himself out of goatskin. He's dressed like a peasant, in blue broadcloth and jackboots. Instead of a waistcoat he's wearing, over his coarse, white linen shirt, another shirt—made from violet flannel, and chequered with red and black squares. The loose, floppy collar of the linen shirt is folded down over that of the flannel shirt. Around his waist he has a leather belt.*

ARCADIPANE (*picking up the bundle from the ground*): See if
you can carry this one as well. Then we'll have finished . . .
Everything'll be out. (*Carefully and considerately he loads the
bundle on to the peasant's back. Meanwhile another peasant
comes in through the door Left, carrying a chest painted green.*
SARA *follows him in. The bells of an approaching carriage can
be heard in the distance.*)

SARA: Is this chest to go on the cart too?

ARCADIPANE: Yes. (*To the peasant.*) But wait till I get there
before you put it on the cart. I'll come and do it myself. I'll
have to find a place to put it. And make sure everything's
strapped down properly. Come on. I'll take the bag. (*He
picks it up*).

SARA: The bag goes on the mule.

ARCADIPANE: Oh, there's a carriage coming. It can't be
them, surely?

SARA: No. It's too soon.

ARCADIPANE: There's nothing more left upstairs?

SARA: Nothing at all. Go and see who it is, will you? But it
can't possibly be them. (*She goes back into the house.
ARCADIPANE leaves the porch, following the peasants, who
have already gone out Back and to the Left. For a moment the
stage remains empty. Then* ARCADIPANE *re-enters Back,
followed by* DR GIONNI.)

ARCADIPANE: Well, here we are! Do come in, Doctor. If
you'd like to go upstairs . . . I don't know if that's what you
want to do . . . My quarters are over here . . . And the boy's up
there . . . (*He points to the staircase Right.*)

GIONNI: No. No. I must be on my way again immediately. I'll
come back, after I've made my visit. I've got to see a
neighbour of yours. Over at Lotti's.

ARCADIPANE: Oh yes, his mother. Yes, I know. Seems she's
in a bad way.

GIONNI: Yes, I'm afraid so. I just stopped off in passing to let
you know that . . .

ARCADIPANE: Wait a minute. I'll call Sara. (*He goes over to
the door Left, mounts the step, and calls.*) Come down a
minute, Sara . . . The doctor's here. (SARA *comes in*

through the door Left.)

SARA (*apprehensively*): What's happened now?

GIONNI: Nothing. Now don't get agitated. I only want to tell Lucio something . . . So that he's prepared . . .

SARA: He must be upstairs. Strange he didn't hear the carriage-bells.

GIONNI: He's probably asleep.

SARA: No. Would to God he were! He doesn't sleep a wink. Believe me, I'm so very worried about him. And now, on top of it all, this accident to his father. . .

GIONNI: Yes, but that's all . . .

SARA: You can have no idea how his poor head . . .

ARCADIPANE: He never gives himself a moment's rest . . .

SARA: Oh, and his eyes . . . I don't know how to put it . . . It's as if they were petrified . . . Yes, that's it! . . . Petrified with grief! . . . And yet . . . They're **blazing** at the same time . . . As though he were in a raging fever. And what he must be thinking! Last night he told me he felt that the hour of his father's resurrection was at hand.

ARCADIPANE: What did he mean by that? Hasn't he risen already? By means of the miracle . . . (*A gesture in the direction of* GIONNI.)

GIONNI: For pity's sake, don't call it a miracle! Don't you call it a miracle too!

ARCADIPANE: But that's what everybody's calling it! Everybody!

GIONNI: And that's what's so harmful! We must put a stop to it!

ARCADIPANE: Harmful, do you call it? Why, we're all still absolutely flabbergasted by it! There's talk of nothing else in the whole countryside hereabouts.

SARA: And you can just imagine what it's like in town!

GIONNI: Oh, yes I dare say! But I'm more concerned about the effect it can have on him.

ARCADIPANE: You mean the miracle of his resurrection?

GIONNI: Exactly. He cannot possibly admit that it's true . . . Believing as he believes, he just cannot admit the possibility of such a miracle as this.

ARCADIPANE: And why can't he?

GIONNI: Because God alone can call the dead back to life.

ARCADIPANE: I still can't see why he can't believe in it. Wasn't this, maybe, the Will of God?

GIONNI: Ah, there you have it! Good for you, Arcadipane! So I'm not a devil in **your** eyes?

ARCADIPANE: What on earth are you saying, Doctor?

GIONNI: I see everybody eyeing me, just as if I possessed the diabolical power of bringing the dead back to life . . .

ARCADIPANE: Well, you know, you have brought **one** back!

GIONNI: Precisely! By means of a miracle! And it's this very man, who ought to be thanking God that I did, who's keeping me on tenterhooks, in case he should get to know what's happened!

SARA: Oh, then perhaps that's why Lucio says . . .

GIONNI: What?

SARA: That his father's true resurrection is at hand?

GIONNI: Does he suppose that in the end his father will admit it himself?

SARA: Perhaps he **hopes** he will.

GIONNI: He'd do well not to build his hopes too high. As a matter of fact I came here on purpose to warn him what attitude to adopt with his father, when he comes. And I'd like to warn you too . . .

SARA: Oh, there's no need to warn us. We shan't be seeing him, Doctor. We shall be gone before he gets here . . .

ARCADIPANE: We're just on the point of going now . . .

GIONNI: Oh, of course, yes. Forgive me . . .

SARA: I'll go up. I'll just go up and call Lucio. (*She crosses the stage and exits up the stairs Right.*)

GIONNI: Ah, yes! I know! I've done you a bad turn, Arcadipane. Naturally, when the news of his death reached you . . .

ARCADIPANE: You mustn't think, Doctor, that Sara and I rejoiced at it . . .

GIONNI: I don't say you **rejoiced** . . . But it's quite certain it left you in a position to . . .

ARCADIPANE: To legalise our union? Ah, yes! We'd have done that at once . . .

GIONNI (*almost to himself*): That's curious!

ARCADIPANE: What is?

GIONNI: You still could . . .

ARCADIPANE: **How** could we? With him alive?

GIONNI: There's the death-certificate.

ARCADIPANE: It'll be cancelled!

GIONNI: But at the moment it's still valid . . . All signed, sealed and delivered by the doctor who made the post-mortem examination. **Legally** he's dead.

ARCADIPANE: You don't mean that seriously . . .

GIONNI: No . . . But . . . In the eyes of the law.

ARCADIPANE: The law, Doctor . . . There's only one law . . . The Law of God.

GIONNI: But your children . . .

ARCADIPANE: It'll be sufficient for them not to be outside God's Law. I've got nothing to leave them, except the example of obedience to that Law. There's only one thing that grieves my heart . . . That I shall never again hear my own voice under the tiles of this roof. It brings back to me . . . Oh, if you only knew! . . . The memory of so many nights. Sitting on that step over there. Gazing over at the staircase. You can't possibly imagine the love that I've been able **to put into** these stones . . . Into this earth . . . Into every tree that I've planted here . . . With her by my side . . . (*He is alluding to* SARA.) She stepped down from being my Master's wife and became my companion. Here she comes now . . . She's coming downstairs with her son. I'll be going. I've never spoken to him in my life. I've never even let him catch sight of me. (*He goes out Back, turning to the Left.* LUCIO *and* SARA *come down the stairs Right.* LUCIO *is twenty-two, slim and very pale, with a face hollowed by the spiritual travail that has kindled a feverish light in his eyes. He has slender, graceful and very sensitive hands. At frequent intervals he wrings them convulsively. He is not at all shy. On the contrary, it's as if he were impelled to speech and action by an anxiety which seems at times to be stimulated by anger. He's rather ill at ease in the clothes he's wearing—a grey, ready-made suit, somewhat clumsy in cut. He looks rather like a schoolboy who's wearing long trousers for the first time. He comes* *hurrying down the stairs with his mother.*)

LUCIO: No, no, Doctor . . . !

GIONNI: Good morning, Lucio . . .

LUCIO: Good morning. I cannot remain silent! I give you fair warning . . . I cannot remain silent! If he comes here . . .

GIONNI: All that I meant was . . . With regard to what's happened.

LUCIO: What is it you want me not to tell him?

GIONNI: . . . This thing that everybody's calling a miracle . . . The help I gave . . .

LUCIO: And why shouldn't I mention it to him?

GIONNI: Because he doesn't know anything about it yet!

LUCIO: He doesn't know anything about it . . . ?

SARA: He doesn't know that it was you who . . . ?

GIONNI: For pity's sake, not a word about **that**! He remembers nothing whatsoever about anything. All he knows is that he was knocked down by a motor-car. He thinks that he was concussed and that his memory of everything has been completely blotted out.

SARA: He doesn't even know about the death-certificate then?

GIONNI: He knows nothing about anything! Nothing at all! I tell you, he hasn't even the remotest suspicion. He's busy thanking God that, apart from the concussion . . . Oh yes, that might very well have proved fatal! . . . He suffered no other harm as a result of being knocked down.

LUCIO: And do you really think it's possible that he won't find out what's happened?

GIONNI: The most important thing is that he shouldn't find out about it for the moment . . . Not in the state that he's in just now. You can imagine the effect it would have on his mind, can't you? . . . His spiritual agony . . .

LUCIO: You don't think it would do him good to know?

GIONNI: Good heavens, no! God forbid! You'd better get that idea out of your head as quickly as possible! He damned me as a sacrilegious scoundrel merely for bringing a dead **rabbit** back to life! Just imagine what he'd have to say now, if he found out that . . . ! I give you my solemn oath, Lucio, that if it hadn't been for your little sister . . . who implored me to

do the same thing for him . . . She was absolutely desperate!
. . . Well, as far as my own predilections are concerned, I'd
have thought twice about it . . . And more than twice . . .
before doing it. Yes, I'd have had serious scruples about
doing it . . . Just **because** of what the consequences were likely
to be . . .

LUCIO: And suppose it's . . . **Those consequences** . . . That I'm
relying on now?

GIONNI: No! No! What on earth are you talking about?
You're **relying** on the consequences . . . ?

LUCIO: I'm relying on those consequences to call him back to
life, and to ensure that God really does accomplish His
miracle . . . not only on my father's body.

GIONNI: You're willing, then, to run the risk of killing him?

LUCIO: Am I . . . ? No, Doctor. **You're** the one that's running
that risk, not I.

GIONNI: How am I? Why do you say that?

LUCIO: You have made his body walk again . . . But is it only
his body that counts?

GIONNI: No. Your father has his faith!

LUCIO: Precisely. And did you show any respect for that faith
of his when you set him on his feet again, using means which
he regards as sacrilegious? The moment he finds out the
truth, **you** will have killed him!

GIONNI: Nonsense! At this very moment I'm doing all I
possibly can to **prevent** . . .

LUCIO: To prevent his finding out? If he doesn't find out
today he'll do so tomorrow.

GIONNI: All I'm asking is that he shouldn't find out at this
precise moment. Do remember that, after all, it was on your
account . . .

LUCIO: You mustn't say that it was on my account! Say
rather that it was so that this supreme test . . . The supreme
test of life itself . . . Which God has been pleased to visit both
upon him and upon me . . . might be met.

GIONNI (*shrugging his shoulders*): Supreme test . . . Supreme
test . . .

LUCIO: Do you mean you think it's something more

important than that? Doctor, you mustn't do anything to
hinder him in any way, if he should come up here today in
order to face it.

GIONNI: But do you really imagine that he's coming here for
that?

LUCIO: **Isn't** he coming up here in order to speak to me?

GIONNI: Yes, but I'm quite sure he's not expecting to have to
face this supreme test you've been talking about! Not in the
least!

LUCIO: What is he expecting then?

GIONNI: **I don't know!** I suppose that . . . Well, that he's
expecting you to retract . . .

LUCIO: To go back on what I've done? And do you mean to
say that you expect me not to tell him what my reasons were
for doing what I have done?

GIONNI (*getting angry*): Oh, go on! Tell him your reasons!
Do whatever you think best! It'll all seem like heresy to him,
anyway! You know, when all's said and done, my dear
Lucio, mine's a rum fate, and no mistake! Look at me!
Doomed! Doomed to get everybody's back up! All the time!
It must be my face . . . I don't know . . . Perhaps it's my voice.
I respect other people's faith, and at the same time people get
annoyed with me on account of my tolerance! I think like
you, I feel like you. And here we both are: you're thoroughly
annoyed with me, and I'm thoroughly annoyed with you . . . !

LUCIO (*smiling*): No. You're wrong there, I'm not the least bit
annoyed . . .

GIONNI: I am, though! And I'm going! I've done my duty as a
doctor. I implore you . . . As a friend . . . To leave your father
in ignorance. Just for the moment. Leave him in ignorance
of what's happened to him.

SARA: Yes! Yes! I agree with what you say! You oughtn't to
tell him anything. Not just for the present.

LUCIO: If you think that it'll do him the slightest harm, I'll
keep silent, even if he forces me to talk about . . .

GIONNI: That's not what I'm saying!

LUCIO: I shall have to, Doctor! He'll want to talk to me about
my loss of faith, and I'll be obliged to tell him it's not true.

I've acquired it, if anything . . . If anything—it has been strengthened . . .

GIONNI: Not as far as he's concerned.

LUCIO: Faith is something everyone acquires for himself.

GIONNI: No . . . I mean . . . Well, the way he looks at things . . .

LUCIO: And do you know how I've acquired it? Simply by denying the reality of that death you're so frightened he'll get to hear about . . .

GIONNI: **Denying** it? How can you deny **death?**

LUCIO: By ceasing to presume that God, simply because this body of mine . . . in the natural course of events . . . will sooner or later fall to the ground, like a withered leaf from a tree . . .

GIONNI: And isn't that death?

LUCIO: Of course it isn't! **Death!** A handful of dust that returns to dust . . .

GIONNI: That's what your father says, too!

LUCIO: Yes . . . But he goes on to assume that . . .

GIONNI: Yes, quite! That his spirit . . .

LUCIO: **His** spirit? How is it **his?** . . . Don't you see that's where he's wrong!

LUCIO: In saying that it's **his** spirit?

LUCIO: Yes, that's it, Mamma! In admitting that it is eternal . . . Infinite . . . And yet assuming that it can possibly be mine . . . Something that belongs to a man who dwells within the boundaries of time . . . A fleeting, momentary form . . . Something that is yesterday's or tomorrow's. You see how it is, don't you? To prevent our little existence coming to an end, we annihilate life. In God's name. And we make God rule over the kindgom that lies beyond this world. No one knows where it is. We make Him rule there too. Over a kingdom of the dead which we have imagined in order that, when we reach it, He may give us our reward or our punishment. We are an insignificant part of the whole existence He has created yet we dare to assume we can decide who is good or evil. We can't bring ourselves to admit that He alone knows what He does and why He does it. Don't you see, Doctor—this wonderful event should be for him—as it

is for me—a true resurrection from the dead. He must deny
that there is death in God. He must believe in this, which is the
only Immortality there is. An Immortality that is not our
own, not something that is in or for ourselves. That is not the
hope of reward or the fear of punishment. He must believe in
the eternal present of life . . . Which is God . . . And then
indeed will God . . . After this experience which He has
granted my father . . . Then will he . . . And He alone . . .
Accomplish the miracle of his resurrection. I shall say
nothing, nothing at all. Nothing, I promise you. I shall let
him say just whatever he wishes to say to me. And . . . Don't
worry, I'll do everything within my power to avoid sharing
your fate, Doctor. I mean, I'll try to say nothing that might
irritate him.

GIONNI (*he is lost in wonder and admiration at what* LUCIO
has said so gently, so fervently and so simply): Exactly!
Provided, of course, that by keeping quiet you don't irritate
him all the more. That's what you might call **my** fate! Take
now, for instance . . . I'm irritated to the point of
exasperation with myself for the advice I've been giving you.
Oh well, don't let's say any more on that subject. Let's hope
that everything turns out well in the end. Good-bye for the
moment, . . . Signora.

SARA: Good-bye. But you must call me Sara . . . Will you be
coming back?

GIONNI: Oh, yes! Yes! Very soon. Good-bye then. (*Exit
Back, taking the left turn. Shortly after he disappears we hear
the sound of his carriage-bells.*)

SARA: And now I'll be going as well . . .

LUCIO (*hearing the sound*): Can you hear, Mamma?

DIEGO: Hear what?

LUCIO: Those bells.

DIEGO: It'll be the Doctor's carriage.

LUCIO: When I was a little boy I used to think that the open
country, stretched out there in the morning sunlight, was
made especially to spread the sound of the bells.

SARA: The country? But, my dear, when you were a little boy. . .

LUCIO: I could see it from the courtyard of the seminary, way up there at San Gerlando. I used to look down on to it. During playtime the other boys . . . used to race about . . . Shouting like mad, and tucking up their cassocks so they could run better. I used to keep in the background. At the end of the yard. Because from there I could enjoy the wide sweeping view of the green valley. With the great wide road that cut through it like a furrow. And I could see the carriages driving out through the countryside . . . they looked tiny . . . Three horses harnessed together . . . And from faraway the sound of the bells would come stealing up on me—just as they're doing now. (*His mother is in tears; he turns to her.*) Are you crying, Mamma?

SARA: Yes, because of the grief I can hear in your voice . . .

LUCIO: Yes, I did feel . . . I did feel a terrible anguish . . . Anguish . . . Regret for life, which might have been so lovely. It seemed to me that I was experiencing all the joys of a drive in the open air . . . Through the countryside . . . Through those green fields . . . All golden in the sunlight. I sense the atmosphere around me . . . And the smells of things. I think of how we used to come out of the seminary, two by two, as we went for our walks. And we'd pass by one of those carriages standing on the rank in the Square . . . Waiting to be hired. You know, I can still smell the reek of stables. I can even see a wisp of straw between the horses' grey lips. I can hear the ring of iron-shod hooves on the cobbles when they stamped. You see, Mamma, when I was a little boy, up there in the seminary, faith was . . . It was **smell** . . . Taste . . . The smell of incense . . . The smell of wax . . . The taste of the Consecrated Host . . . And a terrible dismay at people's footsteps as they echoed inside the empty church . . .

SARA: You were very tiny . . . Your face was so very white even then . . . Oh, how it hurt me, my son, when I saw you come home for the holidays, dressed in your little cassock! **You** used to tuck your cassock up too . . . So that you could run to me . . . And then you'd immediately let it drop again . . . So that the little girls in the street shouldn't laugh at you . . . And shout after you, 'Little priesty! Little priesty!' And it

was as if your eyes were filled with terror when you looked at
me . . .

LUCIO (*covering his eyes with his hands*): No, Mamma! **No!**
Don't remind me!

SARA: Why not?

LUCIO: If you only knew the shame of it all! Why there was
that look in my eyes. All the filth of life! Child as I was, I had
absorbed into myself all the filth of life! It had been put there
inside me by one of the boys . . . One of the big boys. You
know the one I mean, don't you? He went mad later on. His
name was Spano . . .

SARA: You were barely six years old . . .

LUCIO: And I knew everything! And I don't know whether it
was more horror I felt, or **terror**. Terror of that evil beast
who defiled everything with his foul imagination, and who
spared nobody!

SARA: Did he talk to you about me?

LUCIO: You have no idea of how he terrorized me! He did just
whatever he liked with me! He simply terrified me!

SARA: Oh my child . . . I never dreamt that things were as bad
as that!

LUCIO: If only you'd known . . .

SARA: I saw that you were crushed . . . As a child of your age
ought never to be. But I never guessed that that was the
reason. It used to tear my heart to shreds to see you two
children, you and her, the way you were . . . Dear, tender
creatures . . . Wilting away. And it grieved my heart to see
your father so hard, so obstinate, so determined not to admit
that I was right. He would tell me you were both well . . .

LUCIO: **Well!**

SARA: Yes, well. And I . . . I would take your little faces in my
hands and make him look at them. 'Do you still dare to tell
me that they're well?' I couldn't stand life any longer. I felt
the tortures that were being inflicted upon you . . . I felt them
as if they were biting into my own flesh.

LUCIO: Yes. And when, in point of fact, poor Lia . . .

SARA: When I saw them bring her back home to me . . . A
helpless cripple . . . Her life—**finished** . . . And when I saw

that the Sisters . . . The very Sisters who were to blame for my child's being in that terrible condition . . . were to help me look after her . . .

LUCIO: They were . . . ?

SARA: Yes, you understand . . . **They** were to . . . I wasn't to be left to look after her myself! They were the ones who were to . . . ! I hurled myself at one of them, just like a wild beast . . . Oh, I don't know what I did to her! They tore her from my grasp . . . They thought I was possessed by a devil (*She breaks off, so that she may curb the frantic onrush of hatred which she feels once more assailing her. She begins again immediately.*) Lucio, they made me go away . . . They forced me to run away . . . Just as if I'd been a mad-woman! I begged them, I implored them to bring my baby up here to me . . . I was quite sure that I'd have been able to make her well again. But I had have her up here by herself . . . Without him. I couldn't bear the sight of him any longer . . . I'd have killed him! He wanted me back again. Yes, because . . . He posed as a saint . . Set himself up as a tyrant . . . And then . . . Well, what made me furious with him . . . Whenever he came near me . . . Was the feebleness, the softness of the man . . . (*She breaks off with an exclamation and gesture of disgust.*) Oh, God! . . . And yet, I swear to you, Lucio, I'd have made the sacrifice . . I'd have made the sacrifice . . . I'd have overcome the horror that I felt for him from that time on . . . Provided that some good might have come out of it . . . For **you** . . . For you, my children. And I stipulated that you at least should be set free and allowed to come and live up here . . . You and Lia . . . Up here with me. He refused . . . He wouldn't hear of it. And so . . He refused what I demanded, and I refused his demands! You cannot imagine what I suffered! My agony here . . . And yours there in the seminary! And even if I'd sacrificed myself I couldn't have brought you one moment's comfort in that agony of yours.

LUCIO: I know that you applied to the Courts . . .

SARA: And I lost.

LUCIO: They decided against you?

SARA: Yes, they decided against me! They said it was my duty to remain with him and my daughter! And that my claim that you ought to be taken away from the seminary was an unjust one. And, to cut a long story short, that it was *I* . . . I, and not he . . . who was breaking up the family. I was so furious . . . after two years of desperate ferocious struggle . . . that I threw up everything . . . Everything! What else was I to do? I felt such a loathing! You can see the town from up here. I couldn't bear the sight of it any longer. I turned my face away whenever my eyes . . . strayed in that direction! I felt such a loathing for those churches . . . Those houses . . . And the Court that . . . All of them! When they deny a mother the right to look after her own children . . . When a mother who is trying to provide for the health of her own children is condemned in Court . . . You can't help yourself. Life becomes impossible. They condemn you to act as I acted! I threw away everything I possessed and became a peasant. A peasant! Up here . . . Out in the open air . . . Out in the scorching sun! . . . I was seized with the need . . . The overwhelming **need** . . . To be a savage! . . . I felt the need to sink down to the ground at nightfall . . . Like a beast that's been worked to death. Hoeing, treading out the grain on the threshing-floor with the mules . . . Barefoot in the August sun . . . Tramping round and round, with my legs bleeding . . . And shouting like a dunkard! I felt the need to be brutal with everyone who asked me to have compassion on myself . . . You know who I mean! This pure man. He's as pure, Lucio, as a babe newly delivered from the hands of God. This man . . . . Who's never been able to endure my setting myself on the same level as himself . . . And who prevented me from destroying myself . . . By teaching me all the secrets of the countryside . . . All the secrets of life . . . The **true** life that's lived out here . . . Far far away from the cursèd town . . . The true life that is the life of the earth. This life which now I **feel** . . . Because my hands tend it . . . Help it to grow, to flower and to bear fruit. And the joy of the rain that comes just at the right moment. And the calamity of the mist that makes the olives wilt, just as they are about to burst into flower . . . And . . . Have you see the grass that grows on the bank at the side of the lane here? So fresh and green at daybreak, when the rimes's upon it! And the pleasure . . . You know, it's something so wonderful! . . . The sheer pleasure of making bread with the same hands that sowed the corn . . . !

LUCIO: Yes, Mamma! **Yes!** And, as you see, I've come to you . . .

SARA: My son, the joy you've given me, God alone . . . God Who sent you to me . . . He alone could bestow it on me. And I shouted, I shouted in your father's face that I felt myself once again to be blessèd among women . . . **Purified!** You've paid me back in full, my son . . . For everything . . . With your coming. And, as you see, I too can speak to you about everything. Without being puffed up with pride or cast down with shame. Because I alone know what I've had to suffer . . . What price I've had to pay . . . In order that I might become what I now am . . . Something that perhaps nobody any longer knows the meaning of . . . Something . . . **Natural.**

LUCIO: I do. I understand you completely—looking at you. Listening to you.

SARA: I really **have** set myself free. There's nothing I desire, because there's nothing I lack. I hope for nothing, because what I have is sufficient for my needs. My health is sound, my heart's at peace with the world, and my mind is serene.

LUCIO: But, Mamma, you can't, you **mustn't** go away from here.

SARA: I've already gone. All my things are on their way to . . .

LUCIO: No, no! I'll stop it! Yes, this is something that I **shall** talk to him about! And I shan't mince my words!

SARA: You can't do anything to stop it, Lucio . . .

LUCIO: Yes, I can, I tell you! I **must!**

SARA: You cannot and you must not! And, what's more, I don't want you to. **I don't want you to.**

LUCIO: But all that you've done up here . . .

SARA: It wasn't for my own sake that I did it. I should like . . . Yes, it's true—and I said as much to your father . . . I should like to think that what I'd done, I'd done for your sake, yours and Lia's. Yes, that is something you **can** try to stop him

from doing. Stop him letting the farm . . . All the wealth of
this farm . . . Go to rack and ruin. As it most certainly will if
there's nobody here who knows how to look after it. You still
have the right to stop him doing that with the property. If
you can't do it on your own behalf, you can at least do it on
behalf of your little sister. But not for my sake . . . And you
mustn't. I repeat . . . **I don't want you to.**

LUCIO: It shall be as you wish. I'll do it for my own and Lia's
sake. But . . . Where will you go?

SARA: Don't worry about me. We've made all our arrangements. We know where we're going. Just for the present
we're going to stay with one of our friends who's bailiff on a
farm some little way from here—at Le Favare. Then next
year we're going to be leasing a farm . . . It's quite near here.
And then there'll be a chance of making a little for ourselves .
. . Because up to now, you know, we've never kept a penny
for ourselves. But we shall have to start putting something
aside . . .

LUCIO: Yes, you will, because . . . Mamma, do forgive me . . .
I've not yet had the courage to talk to you about it . . . You've
got two children . . .

SARA: Yes, **his** children. You haven't seen them yet, of course.
They're two sturdy little peasants . . . Baked brown by the
sun.

LUCIO: And he . . .

SARA: Oh, if you only knew how apprehensive you make him
. . . How you terrify him . . .

LUCIO: I do . . . ?

SARA: Yes . . . He's afraid, and he's ashamed. He's counting
the seconds. He's simply dying to get clear of this place. He
knows that I'm talking to you at this moment, and I'm quite
sure that he's out there, and behaving just like a bitch with a
litter of puppies! When she sees her master pick up one of
them to show a friend, and she doesn't dare snarl at him!
She just keeps on stealing pitiful glances at them, to see what
they're doing to her baby . . .

LUCIO: Won't you call him in?

SARA: Why? Would you like me to?

LUCIO: Yes. And the children too.

SARA: They're probably just outside . . . They're waiting for me, so that they can make a start. (*She goes to the back of the stage and calls out towards the Right.*) Oh, Roro! Come on in, will you? Yes, in here! Come on! And bring the children! Come on! Come on!

LUCIO: You call him Roro?

SARA: Yes, that's **my** name for him. His real name's Rosario, and I call him Roro. The little one was already up on the mule. As soon as he finds himself in the saddle, he's happy as a sandboy!

LUCIO: What are the children's names?

SARA: Tonotto . . . That's the older one . . . And the other one's Michele. Here they come now. (ARCADIPANE *enters back, leading the two little boys by the hand.*) This is Arcadipane. (*The two boys run to her.* TONOTTO *reaches her first, then* MICHELE.) And this is Tonotto. And this (*she takes the younger boy in her arms*) . . . Is Michele.

LUCIO (*bending down to kiss* TONOTTO, *and then kissing* MICHELE *as he perches there in his mother's arms*): How lovely they are, Mamma! So strong!

SARA: They're healthy. (*To* ARCADIPANE.) You don't remember Lucio, do you?

ARCADIPANE: Oh, yes. I remember him as a little chap . . . No bigger than him. (*Pointing to* ONOTTO.)

LUCIO: I've got a memory of those days too . . . But I don't know whether it's really true or not . . . It's a memory of you too, Mamma. But perhaps it's not really a memory . . . Perhaps it's a vision that came to me . . . I don't know . . . As though from another life . . . Like in a dream you're looking out of a window that's ever so far away . . . And sunk deep in the world of your dream. But seeing you again now . . . I don't know . . . I find myself beginning to doubt whether . . .

SARA: But of course I'm quite a different woman now, as you know very well!

LUCIO: Oh, yes! Of course! But, what I meant was . . . What I'm beginning to doubt . . . to wonder whether that picture of you was not just something that I'd dreamt. It showed you as so very different . . . No, not more beautiful, Mamma, you know . . . Quite the contrary, in point of fact! You're so lovely now . . . So very much, so very very much more lovely! And the woman of my vision . . . She, on the other hand, was so very sad. And the picture of him, too, the one that I carried in my mind . . . But tell me something, Mamma . . . Don't laugh . . . Don't you remember . . . When we were at home . . . When you were still living with us . . . We had a cat . . . She was all white . . . ?

SARA: A white cat? When you . . . ? (*Suddenly she remembers: she sees the picture* . . .) Yes! Yes! We did! We did have a . . . ! But it wasn't a **she**, it was a **tom!** Yes, we did have one . . . Yes! Yes! It was white . . . A lovely big white tomcat: Yes! Yes, I remember!

LUCIO: In that case . . .

SARA: In that case **what?**

LUCIO: The thing I've been remembering all this time must be a picture of you. Yes. A room . . . A dining-room . . . Very large . . . With a low ceiling . . .

SARA: Why, yes! The dining-room of the house we used to live in . . .

ARCADIPANE: At the bottom of the path leading up to San Francesco . . .

LUCIO: I don't remember it at all clearly . . . I've only got . . . Well, a vague impression of that room . . .

SARA: Yes, it had a window looking out on to the vegetable gardens over the road . . .

LUCIO: There was a square table in the middle of the room . . . I can see it now . . . With just one place laid . . . A table-napkin . . . Freshly-ironed and with the folds still showing stiffly . . . A bottle of red wine, with the froth in the neck of the bottle . . . I could catch it on my fingers . . . Just like this! . . . . That sunbeam which was playing down upon it, through a chink in the closed shutters across the window! . . . He's sitting there . . . Where that table-napkin is . . . And eating, with his head bowed over his plate . . . The white cat is sitting there too, perched up on the other side of the table . . . His front legs are stiff, his head high . . . His tail is hanging down

over the edge of the table, and every now and again it moves
. . . Just as if it were moving of its own accord . . . Like a little
snake. And, Mamma, you're talking to **him**, and not paying
any attention to me . . . Suddenly you turn round, fall down
on your knees and take me in your arms . . . And . . . I don't
know why . . . You burst into tears . . . Holding me ever so
tightly to your breast. I stick my head over your shoulder . . .
In order to look at him . . . Just as if the suspicion's dawned
on me that it was he who'd made you cry. I see him get up
from the table . . . Abruptly . . . And his eyes too are red with
tears . . . He goes over to the corner of the room . . . And
dashes out of the room. I'm terribly afraid, and I'm just
going to scream out when, you suddenly let go of me and
rush out of the room after him. I'm left there . . . In a state of
suspense and bewildered dismay. And then I see the cat jump
across to where the plate is . . . Snatch up the meat in its teeth
. . . And jump down from the table. It's curious how vivid my
memory still is of that cat . . . Whilst the pictures I have of
you . . . Of him and of you . . . I can remember very clearly
how you were both crying.

SARA: It was on your account, my son. I was crying because
of you . . . And so was he.

ARCADIPANE: She was crying because of what she was
suffering . . .

SARA: I was in such a state that I just had to pour out my heart
to anyone that came along . . .

ARCADIPANE: Everybody was sorry for her!

SARA: Lucio, there's something I'm going to tell you now . . .
Here in front of him. I've never said it to anyone before . . .
Not even to myself. When, in utter despair, I left the house
and came up here . . . I knew quite well . . . I'd become aware
that, under the compassion that he felt for me, there lay . . .
Already . . . A feeling of affection for me . . . (*Turning towards*
ARCADIPANE.) Tell me . . . Wasn't there? It's true, isn't
it?

ARCADIPANE (*his bashfulness assails him again; he gives
assent more by his nod than by his barely audible*): Yes, its
true . . .

SARA: A woman is very quick to notice such things, even if she pretends not to, and goes on treating the man as I managed then to go on treating **him** . . .

ARCADIPANE: I was her servant . . . And I swear that even what I felt then . . .

SARA: There's no need for you to swear anything of the kind. As you'll remember, I began by telling you that what I'm saying now is something that I'm revealing for the first time to myself . . . And you didn't want to either . . . Did you? . . . You didn't want to admit to yourself that you were in love with me?

ARCADIPANE: I was afraid to . . . !

SARA: Very well then. And now I must confess that it was this very thing, this secret awareness of his love, Lucio, that drew me to the land . . . That made me want to live the life of a peasant. And I was like Roro—I didn't want to admit it to myself either. Rather as if it were some kind of folly that I was bent on committing. But feeling deep down inside me that this was the only way in which I could keep myself from going mad . . . Yes, the only way! . . . By acting furiously the part of a peasant-woman! And that's why I was always so rude to **him** . . . When he still wouldn't understand . . . Still tried to prevent me from doing what I wanted to do! And now it's your turn, Lucio, to realize that . . . Having made a clean break in my life . . . As I was forced to do . . . I can't find any place for you in my present life. You come back to me out of that life, the life that is no longer **my** life, my son, and I can't find any room for you in my present life. It belongs to him and to these two little children. I must, I **must** go with them.

LUCIO: Yes, Mamma, that's only right. And you mustn't think that I want . . . Or hoped that my coming here . . .

SARA: I know, Lucio. I'm only saying all this so as to give him the strength to face up to you. (*To* ARCADIPANE.) And now we must be going.

LUCIO: I know too that I may not even so much as come with you . . .

SARA: No, Lucio, you can't . . .

LUCIO: But I should like at least to . . .

SARA: To what? Tell me . . . Tell me . . .

LUCIO: Well . . . I mean . . . Secretly, if you like, Mamma . . .

SARA: Secretly? . . .

LUCIO: Yes. I want you to give me the strength . . . After I've had my talk with him . . . To set out on my new path . . . Alone . . . As I must be . . . And without any longer having anybody to help me . . . Without even a proper place in society.

SARA: But why . . .? Of course you won't be . . . Why should you? Don't you want to stay . . . ?

LUCIO: Stay where? In the same house as my father? Like this? (*He points to his lay attire.*) You know what he's like!

SARA: But he can't turn you out!

LUCIO: No, he can't turn me out. But he certainly won't want any longer to give me the money to finish my studies . . .

SARA: I'll give you the money if he refuses! No matter what it costs me!

LUCIO: No, Mamma, you can't . . .

SARA: I can . . . Oh yes, I can! No matter what it costs me, I tell you!

LUCIO: No! What I mean is . . . You **can't** . . . For the same reason that I can't come away with you, Mamma.

SARA: But it's not the same thing at all! No! If you were to take the money from him . . . (*A gesture in the direction of* ARCADIPANE.) But you'll get it from me, from what I earn with my work.

LUCIO: You owe everything that you earn by your work to your children. No. And, what's more, perhaps it's all for the best that I should give up studying and make some attempt to free myself . . . Just as you have done . . .

SARA: No! No!

LUCIO: Yes! So that I too may find my own true nature . . .

SARA: No!

LUCIO: So that my life too may become simple and easy in the humility of toiling with my hands . . .

SARA: But you won't be able to . . . !

LUCIO: Oh yes, I shall! I shall . . . !

SARA: You won't be strong enough to . . .

LUCIO: I shall find strength.

SARA: No . . . No . . . You must do good in life in another way. . . . Oh, my son! . . . Using the light that shines here . . . Here behind your brow . . .

LUCIO: I shall still be able to do good in that way, even when I'm toiling away as a humble labourer.

SARA: No, you mustn't. In this matter you're not to take me as your example. No. I was able to do what I've done because that was the only way I could find my salvation. But you're different . . . There are so many paths before you.

LUCIO: At the moment I can't see one single one.

SARA: If you've found yourself unable to follow the path he chose for you when you were a child, it'll be his **duty** . . . Now . . . to give you both the time and the means to find some other path . . . One that is worthy of you . . . One along which you may walk . . . One that will carry you far!

LUCIO: Yes, you're quite right, Mamma. But I didn't mean just talking about me . . . I meant, talking about . . . **Everything**. I stand in need of comfort at this moment, and you alone can bring me the comfort I need. I've come to you, defying everybody and everything, simply in order to beg for that comfort.

SARA: . . . What is this comfort, Lucio?

LUCIO: I want to feel that you're near me—even if you're hidden—when I have my talk with him. Perhaps it's so that I shan't say things which I ought not to say. I need this strength to come to me from you. Don't deny me. Afterwards you can go away. No one will stop you. No one will see you go.

SARA: Very well, Lucio, if that's what you want me to . . .

ARCADIPANE (*apprehensively*): But hidden . . . **where?**

SARA: No . . . Not hidden. Why should I hide? I've seen him already, and talked to him face to face. And, if the need arises, I will talk to him again. I'll wait up there . . . The rooms are all empty. He'll never dream that I'd want to stay here. There's not even a chair left up there. I'll sit on the little ledge under the window, and wait till you've finished your talk.

ARCADIPANE: No, Sara . . . Don't do it!

SARA: What are you afraid of?

LUCIO: I'll answer for her. She'll come away with me. She shall return to her sons and to you. You need have no worries on that score.

ARCADIPANE (*to* SARA): But won't **he** think that Lucio's defending the land for your sake too, if you stay here?

SARA: I've already told him to his face we don't need his farm to keep us alive . . . for we've never taken anything out of it . .

LUCIO: And I shall do nothing to prevent him from disposing of it just as he wishes. Don't worry. I told you, I can't go on living in the same house as him. I shall go away too. Besides, Mamma, it doesn't really matter . . . You go . . . You go on your way . . . With him . . . I'll find my own strength.

SARA: No! No! I'll stay . . . I'll go upstairs. (*The sound of carriage-bells is heard.*) You go on . . . Go on. Wait for me at Lotti's Farm . . . I'll rejoin you there. If it's not Dr Gionni on his way back, it'll be them. Go on! . . . Go on! (ARCADIPANE *and the two little boys exeunt back. The noise of bells comes nearer.* SARA *goes over to the door Left, and before she goes off she says to* LUCIO.) I am here, my son. (*Exit, closing the door behind her.*)

LUCIO *stands there expectantly. Shortly afterwards the carriage stops outside the house.* CICO'*s voice is heard.*

CICO: Here we are! Here we are! I'll help you down! I'll help you down!

DEODATA: No! Take it easy! No! Let me do it, Cico! I know how to lift her.

CICO: Your wheel chair is all ready! There's a good girl! There she goes . . . Racing along as if it was her own two little legs that were carrying her!

LIA *comes into sight in her wheel-chair. She is silhouetted against the sunlight at the back of the stage.* CICO *and* DEODATA *come ruunning in after her.*

LIA: Lucio! Lucio! Where are you?

LUCIO (*running over and embracing her*): Lia!

DEODATA (*her first astonishment is rapidly extinguished by a sense of disillusionment, which is near to contempt*): There he is!

CICO: Oh, look! I didn't even notice . . .

LIA (*freeing herself from his embrace*): Let me look at you! No-No-o-o-o. You look silly! Oh, goodness! You look as if you've shrunk!

DEODATA: You've got the nerve to show yourself in those clothes . . . ?

CICO: He might be just anybody . . .

LIA: You don't look like **you** any longer!

DEODATA: If you only knew the effect you have on people who see you again looking like this, after . . . ! But where on earth did you buy that suit? Can't you see how badly it fits?

LUCIO: What does that matter? Where's my father? Isn't he coming?

LIA: Yes, he's coming . . . With Monsignor Lelli . . . In another carriage. They were waiting for the lawyer.

LUCIO: So that they could settle the transfer of the farm?

DEODATA: Oh, just think of it! The moment he claps eyes on you, looking like that! He won't want to listen to a word you've got to say. And meanwhile, just you take a look at her . . . (*She takes* LIA's *face between her hands, and shows it to* LUCIO.) It's done her good already . . . The first breath of fresh air, and its already done her good. Look at her, she's got quite a colour.

LIA: Oh, it's so lovely up here! So very lovely!

LUCIO: So his mind's still set on it?

DEODATA: Your father's, you mean? More than ever!

LIA: Yes . . . You'll see . . . He frightens me . . . And I fell ever so sorry for him too, Lucio . . . It hurts me to see him . . .

LUCIO: But does he still suspect nothing?

LIA: About what?

LUCIO: About what's happened to him?

LIA: Oh, no! He hasn't even the vaguest suspicion?

DEODATA: Not the slightest!

There is a prolonged pause.

CICO (*his manner is absorbed, for like all the rest he is thinking of the terrible thing that has happened*): And he was dead! Absolutely stone-cold dead! (*A pause.*)

DEODATA: Yes, dead.

LIA: I saw him with my own eyes . . .

LUCIO (*deliberately, meaningfully*): Dead?

LIA: Yes.

LUCIO: Well, in that case, you must tell him! Dead. You too must tell him that he was dead.

LIA: Dead, yes, dead.

DEODATA: We all saw him!

CICO: Dead.

DEODATA: Monsignor Lelli as well!

CICO: Yes, him as well. Dead. He got a good view of him. And then there were the doctors who examined him and *said* he was dead!

DEODATA: One of them wrote out the death-certificate. (*A pause.*)

LUCIO (*to* LIA): It **was** you, **wasn't** it?

LIA: Me? What about me?

LUCIO: It was you who got them to send for Dr Gionni?

LIA: Oh, yes! I started to shout at them! Nobody wanted to at first!

DEODATA: I didn't want to because . . . Well, because I didn't believe it was possible!

CICO: And Monsignor Lelli didn't want to either! He certainly **didn't** want to! I was the one that ran off to fetch Dr Gionni! I wanted to see too . . . I mean, what he'd do . . . With a corpse stuck there in front of him!

LUCIO: And then?

LIA: You know, it happened immediately! Immediately!

LUCIO: What did?

LIA: His heart started beating again! And his face . . . Instead of being all white . . . As it had been . . .

CICO: White as white.

DEODATA: Like wax . . .

LIA: Came back to life again immediately . . . Oh, I don't know how to describe it to you! . . . You could see . . . You could see that the life-blood was beginning to flow again in his veins ..

DEODATA: And the breath was stirring in his breast . . .

CICO: His lips opened again . . .

LIA: Yes! Oh, how wonderful it was! You could just see them moving! Ever so slightly! Oh, the joy I felt then! There he lay . . . Still not conscious of life . . . But he wasn't dead any longer! Joy . . . At the same time . . . Something . . . Something **terrifying!**

DEODATA (*there is sombreness in her voice; her words come slowly, emphatically*): It makes me tremble still, just to think of it.

A long pause.

CICO (*softly, to* LUCIO, *as if in confidence—a diabolical note in his voice*): You were quite right, you know, to throw away your cassock.

DEODATA (*instantly, to* CICO, *her voice loud and harsh*): No! Don't say that! You're not to say that!

CICO: It just slipped out! (*And he puts his hand over his mouth.*)

DEODATA: You promised me you wouldn't say that.

CICO: Yes, I promised you I wouldn't **say** it! But I go on thinking it all right! With a vengeance! (*To* LUCIO.) You do realize, don't you, that ...? **Dead!** ... And he doesn't know a thing about it! Where's he been? He ought to know ... And he doesn't! If he doesn't know he's been dead, that's a sure sign that when we die, there's nothing on the other side ... Nothing at all.

A pause.

LIA (*gives a strange little laugh—it's almost as if she were laughing secretly to herself*): My funny little wings, Deodata ... **M'm?** Those funny little angel's wings. I was to get them so as to make up for not being able to walk down here in this world. It's good-bye, then, to flying about in Heaven!

LUCIO (*moved*): No, Lia . . .

LIA (*gently*): But, if Paradise doesn't exist . . .

There is a pause. Then CICO's *voice cuts into the silence, the words coming slowly, sombrely.*

CICO: The Lord's other house . . . The one up there . . . For all who have suffered in patient resignation down here on earth . . .

DEODATA (*her voice too is slow and sombre*): And who abstained from pleasure that they might not fall into sin . . .

CICO (*slowly, sombrely*): Those who are sore distressed and those who have been cast out from their inheritance . . .

DEODATA (*slowly, sombrely*): The Good Tidings of Jesus Christ . . .

CICO (*his voice still sombre, still slow*): Nothing . . . Nothing left at all.

During these last lines the faint sound of carriage bells has been heard. This sound has now stopped. There is a moment of expectancy, filled with dismay and anguish. DR GIONNI comes in up Back.

GIONNI: Shh, everybody! Shh! Shh! He's coming. He knows.
LUCIO: He's found out?

GIONNI gives an affirmative nod of the head. Into the silence that falls on-stage—a silence heavy with the weight of all that dismay and anguish—DIEGO SPINA enters. He comes in up Back and advances down-stage, followed at some distance by MONSIGNOR LELLI and MARRA, the notary. He sees no one. He steps off the raised portion between the two pillars, comes over to the table, and falls into a seat beside it. He is white with terror, and his eyes are wide open, gazing into vacancy. Everybody looks at him in an agony of suspense and dismay, continuing to maintain that silence which is, in fact, the utterly terrified silence of life when it is brought face to face with death.

CURTAIN

ACT THREE

The scene is the same as in Act Two, a few minutes later.
When the curtain rises the audience sees once again the same
tableau as that on which the preceding act concluded... That's to
say, the same characters are in the same positions and caught in
the same attitudes. Only DIEGO SPINA *and* LUCIO *are*
missing. Shortly after the curtain goes up LUCIO *comes down the*
stairs Right and everyone turns and looks at him anxiously.

LUCIO: He's locked himself in.

LIA: Did you call him?

LUCIO: I tried to get him to open the door and let me in.

MONSIGNOR LELLI: Wouldn't he?

LUCIO: No.

DEODATA: Didn't he even answer you?

LUCIO: Well, when I kept on and on calling him he shouted,
  'Go away!'

Pause.

GIONNI (*apprehension in his voice*): You go up, Monsignore!
  You go on up and try!

LUCIO: No, Monsignore. From the tone of his voice when
  he ordered me to go away ... Well, I'm quite certain that at
  this moment he'd refuse to see you, too. Don't go up.

Pause.

MONSIGNOR LELLI: It's terrible.

Pause.

LUCIO: Perhaps it's all for the best that he should be alone while he sounds the abyss into which his faith has plunged. And then God will rise again in him.

MONSIGNOR LELLI (*shocked, severe*): God? What God do you think is ever likely to rise again in him?

LUCIO (*simply*): That God who dwells in all of us, Monsignore, and who has set us upon our feet.

MONSIGNOR LELLI (*in his pulpit-voice, but sincerely*): Upon our feet? What do you mean, upon our feet? Can't you see? Here we are, our knees trembling with terror! And your little sister here . . . Look at her! . . . She is not on her feet. You make the earth fall away beneath us . . . Set a yawning abyss under every one of us . . . And then you say we are on our feet! Look at that woman! (*A gesture in the direction of* DEODATA.) Look at that old man! (*A gesture in the direction of* CICO.)

CICO (*trembling all over*): You can leave me out of it, Monsignore! You can leave me out of this! To Hell with your God! (*He tears his red cap from off his head and flings it on to the ground.*) I've got my own devil inside me! I have, I tell you! And from now on nobody's going to bottle him up . . . Never again! (*He picks up his cap again and replaces it on his head.*) There! That settles that! And don't call me **old**! Old, my . . . *Foot!* (*Suddenly turning towards* DEODATA.) D'you want me, Deodata? I'll marry you! (*He runs over and embraces her.*) I'll marry you! I'll marry you, Deodata!

DEODATA (*trying to free herself.* MARRA, *all the while, splitting his sides with laughter.* LIA *is laughing too—but hers is a different kind of laugh, almost involuntary*): Take your hands off me! Let me go, you lunatic!

CICO (*still hanging on to her frantically*): I'm going to marry you now! Here and now! We won't bother about the law and the sacraments! We'll get married the way the dogs do! And you'll soon see that there's no sin in having your bit of fun!

MONSIGNOR LELLI (*asserting his authority—*GIONNI *mean-while has hastened over and, with a thrust of his hand, pushed* CICO *away*): That will be enough of that, Cico!

DEODATA (*freeing herself*): Oh, you're a dog all right! Leave me alone!

GIONNI: Let go of her!

CICO (*rounding on* GIONNI): Who asked you to poke your nose in, anyway?

GIONNI: We're not beasts! We're **men**!

MONSIGNOR LELLI (*to* MARRA, *who's still laughing*): And you too, Marra! Stop laughing! Don't let's all take leave of our senses!

While this has been going on LUCIO *has covered his face with a hand.*

GIONNI (*to the notary*): Do remember that everything can be heard upstairs! And it was you . . . Yes, it was you who . . .

MARRA: Quite unintentionally . . . Now, you must grant me that! I was absolutely ignorant of the fact that he didn't know anything about it . . .

GIONNI (*to* MONSIGNOR LELLI): And to think that I'd come dashing over to warn his son! But how on earth was I to know that . . . Today of all days! . . . When he was coming over here for the very first time . . . Well, I imagined that it was to have a talk with him. (*A gesture in the direction of* LUCIO.) How was I to know that he'd bring the notary with him?

MARRA: Ah, you see . . . Since he wanted to draw up the deed of gift relating to the farm . . .

GIONNI: Clear as clear! He'd have to be told! I repeat, I thought that he was coming over to persuade his son not to break his heart by renouncing his . . .

MARRA: Oh, no! No! What I meant was . . . Well, he was bound to find out what had happened. He has to sign the deed of gift. And how could I ask him to sign it if, according to the Registrar, he's legally dead? I thought he knew. So I laughingly ask him, 'Oh, by the way, have you got them to rub your name out in the Register of Deaths?' No sooner have I got the words out than I see Monsignor Lelli signalling to me . . . And there **he** is . . . With his face as white as a sheet . . . Frowning away . . .

GIONNI (*to* MONSIGNOR LELLI): But didn't you try to . . . ?

MONSIGNOR LELLI: Yes, I tried . . . But he (*a gesture in the direction of the notary*) without realizing . . .

MARRA: What you mean is . . . Without having the faintest idea . . .

MONSIGNOR LELLI: Began to talk about the miracle you'd performed . . .

MARRA: But I mean to say . . . Well, let me put it bluntly . . . All this fuss and nonsense! . . . Oh yes, I realize what it must have been like for him . . . To hear about it all of a sudden, the way he did! But, when all's said and done . . . Well, if it had happened to me . . . Even if it had been a question of being dead . . . for . . . half an hour . . . How long was it in fact? . . . Three-quarters of an hour . . . Why worry? If I can give myself a pinch here and now and say, 'I'm alive' . . .

MONSIGNOR LELLI (*drawing himself up, sternly*): So you think that that's all there is to it? **Alive?** (*Spreading the syllables one from another.*) What do you mean, '**alive**'?

MARRA: Why . . . **Alive!** You're not trying to deny that, **are** you? Does it matter **in what way?**

MONSIGNOR LELLI: It matters more than anything in the world!

MARRA: Well . . . The doctor here knows **in what way** . . . In fact we all know really.

MONSIGNOR LELLI: But we are not put into the world merely to live! No! And the other thing that we must all of us do . . . **Die** . . . It's the sort of thing that . . . Well, you've seen for yourselves . . . To know nothing about it . . . To be unable to say anything about it . . . It means . . . that one feels immediately that life is extinguished . . . It means that one is annihilated.

Pause.

DEODATA (*breaking the silence*): Utter despair.

Pause.

CICO (*breaking the silence*): His soul, as soon as it had left his body, ought to have appeared before the Seat of Divine Justice. It didn't. So what does it mean? That there isn't any

Divine Justice. There's nothing when you get to the other side. (*Pause.*) So, Monsignore, it's Good-bye, Church! Good-bye, Faith!

Pause.

LIA (*breaking the silence. Her voice is light and clear and in it there almost seems to smile—so greatly does it tremble—that anguish which is prompted by a sense of desperate need*): God must . . . **Must!** . . . Exist there too!

LUCIO (*as if transfigured by a sudden tremendous onset of divine emotion*): Yes, Lia, He is there! He is there! Now I feel that He *is* there . . . That He **must** be there! **That He must be there!** Yes, Monsignore, He must be there so that He may give back their wings to those who, on earth, lacked the power to walk upon their feet! . . . He *is* there! He *is* there! . . . Now I understand, now I feel, really feel, the meaning of Christ's word, CHARITY! Because men cannot always stand upon their feet . . . Not all of them! God Himself has resolved to build His House here upon earth, so that it shall be promised to man of the true life that lies beyond the grave. His Holy House, where the weary, the wretched, and the weak may go down upon their knees . . . Where every kind of sorrow and every kind of pride may kneel down. Yes, Monsigore, like this . . . (*He kneels.*) Just as now I kneel down before you . . . Now that I feel myself worthy once again to put on my habit in the name of the divine sacrifice of Christ and of the faith of my fellow-men!

MONSIGNOR LELLI (*stooping and laying his hands on* LUCIO's *head*): My son, blessèd are you, for God has stepped down from your mind and once again has entered into your heart!

DEODATA (*in joyous amazement*): He's going to put on his cassock again?

CICO (*almost ferociously*): But what about what happened? What about **that?**

MONSIGNOR LELLI (*still stooping over* LUCIO): What do you mean, 'what happened'?

CICO: To him . . . Him that's up there! . . . Came back to life, and doesn't know a thing about what's on the other side.

MONSIGNOR LELLI: And who told you that God allows those who return from beyond the grave to **know?** It is your duty to **believe**, not to know!

LUCIO (*getting up*): In God there is no death!

LUCIO *makes his way, radiant, to the stairs Right, so as to go up and put his cassock on again. SARA, who has remained hidden, listening to all that has just happened, opens the door Left at this moment and reveals herself. She is trembling all over with emotion. She calls out to* DR GIONNI.

SARA: Doctor . . . Doctor . . . (*They all turn in utter amazement.*)

GIONNI (*going over to her*): Oh, it's you, Signora Spina? You were in there?

SARA: Yes. Just as my son wished.

GIONNI: Lucio?

SARA: Yes. So that I might give him strength. But he's found it . . . He's found it in himself . . . **For** himself . . . He's found the strength he needed to carry out the sacrifice . . .

GIONNI: That had to be made if his father was to be saved. Now perhaps . . . Up there . . . When he sees him dressed in his cassock again . . .

SARA: Yes! Yes! I'm trembling all over . . . Oh, you can see for yourself! Now he no longer has any need of me. So I can go away. Tell him that I bless him for what he's doing. No one can possibly know better than I do just what it is that he's doing. He's talked to me about life . . . About how he **feels** it! How he feels it! How he would **live** it! He's renouncing it! He is going now to put on his cassock again . . . Once again he will die.

GIONNI: He himself said that in God there is no death.

SARA: Yes. It's true . . . In this particular sense . . . Yes, you see . . . It's true in this way . . . There are saints even on earth.

MONSIGNOR LELLI: To rekindle in the darkness of death the divine light of Faith . . . That Faith which is charity towards all those to whom every good thing has been denied in life.

DEODATA: He might have kept that light burning in himself, without waiting till he saw his father lying dead . . . And his father and all the rest of us absolutely out of our wits with despair.

MONSIGNOR LELLI: And then you wouldn't have seen how God recalled him unto Himself. Neither would you have seen how he came to realize how great was his need of Faith.

CICO (*utterly fed-up*): Now don't say another word! Not another word! As far as I'm concerned what you said just now is good enough for me . . . That God can't allow those who come back from beyond the grave to know anything about it . . . There, you see . . . That's good enough for me. (*And immediately, in an undertone, just as if there were really someone else speaking from within him.*) Although, all the same, He might allow it . . . He might let us know . . . Seeing that we've got someone here who **has** come back!

MONSIGNOR LELLI: It would be the end of life.

CICO: Why would it be the end of life?

MONSIGNOR LELLI: Because life is given to you on condition that you live it out without **knowing** . . . Simply **believing.** And woe betide the man who believes that he knows! God alone knows everything, and man when he appears before Him must bow his head and bend his knee.

At this moment the deafening report of a gun is heard. The noise comes from upstairs, but it re-echoes and reverberates at the back of the stage Left. Everyone is shocked into speechlessness. Their first reaction is to think that DIEGO SPINA has killed himself. They all turn and look up the stairs.

DEODATA: Oh, God! What's happened?

CICO: He's killed himself! He's killed himself!

LIA: No! Papa! Papa! Hurry! Hurry!

MONSIGNOR LELLI: Lucio's up there! Can he really have . . . ?

GIONNI (*holding* CICO *back*): No, the sound came from over there! (*He points in the direction of Back Left.*)

And, as a matter of fact, ARCADIPANE *appears up-stage Left.*

He is in evident distress. He is lightly wounded in the scalp, and he is holding his left temple in his bloodstained hands. As soon as SARA catches sight of him she screams and rushes over to him, terrified. Everybody speaks at once.

SARA: Oh! It's you. Who did it? What have they done to you?

MONSIGNOR LELLI: Did he do it?

ARCADIPANE: He fired at me. From the window. Oh, it's nothing! It's nothing! Look . . . Here . . . Only a scratch!

GIONNI: Let me have a look at it! Let me look at it!

MARRA: Has he gone out of his mind? After all these years?

LIA: What happened? What happened?

DEODATA: Your father! He shot at him from the window!

CICO: He tried to kill him!

SARA (*to GIONNI, who is examining the wound*): Is it very bad, Doctor? Is it?

GIONNI: No, as good luck would have it! Nothing at all! Barely scratched him!

At this moment DIEGO SPINA comes hurtling downstairs like a madman. He is still armed with the gun and is grappling with LUCIO, who is trying to hold him back. LUCIO is dressed once more in his priest's cassock. At DIEGO's appearance there is a burst of simultaneous cries of horror, terror, entreaty, protest.

ALL: Oh, my God! Here he is!

No! No!

Papa! Papa!

Merciful God!

Hold him, Lucio! Hold him!

Everyone is perplexed, hesitating between courage and fear, wondering whether to fling himself upon SPINA and disarm him, or to get out of range of his gun. Meanwhile DIEGO SPINA points the gun at ARCADIPANE, raises it and takes aim, shouting to LUCIO, from whom he has managed to free himself.

DIEGO: Leave me alone! (*And to the others.*) Get out of my way! Get out of the way! First of all I'm going to kill him! Then you can arrest me!

SARA (*leaving* ARCADIPANE *and going over to him*): Who are you going to kill? Why should you want to kill him?

LUCIO (*running forward to shield her*): No, Mamma!

And at the same moment ARCADIPANE, *freeing himself from the restraining hands that are trying to hold him back and out of harm's way, says.*

ARCADIPANE: No! What are you doing, Sara? Let me go!

But when SARA *has uttered her challenge* CICO *has leapt forward and hurled himself on the gun which is levelled at* ARCADIPANE. *He forces the muzzle down and grabs hold of* DIEGO SPINA *round the waist.* SPINA *struggles to free himself. They all talk at once.*

CICO: Now keep still! Are you out of your mind?

DIEGO: Take you hands off me! (*To* SARA.) No, it's not you I want to kill! Get out of the way! He's the one I want to kill!

SARA: You'll have to kill me first!

MONSIGNOR LELLI: Well done, Cico! Hold him! Hold him tight!

GIONNI (*rushing over*): For pity's sake, Signor Spina!

MARRA (*rushing over*): You don't mean that seriously, do you? After all these years?

DEODATA: Your daughter's here! Your *daughter*!

LIA: Papa! Please, Papa!

DIEGO (*just going on with what he was saying, turning to* SARA *and then to the others as he speaks*): He mustn't live one moment longer! **He must not live one moment longer!** Let me go!

SARA (*confronting him*): Yes, let him go! I am here! Let him go, Cico! I want to see what he'll do!

ARCADIPANE: Don't provoke him, Sara!

SARA: You stay where you are!

LUCIO: Mamma!

SARA (*to* LUCIO): And you, don't stand in the way! All of you, let him talk ... To **me**! (*To* DIEGO.) What is it you want to do?

DIEGO: I don't know! I don't know! I can do anything I like!

SARA: You can do nothing!

DIEGO: I can do anything I want to! **Anything!**

SARA: Because you no longer believe that God sustains and holds you up . . .

CICO: We're the ones that're holding you now! Holding you **back!**

SARA: Because of this, you've become a beast and **kill?** But not even the beasts kill in this fashion.

DIEGO: I've lost all sense of reason! I see neither rhyme nor reason in anything! There's nothing I can't do! (CICO *hasn't slackened his grip upon him. Now* DIEGO *says to him, in a tremendous outburst of rage and handing him the gun at the same time.*) Take the gun, and let go of me! (CICO *lets go of him, keeping hold of the gun.*) There you are . . . Now I'm disarmed! Go on, arrest me! There he is, over there . . . Wounded. Yes, I tried to kill him . . . The moment I caught sight of him out of the window . . . Standing down there . . . On the ground . . . On this earth that . . .

SARA: He was waiting for me . . . We were going away together . . .

DIEGO: No . . . I mean . . . On the ground . . . This earth . . . Down on to which I've fallen, out of the cloud of falsehood up there . . . The earth . . . Things . . . You, you've been living here with him . . . Oh, but you're not going to live with him any longer, you know! Oh no, not now! Not now! (*And once more he springs forward, intent upon seizing her, but at once he is caught and held back again, just as at the self-same moment* ARCADIPANE *springs forward in his turn. Once again everybody is talking at the same time.*)

CICO (*on this side of the stage—he and* MONSIGNOR LELLI *and* MARRA *are grouped around* DIEGO SPINA): Trying it on again, eh? Oh, I shan't let you go again!

MONSIGNOR LELLI: Aren't you satisfied with what you'e done already?

MARRA: This is utter madness!

DIEGO: Neither I nor he shall have her! I can't bear the sight of him any longer! Neither I nor he shall have her! Yes! Yes!

I'm mad!

ARCADIPANE (*who is being held back by* SARA, LUCIO, *and* DEODATA): God help you if you so much as try to lay hands on her! Huh, so you'd like to take her back now, would you?

SARA: No! Now be quiet! Stay where you are! This is my affair! And I'm going to deal with it myself!

LUCIO: Let him say what he has to! You must show him some consideration!

DEODATA: He's not himself! No, he's not himself any longer!

DIEGO (*carrying on with what he was saying, turning to the three of them who are holding* ARCADIPANE *back*): Yes! Why yes, let him! Let him kill me! Let him kill me! It'd all be all for the best! He's got the right to! I tried to kill him! All the crimes in the world and this as well! Only . . . There's this, you see . . . You don't have to pay for what you do . . . Not a thing! . . . Not if you pay for everything here! Prison? The whole world's a prison, a prison there's no escaping from! And there's nothing on the other side! I **know**! (*Suddenly addressing himself to* GIONNI.) Doctor, did you enjoy yourself? Was it a wonderful joke, sticking a needle into my heart, like a rabbit?

GIONNI: But it was your daughter who . . . Look at her!

LIA (*in anguish*): Papa . . . Papa! . . .

DIEGO (*flinging himself down by* LIA *and embracing her as she sits there in her chair*): Oh, my darling child, why did you do it? Was it because you wanted to make me see the havoc . . The havoc I've made of my life? (*Getting up again and turning towards the* DOCTOR.) But you, you who knew all the horror that I should find confronting me when I opened my eyes again, how could you possibly bring yourself to do it? Because I was dead . . . As you know . . . You all saw me . . . Dead . . . Dead . . . You saw me too, Monsignore! . . . Dead . . And another doctor . . . Not he . . . Another doctor examined me and said that I was dead . . . Signed the certificate! . . . And then he . . . thrust me back into life again . . . Like a rabbit . . . And I knew nothing at all about it . . . **I know** nothing about it! I know nothing about it now, Monsignore! Bankruptcy . . . If life were a business, I should be bankrupt! I can cry it aloud to the whole world . . . Bankrupt! I say it and I know! If yours is a faith that is sincere, as mine was, then abandon it! Lose your faith! Lose it!

MONSIGNOR LELLI: But your son . . . Look at him! . . . He has regained his faith!

DEODATA: He's put his cassock back on again! Look, he's put his cassock back on again!

MONSIGNOR LELLI: Once more he dwells in the light of God!

DIEGO (*caught in surprise, to* LUCIO): You?

LUCIO: Yes, father.

SARA: For your sake!

MONSIGNOR LELLI: For all our sakes!

DEODATA: Yes, for all our sakes, for all our sakes, for the sake of his little sister.

DIEGO: But how? Why? Now? Now that I know . . . ?

CICO: No! No! You know nothing at all! God can't allow anybody that comes back from beyond the grave to know anything! So what's happened to you is no proof of anything! No proof of anything at all!

DIEGO: What do you mean, it's 'no proof of anything at all'? I was dead, and my soul . . . My soul! . . . Where was it during all the time that I was dead?

LUCIO (*simply and gently*): With God, father. Your soul is God, father. And you call it yours. It is God, don't you see? And what can you possibly know of death, if God now, by means of one of His miracles . . .

DIEGO: One of *His* miracles? . . . But it was **he** who did it! (*Pointing to* DR GIONNI.)

LUCIO: It was not he! Do you really believe that all the dead can be called back to life by anything that a doctor can do? He himself recognizes that it was a miracle!

DIEGO: Yes, a miracle of his science!

LUCIO: If our soul is God within us, what else would you call his science and a miracle achieved by means of it, if not of His miracles, wrought when He would have it accomplished?

And what can you possibly know of death if there is no death in God? And if He is now once again to be found in you, as He is still to be found in all of us here . . . Eternal, in this moment of our life which only in Him is life without end?

DIEGO: You . . . You're talking to me like this? Now? You, for whose sake I . . . ?

LUCIO: Yes. So that you may rise again from your death, father. Do you see? You had shut your eyes against life, in the belief that you were bound to see the other life that lay beyond the grave. This has been your punishment. God blinded you to that other life, and now He makes you open your eyes again to this life . . . Which is His life . . . In order that you may live it . . . And in order that you may allow other people to live it . . . Toiling and suffering and rejoicing like everyone else.

DIEGO: I? And your sister? And what about you? I tried to . . . I meant to kill . . . And all the evil that I've done . . .

LUCIO: I take it upon myself, father, and I redeem it! If now I take up the burden of all this evil that you have done, and if I feel it . . . If I feel it to be good . . . To be a blessing upon me . . . Then that is God! Do you see what I mean? That is God's doing . . . God who sees you with your own eyes . . . Who sees what you do . . . What you have done . . . and what you must do now.

DIEGO: What must I do?

LUCIO: You must live, father. In God . . . In the works that you will perform. Arise and walk . . . Walk in the ways of life. And leave to this man, (Pointing to ARCADIPANE.) leave to this man the woman that is his. To this mother you must yield her daughter. But you mustn't just sit there waiting, Lia . . . I feel, my dear little sister . . . I feel that you mustn't wait for me to go back . . . You mustn't wait for me to make the organ sing out . . . In Lia's name . . . Filling the church with all the glory of God's Heaven! (He turns to his mother.) Mamma! Mamma! Call your daughter to you!

SARA (is transfigured, as if reflecting the divine exaltation of her son. She holds out her hands to LIA): My daughter! My daughter!

LIA (*she rises from her chair at her mother's call, and runs over to her on her still unsteady legs*): Mamma! Mamma!

LUCIO *appears as if bathed in a divine light.*

CICO: *This* is a miracle! This is the **miracle!** (*And he falls down on his knees.*) She's walking . . . She's walking . . .

And all the others too, dumbfounded with joy, stand there, their lips shaping the word:

Miracle.

CURTAIN

BIBLIOGRAPHY

The following is a list of Pirandello's plays with the date of the first Italian performance. The English title is given where the play has been translated:-

1910   *La morsa* (The Vise)
        Lumie di Sicilia (Sicilian Limes)
1913   *Il dovere del medico* (The Doctor's Duty)
1915   *Se non cosi*
1916   *Pensaci, Giacomino!* (Think it Over, Giacomino!)
        Liolà (Liolà)
1917   *Cosi è se vi pare* (Right You Are, If You Think You Are)
        Il berretto a sonagli
        La giara (The Jar)
        Il piacere dell 'onesta' (The Pleasure of Honesty)
1918   *Ma non è una cosa seria*
        Il giuoco delle pacti (The Rules of the Game)
1919   *L'innesto* (The Grafting)
        La patente
        L'uomo, la bestia, e la virtu'
1920   *Tutto per bene* (All for the Best)
        Come prima, meglio di prima
        Cece' (Chee-Chee)
        La Signora Morli, una e due
1921   *Sei personaggi in cerca d'autore* (Six Characters in Search of an Author)
1922   *Enrico IV* (Henry IV)
        All'uscita (At the Gate)
        L'imbecille (The Imbecile)
        Vestire gli ignudi (Clothe the Naked)
1923   *L'uomo dal fiore in bocca* (The Man with the Flower in his Mouth)

La vita che ti diedi (The Life I Gave Thee)
L'altro figlio (The House with the Column)
1924 *Ciascuno a suo modo* (Each in His Own Way)
1925 *Sagra del signore della nave* (Our Lord of the Ship)
1927 *Diana e la tuda*
L'amico delle mogli
Bellavita (Bellavita)
1928 *Scamandro*
La nuova colonia
1929 *Ò di uno ò di nessuno*
Lazzaro (Lazarus)
1930 *Come tu mi vuoi* (As You Desire Me)
Questa sera si recita a soggetto (Tonight We Improvise)
1932 *Trovarsi*
1933 *Quando si e'qualcuno*
1934 *La favola del figlio cambiato*
1935 *Non si sa come*
1936 *Sogno (ma forse no)* (Dream, But Perhaps Not)
1937 *I giganti della montagna* (The Mountain Giants)